JUDY

*THE UNFORGETTABLE STORY OF A
DOG WHO WENT TO WAR AND
BECAME A TRUE HERO*

Judy

The Unforgettable Story of a Dog Who Went to War and Became a True Hero

Damien Lewis

Quercus

New York • London

Quercus

New York • London

© 2015 by Damien Lewis
First published in the United States by Quercus in 2014

Any member of educational institutions wishing to photocopy part or all of the work for classroom use or anthology should send inquiries to permissions@quercus.com.

ISBN 978-1-62365-667-6

Library of Congress Control Number: 2014951598

Distributed in the United States and Canada by
Hachette Book Group
1290 Avenue of the Americas
New York, NY 10104

Manufactured in the United States

10 9 8 7 6 5 4 3 2

www.quercus.com

Minitus acuminae—"Protected with a sting."
—Motto of the Yangtze River gunboat HMS *Gnat*

". . . even the mosquito was sick of the taste of blood."
—Alice Renshaw, pupil at Pensby High School for Girls,
on the Japanese POW camps of the Second World War

Acknowledgments

Special thanks are due to the following for their help in bringing this book to fruition. My literary agent, Annabel Merullo, her assistant, Laura Williams, and all the team at PFD, including but not limited to Rachel Mills and Alexandra Cliff. My film agent, Luke Speed. Richard Milner and Josh Ireland, my editors at Quercus, plus the entire team there—including but not limited to David North, Patrick Carpenter, Jane Harris, Caroline Proud, Dave Murphy, and Ron Beard. Heartfelt thanks to you all. Thanks also to Simon Fowler, for your expert and tenacious research capabilities, and to Tean Roberts, for reaching out as you did to survivors and their families.

Special thanks are due to the following who gave freely of their time, their expertise, and/or their life experiences to enable me to bring this story to life on these pages. First and foremost Rouse Voisey, who shared his incredible life story with me. Rouse, I am hugely and forever in your debt. Captain George W. Duffy, for sharing your incredible life story, for your fantastic written work, and for the ongoing assistance and encouragement. Peter Fyans and Fergus Anckorn, author and subject of the book *The Conjuror on the Kwai*, which tells the story of Fergus's life and his extraordinary survival as a Japanese prisoner of war. Thank you for your time, your memories, and your help. You were and remain an enormous inspiration to me. Lizzie Oliver, for your inspiration and enthusiasm and for your grandfather's sketches and memories and for reading various drafts. Meg Parkes, for your peerless expertise and your father's diaries and for your continuing assistance unto the very end. Phillip Wearne, for reaching out to some of the key people on my behalf, which proved invaluable. Adrienne Howell, of the Mere Literary Festival, for the generous introductions to those who were able to be of so much help in the writing of this book. David Tett, for the excellent volumes of postcards and correspondence from the POW camps. Heñk Hovinga, for your persistence in getting your book to me and your steadfast help and advice. Les Parsons, for sharing some of your great uncle's experiences as a prisoner of war of the Japanese. Imogen Holmes, for sharing some of your father's experiences as a prisoner of war of the Japanese. Tony Spero, also for sharing some of your father's experiences as a prisoner of war of the Japanese. Tyson Milne, for sharing some of your grandfather's experiences as a prisoner of war of the Japanese. Amanda Farrell and Jonathan Moffatt, for your assistance in the research and for providing invaluable contacts. My thanks are also due to those others who were of assistance to me but preferred to remain unacknowledged.

Finally, special thanks to my wife, Eva, and to David, Damien Jr., and Sianna-Sarah, for putting up with Dad's grumpy hours spent locked away in his study writing. Again.

Author's Note

During the Second World War and the years leading up to it, Judy, the dog whose story is told in these pages, adopted many human companions. However, there are sadly few if any survivors from those years. Throughout the period of the research for and the writing of this book I have endeavored to contact as many of Judy's adopted human companions as possible, plus surviving family members of those who have passed away. If there are further witnesses to her incredible story who are inclined to come forward, please do get in touch with me. I may be able to include further recollections of this wonderful dog in future editions.

Particularly when dealing with the prisoner-of-war years there are few written accounts of what took place. So many people remember Judy, her companions, and their adventures: so few documented those memories. This is understandable. The time spent by Allied servicemen as prisoners of war of the Japanese was terribly traumatic, and many did not want to speak about it. Many chose to take their stories to their graves. I am very grateful to those few still living who felt able to speak to me. Moreover, memories tend to differ, and apparently none more so than those from an environment like the Far East prisoner-of-war camps, in which so many days felt like a repeat of the hellish days that went before. There were so few milestones with which to mark the passing of time or to anchor the memories.

The passage of the decades has also served to further obscure memory. The few written accounts that do exist also tend to differ in matters of detail. Locations and time scale are often somewhat uncertain. That being said, I have done my best to provide a comprehensible sense of place, chronology, and narrative to the story as told in these pages. In the POW years in particular the methodology I have used to reconstruct where and when events took place is the "most likely" scenario. If two or more testimonies or sources point to a particular time or place, I have opted to use that account as most likely. Where necessary I have re-created small sections of dialogue to aid the story's flow.

The above notwithstanding, any mistakes herein are entirely of my own making, and I would be happy to correct any in future editions. Likewise, although I have endeavored to locate the copyright holders of the photos, sketches, and other images used in this book, again this has not always been straightforward or easy. I would be happy to correct any mistakes in the future editions.

*Dedicated to the members, coaches, players and gladiators of
Dorchester Rugby Foodball Club, Dorset, England.*

Preface

Only one animal ever achieved the dubious accolade of being made an official prisoner of war of the Japanese in World War Two. It was a dog. She was a beautiful and regal-looking English pointer and perhaps one of the most extraordinary of our canine companions ever to grace this earth.

In September 1942 she was given Japanese prisoner-of-war number 81A-Medan.

Her real name was Judy, or Judy of Sussex as her shipmates came to call her, for she spent most of her service life as the mascot of the Royal Navy gunboats the *Gnat* and the *Grasshopper*. But Judy of Sussex was much, much more than just a ship's dog. The way in which I came across her story drew me to it inexorably, convincing me that this was a tale that absolutely had to be told.

In the spring of 2013 I wrote a book called *War Dog* (although I prefer the title my American publishers gave it, *The Dog Who Could Fly*). It tells the story of Ant, the extraordinary German shepherd puppy rescued from no-man's-land who went on to fly numerous sorties with the RAF in the Second World War. In recognition of his heroic wartime exploits Ant—or Antis as he was renamed—was awarded the Dickin Medal, more commonly known as the Animal VC.

Ant's master was the Czech—later British—airman Robert Bozdech, with whom he flew into battle with RAF Bomber Command, was wounded, crash-landed, and faced death countless times. In among the photos of the postwar Dickin Medal ceremonies, I found one that appeared to show Antis receiving his medal along with two other dogs. The animal to the right of the photo was a striking-looking liver-and-white English pointer.

There was something compelling about that image and the animal it portrayed—a sense somehow of the dog's extraordinary courage and spirit that spoke across the decades. When next I met the Bozdech family—Robert Bozdech's surviving children—I showed them the photo and asked who the mystery dog might be. We were at Pip's—the eldest daughter's—lovely Devon farmhouse, having a family get-together to celebrate the publication of the book telling their father and Antis's story.

Pip took a look at the photo. "I think that must be Judy. Yes, it's got to be her. Isn't she lovely? She's another Dickin Medal winner, and she has the most wonderful story . . ."

Pip told me the little she knew of Judy's wartime exploits. Indeed, it did sound quite remarkable. My curiosity piqued, I made a promise to myself to try to find out more about the dog—but I was working on another book at the time, and any thoughts of looking into Judy's history fell by the wayside. That was until a second chance happening.

Some months later I was giving a talk at the fantastic Mere Literary Festival in green and leafy Wiltshire, in the south of England. At some stage after the talk I happened to mention to the festival organizer, the delightful Adrienne Howell, my interest in the story of the only animal ever to become a prisoner of war of the Japanese. She threw me a shrewd look, as if trying to assess just how much she should reveal to me.

"Well, you know, Mere has a long history associated with the prisoners of the Japanese in the Far East," she remarked. Adrienne paused for moment and then went on: "In fact, my uncle was one . . . And there are any number of other POW families in the area. But the man you should really speak to is Phillip Wearne. His father, the Reverend Wearne, was a prisoner along with my uncle. He buried my uncle and brought the news of his death back to my grandparents."

Adrienne very kindly offered to put me in touch with Philip Wearne, who she explained was very active in the FEPOW (Far East Prisoner of War) community.

"Of course," she added, "we've all heard of Judy's story. She was simply a wonderful dog. Extraordinary. What she did on the ships and in the POW camps—well, there's nothing quite like it."

Two chance conversations; two people telling me the same thing—*this dog was absolutely out of the ordinary*. My appetite for the story quickened. As Adrienne had predicted, Phillip Wearne was most forthcoming and helpful. He advised me that among others, I really needed to talk to one Lizzie Oliver. Her grandfather, Stanley Russell, was in the same camp as Judy, one of her many POW companions. And although it almost beggars belief, he'd somehow managed to keep a secret diary of his time in the camps, which, had it been discovered, could well have cost him his life at the hands of the Japanese and Korean guards.

Lizzie and I duly met at the Frontline Club, a London venue for those who write about, report on, or otherwise deal with the field of the front line and war. In the refined quiet of the wood-paneled club room, Lizzie explained to me that she was in the final stages of completing her Ph.D. on the Far East POW camps, much of which was inspired by her grandfather's diaries.

Her next comment to me was this: "Whenever you mention the Sumatran railway or the camps, everyone says: 'Oh, you mean the railway with the dog? Judy, wasn't it?' It's amazing: absolutely everyone you talk to remembers her with such affection." She laughs. "There were *people* suffering there also, as well as a dog, but she seems more famous than the railway or the camps! That gives you a sense of just how much she was loved by all who came across her."

Lizzie had a point. After serving for several wild, war-torn years as a ship's dog on the Royal Navy's Yangtze River gunboats, Judy had been bombed and shipwrecked repeatedly before ending up in the POW camps of north Sumatra, part of modern-day Indonesia. She and her fellow POWs had been forced to work on the so-called hell railway, driving a single-track railway through impossible jungle and knife-cut mountains in the center of what was then a land of utter wilderness, a veritable world lost in time.

This wasn't the Thai–Burma Death Railway, which is relatively well known today—the one immortalized in the 1957 film *The Bridge on the River Kwai* and more recently in the movie *The Railway Man*, starring Colin Firth. This was the *other* death railway—one built over 2,000 kilometers away, in Sumatra, by the Japanese, using Allied POWs and locals as slave labor.

If anything its story is even darker. Today, few if any have heard of Sumatra's hell railway or the terrible horrors endured there. But people might just have heard of the camp's dog—Judy!

With some reverence, Lizzie produced from her bag a large and heavy bound book—her grandfather's diary. "There's something I want to show you." She opened the diary at a place that she'd bookmarked. "There." She pointed at the page proudly. "Recognize it? So, who d'you think that is? It's unmistakably Judy. What other dog would ever look like that?"

Taking up half of one page was a hand-drawn sketch of a beautiful liver-and-white English pointer. She was snuffling about in the tropical undergrowth, seemingly searching for a rat to catch among the bamboo huts in which the prisoners were forced to live, packed in there like sardines.

"It's something that's almost never been written about," Lizzie explained. "There's so much told about the horrors of the camps: the brutality, the unspeakable things that were done to the POWs. But those are the things they were forced to suffer. They had no choice, of course. That wasn't how they survived. In part they survived by the choices they made—and keeping a dog or another pet was something that helped keep them going. It was a thread that pulled them back to a little piece of normality. It was something extra to keep alive for during a hard day's labor and to come back to at the end of the day. It offered a hint of home life, of family, of domesticated pets in the home."

Lizzie told me I really had to go and see Rouse Voisey, a ninety-two-year-old veteran of the Japanese prison camps. As far as she knew, he was the last living British survivor of the Sumatran railway, and no one would be better qualified to add layers of richness and texture to the story of the forgotten death railway and its celebrated dog. But before doing so I should meet Meg Parkes, she said. Meg's father had been a Japanese POW, and again, in a way that almost stretches credulity, he had managed to keep incredibly detailed diaries of his time in the camps.

The way in which a handful of POWs managed to keep these diaries is a gripping story in itself. More often than not they used scraps of paper scribbled on in the dead of night and then secreted in old jars or cans, which they buried in the camp graveyard. The two things the Japanese guards seemed utterly fearful of were insanity and death. Those POWs who had lost their minds were shunned by the Japanese, and anything to do with death was also to be avoided. It was their extreme necrophobia—their fear of death and dead bodies—that made the graveyard such a perfect hiding place for the illicit diaries.

In due course I did meet with Meg, and she very kindly gave me a copy of her father's diaries, writings that spoke of the extraordinary relationship he had with a pet cat in the camps, among other animals. Meg echoed Lizzie's sentiments—that the whole history of how the POWs relied upon animals to help get them through their hellish ordeal had never really been written about. There were even camps wherein the POWs tamed and then trained pigeons to carry messages to and from the outside world either to secure news or to let the world know they were still alive.

Simply extraordinary.

Meg was involved in a fantastic school project with Pensby High School for Girls, in Wirral, in the northeast of England. Tom Boardman, then a ninety-two-year-old survivor of the POW camps, had come to the school to talk about his experiences. The eleven- and twelve-year-olds were asked to write short poems, imagining themselves to be an animal—any animal—in the camps. Meg gave me a copy of the booklet they'd produced with snippets of their poems. They were incredibly poignant.

"And the cat said . . . the prisoners stroke me and think of home. I like it, but I am afraid of the hunger in their eyes." —Elena Davies

"And the dog barked . . . why are we here? And why do some of us disappear?" —Sophie Burns

"And the pigeon said . . . I'll carry their sad messages. I am their family and they are mine." —Alice Renshaw

But there was no story to rival Judy's, Meg added. She was truly a dog in a million. Meg, like Lizzie, advised me that the one person I really did need to meet was Rouse Voisey. In due course I drove up to rural Norfolk to meet the man himself. My GPS took me to a pretty bungalow that looks out over wild woods and rolling fields lying to one side of the neat row of houses in which he has his home.

Rouse had clearly been awaiting my arrival. He greeted me on the garden steps—an incredibly sprightly and sharp-looking ninety-two-year-old. We shook hands. He scrutinized me with a quick, piercing look, as if trying to appraise the caliber of the "young man" who had driven such a long way to speak to him about events that lay some seven decades in the past.

He glanced at the scenery, which was lit by a bleak winter's midday sun. "You know, on some days the birdsong is so loud that I can't hear myself greet my neighbors across the fence." He smiled. "I love it here. You're very welcome." He gestured to his half-open door. "Please, come in, come in."

Rouse was a remarkable man, to put it mildly. Not only was he a survivor of Sumatra's railway hell, he'd lived through what by his own admission was a "worse" slave-labor project under the Japanese. He was among a group of Allied POWs who were forced to clear the coral island of Haruku of its jungle in order to hack out a landing strip from the bare rock—in preparation for Imperial Japan's planned invasion of Australia, something that of course never happened. Haruku is an island in the Moluccas—the so-called Spice

Islands—but under the blistering sun and in the scorching heat and dust, building that runway had all but killed Rouse and so many of his fellows had died.

If that wasn't enough, he had then been loaded aboard one of Imperial Japan's so-called hell ships—rusting death traps used to transport POWs like slaves of old from one forced labor project to another—for a journey that he feared would be his last. So ill was he that he could remember little of the voyage prior to the sinking of the ship, the *Junyo Maru*, by a British submarine. It was, at the time, the worst maritime disaster in history in terms of confirmed loss of life: some 5,600 Allied prisoners of war plus local slave laborers perished at sea.

Somehow Rouse survived the shipwreck. In doing so he made it to Sumatra to join the many hundreds of POWs slaving in that living hell. It was then that he first heard about Judy, the de facto mascot of the trans-Sumatran railway. As with all those who'd spoken before him, Rouse was unable to mention Judy's name or recall her memory without a warm smile. He glanced at a photo of his own dog—now deceased—hanging on the living room wall.

"That was my dog, Shona. She was a tricolor English setter. She was the most loving, wonderful companion you could ever wish for. I used to take her to the office where I worked—she'd sleep under my desk. She had the most lovely nature. I put the leg of my chair on her ear once by accident. She didn't snarl or bark at me. She just rolled her eyes and whined, as if to say, *Hey, that really hurts, you know*. I never got another dog after Shona. I couldn't—not after her. And Judy—she was exactly that kind of a dog. There wasn't another like her."

Rouse went on to share with me stories from his time in the prison camps, with his fellows and their camp dog—ones that perhaps he'd never discussed with anyone before, not even his recently deceased wife. He ended our chat with this:

"I was amazed that a dog could survive it all. That Judy outlived the hell of that place—it was incredible. The Korean camp guards in particular—they used to eat dogs. And they had the power of life or death over us all. It makes you wonder how anyone got away with it—keeping a dog like Judy. It's all part of the wonder of her story."

I left Rouse's little bungalow with a box heaped full of yellowing newspaper articles, dog-eared books, photos, and reports from the POW camp survivors—much of the "library" that Rouse had built up over the years.

"Yes, yes—take it all," he reassured me as I asked again if he really was happy with me borrowing his library for a while. "I've got little use for it at my age. And if you need to come talk to me again, please do. I'm here on my own with nothing much to do other than watch the box—and there's never anything on but repeats these days!"

I loaded the precious container onto the backseat of my car, but as I went to say a last good-bye, Rouse held out a hand to restrain me. "You know, there's one question you never asked that people always tend to: *After what happened, do you hate the Japanese?* I rather like it that you felt you didn't need to ask that of me."

Rouse shook his head, his eyes lost in memories of the past. "No, no—I don't hate the Japanese. How can you hate an entire people? I hate the guards who did those unspeakable things to us. But I could never hate an entire people. I think the hate would eat you up. It would consume you." He laughed. "So that's probably how I've lived to such a ripe old age!"

After visiting Rouse I spent time with other survivors of the POW camps and their relatives and families, learning more about the story that was beginning to captivate me. Fergus Anckorn, the irrepressibly youthful ninety-five-year-old who survived the POW camps through his use of magic—he was once the youngest and is now the oldest member of the legendary magic circle—told me about his own incredible relationships with pets in the POW camps, including a dog, monkeys, and even a chameleon! The chameleon would lie on his chest at night while he was sleeping and flick out its tongue to catch mosquitoes. It was his de facto mosquito net!

"Those pets—they kept us sane, you know. They were a little tiny slice of the familiar, of what we knew—of home. And somehow, you knew you had to stay alive and return at the end of a day's hard labor to look after your dog or monkey or whatever was waiting faithfully for you! You had to stay alive for *them*."

Fergus told me about the value of those pets in sustaining the prisoners' morale—or, more accurately, their will to live. In many cases, individuals opted to share some of their meager ration with their pet animal rather than allowing another living being to starve to death. Fergus loved dogs. He had a relationship with them that went very deep and was incredibly enduring. He was a cat lover too.

"Once I spotted a tiny bird like a sparrow on a bush," he told me, a rare sadness creeping into his mischievous, fun-filled eyes. "I stalked up to that bird on hands and knees. On the other side of the bush was an emaciated cat. It was a race between the two of us. I saw the cat spring, the bird took off to escape, and—*pow!*—I caught the tiny bundle of feathers in midair. I cooked that little bird and ate it that very evening. But when I looked at the pile of bones afterward, I felt so guilty that I'd left the cat to starve. I never could forget it or forgive myself."

Like Rouse, Fergus believed that those POWs who hated the Japanese were eventually consumed by their hatred. Those who forgave lived longer and happier lives. And Fergus was one of many who'd go on to explain to me the vital role that pets played as the unsung heroes of the prison camps. It was a story that few had told and one that Judy epitomized more than any other animal that had made it through the hell of the prison camp years.

This, then, is Judy's tale. It opens in Shanghai several years before the start of the war, when British gunboats still cruised the mighty Yangtze River, guarding British interests far into the heart of China. It commences with a tiny bundle of curiosity that ran away from home and ended up serving as the mascot of the doughty Royal Navy gunboat the *Gnat*. It follows Judy and her fellows' extraordinary adventures over the years—from the Yangtze River to the Sumatran hell railway and everything in between.

People often say that truth is stranger than fiction. Undoubtedly, Judy of Sussex's story is one that anyone would find distinctly challenging to make up.

It is certainly one that I feel privileged to have been able to tell.

Damien Lewis,
Cork, Ireland, December 2013

CHAPTER ONE

The tiny puppy wiggled her nose a little farther under the wire.

Blessed with a gundog's excellent peripheral vision, she was keeping one eye on those to her rear—her fellow siblings, plus the kennel staff, who would little appreciate yet another escape attempt. Ahead of her, just a breath away, lay the outside world—the teeming hustle and bustle of life that lay all around but that she and her fellow pups were seemingly forever forbidden from experiencing.

It was all just so tantalizingly close.

The English-run Shanghai Dog Kennels had bred the beautiful liver-and-white English pointer puppies to serve as gundogs for various English gentlemen then resident in Shanghai. But this one pup, it seemed, had other ideas. The kennels were like an island of calm amid the sea of chaos that was 1936 Shanghai—chaos to which the puppy poised halfway under the wire felt irresistibly drawn.

Before her very nose rickshaws—ancient-looking wooden carts pulled by human bearers—tore back and forth as they weaved through the dusty streets, carrying the better-off Shanghai residents trussed up in formal-looking top hats and dress coats. Those rickety carriages fought for space with streetcars and buses, chugging their ponderous way past roadside stalls selling freshly fried and spiced delicacies. And everywhere bright red cloth banners hung from the shopfronts, advertising their wares in exotic-looking Mandarin and Wu calligraphy.

Why it was only she of her siblings who felt this insatiable urge to see, to smell, and to taste the wider world—*to escape*—she didn't know. But ever since birth, curiosity had seemed to get the better of this still nameless puppy. And now here she was, glistening nose thrust under the wire and twitching at the bewitching smells that assaulted it, round and chubby backside still within the safe confines of the kennel, but with only a few more wriggles and a final squeeze required to break free.

Doubtless, one voice inside the pup's head was telling her: *Don't do it!* But another, equally strident voice was urging—*Go for it, girl!* In that moment of indecision as she peered beneath the wire the little puppy heard a yell of alarm from behind. *She'd been spotted!* It was the cry of Lee Ming, the local Chinese girl whose mother lived and worked at the kennels, raising the alarm. Lee Ming was quick and nimble and would be on her like a flash unless she got a move on.

Tiny forepaws thrashed and scrabbled at the dirt as she fought to squeeze her way under the wire. The wrinkly folds of puppy fat rolled and gave beneath her as she got her belly down even lower and wriggled like a fat fish stuck on an angler's hook. The bare stub of a tail, sticking out behind her like a long and rigid finger, twitched to and fro as she strove with all her might to break free.

Behind her Lee Ming came to a sudden halt and reached to grab the disobedient puppy, but as she did so the tiny ball of irrepressible energy gave one last Herculean effort and she was through. An instant and a scamper later and—*poof!*—the diminutive four-legged figure was gone, paws flying as she was swallowed up into the noise and dust and utter disorder of downtown Shanghai.

For a horrible moment Lee Ming stared after the puppy that had disappeared, in complete dismay. There were so many dangers stalking those city streets that she didn't have the heart to imagine the half of them. If there was one thing the little puppy wasn't, it was streetwise. In her headlong confusion she might be run over by a rickshaw. In her fright she might tumble into one of the city's myriad open sewers. But worst of all, a roly-poly puppy like her would offer a tantalizing meal to those partial to dog meat—which included a large majority of the city's native population.

In 1936 Shanghai the flesh of man's best friend was much sought after, being seen as something of a "sweet"-tasting delicacy. A young and tender dog that no one seemed to own or to care for would be fair game. Lee Ming turned back toward the large colonial-style house that lay in the center of the kennel compound. She headed for reception to report the bad news and to help raise whatever search party they would send after the wayward pup. But her heart was heavy, and a dark foreboding lay upon her.

She feared very much that this was the last they'd ever see of the puppy that had run away.

The Shanghai that the puppy had made a break for was no place for any defenseless being, let alone an English pointer barely a few weeks old. Then a city of some 3 million inhabitants, Shanghai—a port city lying in the very center of China's coastline—was a bustling metropolis red in tooth and claw. Because of its position at the mouth of the mighty Yangtze River—Asia's longest and a vital conduit for trade and commerce into China's vast interior—the great powers of Britain, America, and France had long-established trading settlements in the city.

For decades, Shanghai had been known as the Paris of the East, but in recent years it had become a city beset by troubles. Weak leadership and infighting in the Chinese government had allowed vicious gangs of bandits to thrive. Warlords had taken control of large tracts of the nation's interior. Increasingly, Britain, America, and France had been forced to send gunboats far into the interior on the Yangtze in an effort to dissuade those lawless elements from disrupting their lucrative trade in silk, cotton, tea, and other valuable commodities.

Recently, trouble had piled upon trouble, in particular with the resurgence of China's age-old enemy—Japan. In an escalating series of bloody skirmishes the Japanese Navy had bombarded Shanghai. As they had with the British and the other "great powers," the

Chinese were forced to sign a treaty with Imperial Japan, allowing the Japanese to establish a permanent presence in the "treaty port" of Shanghai. Imperial Japan made little secret of its desire to conquer and subjugate the entire Chinese nation, and Shanghai was the gateway to China's then capital city, Nanking.

This then was Shanghai, the city that the escapee from the kennels had absconded to—one menaced by gangland banditry, whose streets were increasingly plagued by soldiers from Imperial Japan, who showed ill-disguised contempt for the local inhabitants. So it was something of a miracle that several weeks after her dramatic breakout, the puppy who had run away was still very much alive and breathing.

The silky chubbiness was long gone, of course. Instead, adolescent ribs poked through a liver-and-white coat that had lost much of its shine and luster. Her nose was dry and cracked, a sure sign that she was in a dreadful condition. Only her eyes seemed to demonstrate their signature brightness, betraying a strength of character that had distinguished her from birth and perhaps led to her present, unenviable predicament. They shone with a burning curiosity and a zest for life despite all that she had suffered since her ill-fated escape. But there was something else now in her gaze—uncertainty and vulnerability, a sense that the young dog had realized to her cost that not every human was her natural friend and ally.

How stupid she had been, she now recognized, to run away. She had traded the comfort and luxury of the kennels for a battered old cardboard box lying in a smelly, flyblown Shanghai alleyway. She'd traded the companionship and playfulness of her brother and sister puppies for the loneliness of life on the streets. And in place of the English kennel owner's natural love for and protection over her dogs, she'd faced cruelty and abuse at every turn in this overcrowded human zoo of a city.

All apart from one individual—Soo. For whatever reason, Soo the Chinese trader was an unreconstructed lover of dogs. Her shabby box-cum-home lay to the rear of his store, and ever since the puppy had found her way to it Soo had taken it upon himself to deliver tidbits of food to her of an evening when his long day's work was done. It was hardly the kind of diet she'd grown accustomed to at the kennels, but at least it had served to keep her alive.

Like many Chinese, it wasn't in Soo's nature or family tradition to keep a dog at home as a pet. In the China of 1936 dogs had to earn their keep as working animals, or they were invariably for the pot. In fact, the eating of dog meat in China had a history stretching back thousands of years, the meat being thought to possess mystical medicinal properties. There were even some breeds of dog that were kept specifically for human consumption, especially in times of seasonal hunger.

Fortunately, Soo wasn't one of those who were partial to having dog on the menu, and the lost puppy from the Shanghai Dog Kennels was lucky indeed to have fallen by chance under his protection.

But tonight, all of that was about to change.

With a sixth sense that was to become her absolute trademark, the lonely pup detected the danger before it was audible or visible to any human ear or eye, Soo's included. A Japanese gunboat had docked in the port of Shanghai, and the sailors of His Japanese Imperial Majesty's ship were making their noisy way along the very road upon which Soo's shop was situated, no doubt in search of alcohol and some locals on whom to vent their aggression. It was late evening, but the hardworking Soo was still there, his being one of the few stores on the street remaining open.

That alone offered enough of an excuse for the gunboat crew to pounce.

As the Japanese sailors started verbally abusing Soo and helping themselves to his wares, he of course protested. Voices were raised in anger, but the Japanese sailors didn't stop there. Within minutes Soo's shop had been plundered, its rickety wooden shelves torn down and smashed to pieces. As for Soo, he was set upon by the Japanese sailors, who were working themselves into a towering rage.

Hearing her one protector in the world being so cruelly assaulted, the adolescent pup had stolen out of her alleyway and snuck around the corner to see if there was anything she could do to save him. Inching forward on her belly, she alternately whim-pered in fright and tried to muster her most threatening growl as the strange figures in their baggy pants over knee-high black boots kicked and punched her protector.

Then one of the aggressors spotted the cowering dog. He stepped away from Soo and took a few paces toward her. Moments later one of those perfectly polished boots was swinging toward the adoles-cent puppy's midriff. The powerful blow lifted her from the cobbles and flung her across the street into a pile of trash on the far side. There she lay, whimpering and in agony and hoping beyond hope that these cruel men in their strange uniforms wouldn't come for her again.

By the time their oppressors had departed, Soo had been beaten so badly that he had to be helped away from the scene. The dog that had until now had viewed him as her protector was forced to take refuge in the empty shadows of a nearby doorway. Into it she crawled, body sore from the kicking, her belly sore from that and the ravening hunger, and her spirit numbed by the trauma and the cold of the long night that lay ahead.

Even though the Japanese sailors were long gone, the lonely puppy sensed that tonight her dream of escape from the Shanghai Dog Kennels had descended into the blackest of nightmares—but as is so often the case, the darkest moment is just before the dawn.

As the sun crept above the city's grand colonial-style skyline, a familiar figure began to pad her way along the street on which the young dog lay. The lone puppy was shivering and crying to herself and lost in misery—so much so that she almost didn't notice the pitter-patter of footsteps come to a halt or hear the words uttered in amazement in her direction.

"Shudi? Shudi? Oh, Shudi! What happened? Where have you been?"

The stubby tail of the pointer—now stained off-white with the dirt and soot from her streetside existence—almost failed to wag in any sign of recognition. But the young dog *had* recognized the soft tones of the voice, just as surely as the little girl from the kennels had recognized the distraught puppy. Her distinctive markings—a sleek liver-brown head, a similarly colored saddle-like marking thrown across her shoulders, plus the large formless splotch of color splashed across her rear right flank—had been instantly recognizable to Lee Ming.

No doubt about it—this was the one that had run away!

In a sprawling city of some 3 million inhabitants the girl from the Shanghai Dog Kennels had by chance chosen to walk that morning past the very door where the lost and injured dog was sheltering. Lee Ming bent, scooped the puppy up, and thrust her deep inside her jacket. With that she ran and skipped through the largely deserted streets, eager to announce her find to the English lady who ran the kennels.

By the time she had reached the big house that lay inside the compound and unzipped her jacket, the puppy had fallen fast asleep.

"Look! Look! I find Shudi!" the little girl announced ecstatically.

The Englishwoman peered doubtfully over the high desk behind which she sat. Spying the puppy, she reached out uncertainly and took the little dog from the girl's outstretched arms. She pulled her closer, stroked her, and fondled her just behind the ears as she studied the markings and tried to compare them with those in her memory. The puppy opened one lazy eye, saw where she was, seemed to smile exhaustedly, and then slipped back into a sweet sleep.

It was the turn of the Englishwoman to smile. "*It is her*. It really is the one who ran away." She glanced at Lee Ming, who was beaming with happiness. "So I think it's time you gave her a good bath and a dinner, don't you?"

Lee Ming nodded enthusiastically. There was nothing she'd like more than to feed and comfort the wayward pup. She held out her arms so Shudi could be returned to her and she could whisk her off for some much-needed tender loving care.

The woman handed the pup across. She glanced at Lee Ming curiously. "But tell me, why do you call her Shudi?"

Lee Ming placed the warm but exhausted bundle back inside her jacket. "I always call this one Shudi," she replied shyly. "*Shudi* means 'peaceful.' Peaceful is how she looks, yes?"

The woman reached out and caressed Lee Ming's face. "She does. Yes, she does. And Lee Ming—that shall be her name from now on: *Judy*."

So it was that the puppy who had run away and come back again against all odds was given a name perhaps most ill suited to her nature: the Mandarin word for the peaceful one—*shudi*—rendered into "Judy" for whichever lucky Englishman might be her future master.

As the little girl carried Shudi—Judy—off for a good pamper, little did she realize how a dog with such inauspicious beginnings would go on to distinguish herself in the coming bloody and all-consuming conflict . . .

Lee Ming could have no idea how famous the English pointer from the Shanghai Dog Kennels would become once the Second World War drew to a close.

CHAPTER TWO

Even in the summer of 1936, four years prior to the start of the war, the signs of Japanese imperial aggression were sweeping through the streets of Shanghai and across wider China.

Using her military might, Imperial Japan would strike a hammer blow through Shanghai and into the Chinese capital, Nanking—a name that would become synonymous with unspeakable terror and brutality. But for now such dark horrors lay far in the future, and much of the city of Shanghai and the Yangtze River remained under the stewardship of the British and Allied gunboat fleets.

The British gunboats were of the Insect class, a name that belied their true purpose, which was to patrol the shallow seas and rivers across the more war-torn reaches of the British Empire. Built by the Lobnitz shipyard on the Clyde, the Insect class ships had initially seen active service during the First World War in what was then Mesopotamia (modern-day Iraq), patrolling the Tigris and Euphrates rivers.

By 1936 they were two decades old and were by no means state-of-the-art warships. But they remained relatively fast, nimble, and well armed. With their flat bottom and shallow draft, they were designed specifically to operate in rapidly flowing rivers like the Yangtze. Known colloquially as the "large China gunboats," they boasted two Yarrow engines and boilers, each driving a separate propeller set in a shaft sunk into the hull to minimize the chance of snagging in the river shallows.

As Shudi—Judy—settled into the blissful comfort of kennel life once again, one of those British gunboats was just completing her annual refit at the Shanghai docks. She was preparing to return to patrol duties, deterring piracy and banditry on the lower reaches of the Yangtze—covering a length of river stretching almost a thousand miles inland.

HMS *Gnat* had not been a particularly happy ship of late, and much of the crew's angst centered on two key aspects of ship's life that were in distinctly short supply right then. The first was the ship's stocks of beer. The China gunboats were unique in the Royal Navy in that they carried with them a stock of beer from which, when on operations, every crew member got a daily allowance. But as the captain of the *Gnat*, Lieutenant Commander Waldegrave, had commented in the ship's log, there was only a few weeks' supply of the precious brew remaining, even with strict rationing in force.

Recently a United States Navy gunboat had docked alongside the *Gnat*. The officers and crew had been invited to share in the British gunboat's hospitality—chiefly her beer—but only once a week on Saturday nights in an effort to preserve stocks. In exchange, the officers and crew of the *Gnat* had been invited to the thrice-weekly movie screenings held in the American ship's cinema.

The second problem was unique to the *Gnat* among the British gunboat flotilla then on the Yangtze: she lacked a ship's mascot, which if anything was even more unthinkable than running out of beer. On her sister ships HMS *Cricket, Cicada,* and *Ladybird* and the flagship, the *Bee,* there were variously cats, dogs, and even a ship's monkey. But the crew of the *Gnat* possessed no furry, four-legged, or even feathered friend, and so it was that the ship's captain set his junior officers the task of finding one.

The junior officers had in turn called upon the resources of the *Gnat*'s canteen committee in an effort to decide which would be the most suitable species of bird, mammal, or reptile to grace the vessel's deck. The nominations had flooded in, but many—Chinese soft-backed river turtles, giant pandas, and alligators included—were judged as being somewhat impractical and inappropriate, if good for laughs.

The canteen committee decided that any mascot for the *Gnat* had to possess three essential qualities. First, as the ship's officers and crew could really do with some female company, she would have to be distinctly feminine. Second, she would have to be easy on the eyes. And third, for practical reasons she would need to be able to earn her keep. So it was that on an early November afternoon in 1936 a delegation of junior officers left the *Gnat* to pay a visit to the Shanghai Dog Kennels.

Like most gundogs, English pointers are blessed—or cursed—with a surfeit of energy. They have been bred to be powerful, alert, and absolutely tireless no matter what extent of terrain they are tasked to cover. Such are the qualities required of a dog whose purpose is to locate, chase after, flush out, and—very often—retrieve game. Essentially a hunting dog, a pointer should be always at the ready to let fly.

Judy had certainly proved herself ready to let fly when she'd squirmed under the kennel wire and run away. Even for an extremely high-energy breed like pointers, she'd shown herself to have an extraordinary abundance of get-up-and-go. On first consideration, these weren't perhaps the ideal qualities for a ship's mascot—one that was going to be constrained to the confines of a vessel that measured 237 feet from stem to stern and 36 feet across. But as soon as they'd spotted her, the junior officers of the *Gnat* seemed oddly convinced that Judy was the one for them.

By now she was approaching six months old and had fully recovered from her stint as a Shanghai street dog. She was striking-looking, holding herself with a poise that seemed to mark her out as a true aristocrat of the breed. She carried her head high on a graceful but powerful neck, and her dark eyes—like glistening coals—were set well back from her long, sweeping muzzle. She gazed at these strange men in their smart uniforms who had come to inspect her, displaying the shy reserve natural to a female of the breed.

To the delegation from the *Gnat*, blissfully unaware of Judy's epic escape and long sojourn in the back alleyways of Shanghai, she seemed like the perfect lady. As an added bonus she was a gundog, which would mean that any shooting parties sent ashore to secure meat for the galley would have a dog to root out and retrieve game. Though not specifically bred as retrievers, pointers can be trained to chase down and gather anything that has been shot—or at least that's the theory.

Back at the *Gnat* the last of the ship's stores and ammunition was being stowed away belowdecks in preparation for pending departure—including supplies of bread, beef, and fuel (gas and kerosene), plus coal. The last licks of paint were being applied to cover the odd patches of rust on the superstructure. The Chinese mess boys—locals employed to help cook and make tea in the galley—had returned from their shore leave, and they were preparing the first brews back aboard ship.

A gaggle of seamen were milling about on the mess deck, situated in the ship's bows, preparing to change into fresh white uniforms for one of their final nights ashore. It was then that the head of the coxswain—the officer in charge both of steering the vessel and of managing the ship's crew—appeared through the open hatch from the main deck above and made an announcement.

"All hands on deck in ten minutes!"

As the sailors pulled on their uniforms, they wondered what on earth might be up. Surely not something that would prevent them from having one of their last nights ashore? In keeping with its wild and exotic reputation Shanghai was a party town par excellence, and no one wanted to be kept from the bars where the beer flowed freely—as opposed to the dwindling supplies aboard the *Gnat*.

The men gathered anxiously on the foredeck, forming two ranks beneath the long canvas awning that stretched practically from one end of the ship to the other. It lent the vessel a somewhat odd appearance, the lengthy covering resembling almost a roof and making the *Gnat* seem from a distance like an elongated streetcar at sea. But the awning had proved hugely useful during long patrols up the Yangtze, providing shade to the main deck and shelter from the monsoon rains that would sweep the length of the great river.

"Atten-shun!" the ship's coxswain called once all were present. "Ship's company mustered, sir," he reported to a figure standing close by.

The *Gnat*'s first lieutenant, R. Haines, stepped forward and mounted an empty wooden ammunition crate, one that would normally carry rounds for the ship's .303-caliber Vickers machine guns. Three of these light machine guns—a weapon that had become synonymous with the projection of Great Britain's colonial power—were positioned on either side of the boat, giving her impressive all-around firepower. But right now it was far less warlike matters that the first lieutenant had on his mind. Having given the order to stand easy, he began to address the men, the faint suggestion of a smile flickering across his normally inscrutable features.

"A few weeks back the canteen committee, with myself as chairman, passed a resolution to the effect that we would have a ship's pet." He paused, as if checking a sheet of paper in his hand, and then continued, the smile creeping farther into his eyes. "To remind you, we decided on having some female companionship, a lady who would be attractive and could earn her keep. I have studied your very interesting suggestions, most of which I regrettably had to discard."

The first lieutenant eyed the men ranged before him. "On the *Bee* they have two cats," he continued. "The *Cricket* has a dog—of sorts. The *Cicada* has a monkey—heaven help them!" A long, weighty pause. "As for the *Gnat*, from this moment onwards no shooting party will be able to return to ship claiming to have shot twenty-three quail but only one could be found."

He turned and let out a cry: "Quartermaster!"

A figure emerged from the door behind him, one that led into the ship's superstructure and up to the bridge. A few paces to his rear a head appeared at knee level, peering curiously around the door frame. As the quartermaster—the ship's storekeeper—pulled gently on a leash, the rest of the figure stepped into the light. It was a four-legged creature—a white English pointer with dramatic liver-colored markings across her head and body.

The quartermaster moved to where everyone could see. All eyes were on the dog. Not yet fully grown, she had an odd, endearing, floppy kind of a walk as she padded across the deck on paws that still seemed too big for her body. Man and dog came to a halt between the first lieutenant and the phalanx of ship's crew ranged before him. Judy proceeded to plunk herself down, her well-bred ladylike air evaporating as a large floppy pink tongue lolled out from what appeared to be a decidedly goofy grin.

It was as much as the men could do not to dissolve into laughter.

The first lieutenant swept his arm theatrically across the dog now squatted before him. "Here she is, then, gentlemen. Meet the first lady of the gunboats. Meet Judy—RN!"

Judy was given a right royal welcome by the crew of the *Gnat*. They picked the nickname Judy of Sussex for her in keeping with her purebred, aristocratic kind of attitude. Sussex was chosen for no other reason than that it was a very long way from Shanghai and because several of the ship's crew hailed from that part of England.

The natural choice for the important post of Keeper of the Ship's Dog fell to Able Seaman Jan "Tankey" Cooper. Tankey was in charge of the ship's food stores and fresh water, but more important, he was also the ship's butcher, which meant he was able to lay his hands on a regular supply of bones.

Via Tankey, Judy was allotted an open-topped box—an empty ammunition crate—positioned near the ship's bridge, plus a ship's blanket, as her sleeping quarters. But in the coming weeks and months she would be found as often as not elsewhere, so much preferable was it to be curled up fast asleep with one of the ship's crew.

Judy was even given an official ship's book number. Every man serving in the Royal Navy had a unique set of letters and numerals assigned to him, for example, JX125001. It identified him as serving in one of four pay grades: 1. Seamen and Communicators, 2. Stokers, 3. Officers, Cooks, and Stewards, 4. All others. Judy's number identified her with the "MX" prefix, meaning she was an "All others" and that she had joined the service after 1925, before which a different system of numbering and lettering was in place.

Judy's ship's number didn't confer any wage-earning status on her, for it hadn't been formally logged with the Admiralty yet. But had the officers of the *Gnat* so desired, they could doubtless have gotten away with it, for the ship's number system was famously confused and confusing. Many a Royal Navy sailor had the same number as another, only one letter in the prefix differentiating the two.

But in any case, Judy would have little need of money now she was aboard the *Gnat*. Life as a ship's dog was going to prove as fine an approximation to doggie paradise as any—or at least in the early months it would. On the *Gnat*, Judy of Sussex was going to have everything she could wish for or that money could buy, including a surfeit of food, good company, warmth, and companionship.

Being a gundog and one intended to earn her keep, Judy was supposed to be kept away from the crew, in the officers' quarters positioned—unusually—toward the front of the ship. Indeed, it was the ship's captain, Lieutenant Commander Waldegrave, plus the chief petty officer, Charles Jefferey, who had forked out the money to buy her on behalf of the ship's company. As such, they reckoned they had every right to keep her to their quarters and to train her "for the gun"—to act as a ship's officers' gundog.

Pointers are bred to do just as their name suggests—to point out prey. A pointer is supposed to adopt a rigid pose whenever a game animal is scented. Though it can differ from dog to dog, classically speaking, an English pointer is supposed to adopt the following pose: head lowered, tail held horizontal in line with the head, one leg raised and bent at the wrist, paw pointing to guide the hunter to the target.

But as the officer's mess boy aboard the *Gnat* was among the first to point out, in Judy's case there seemed to be a fatal flaw in her pointing abilities. In her first forty-eight hours aboard ship she seemed to go rigid or to point at only one thing: whenever she could smell the delicious aroma of dinner wafting around the *Gnat*, she'd point unerringly at the ship's galley!

No problem, the ships' officers argued. They'd train her to point at the right kind of thing—chiefly the duck, quail, antelope, and gazelle that they were keen to hunt along the Yangtze. But there just seemed to be no way of controlling where this taut bundle of energy would be found next aboard ship. Her inquisitive nose took her to just about every nook and cranny, and it was only ever from one quarter—the Chinese mess boys and cooks—that she seemed to receive anything other than a rapturous welcome.

No matter what the officers' intentions, from the very start the ship's company treated Judy as a much-favored pet. It was as if she was everybody's companion—which, indeed, as ship's dog arguably she was supposed to be. Owned by nobody, she was everyone's dog, and therein lay the impediment to any serious attempts to train her for the gun. Likewise, Tankey Cooper's strict efforts to regulate her meals proved equally frustrating. Whenever his back was turned, squares of chocolate and even the odd glass of beer were slipped in the young dog's direction.

By the time HMS *Gnat* was ready for departure from Shanghai, in the second week of November 1936, the ship's captain and chief petty officer—those who had originally procured the dog—had accepted Judy's shortcomings with reluctant good grace. She was first and foremost a ship's dog and not a gundog, and in that she was proving herself wildly successful. Not a man among the *Gnat*'s crew hadn't warmed to her, and Judy's presence aboard ship had proved a much-needed boost to morale.

Having survived the menacing streets of Shanghai, Judy appeared to be set for a long and happy career aboard HMS *Gnat*, gallant ship of the Royal Navy's Yangtze gunboat fleet. But as chance would have it, Judy's next close encounter with mortal danger was but a few turns of the ship's screw away.

And once again, it was curiosity that would almost prove the death of her.

CHAPTER THREE

For decades the scientific study of dogs—and much of the theory around their training—has relied upon the example provided by their ancient ancestor, the wolf. Unlikely as it may seem, all modern-day dogs—from Pekingese to Great Danes—are descendants of one species, *Canis lupus*, the gray wolf. Dogs share 99.96 percent of their DNA with the wolf.

But those genetics have been overlain with up to 30,000 years of selective breeding and, more important, domestication. Many millennia ago humans and dogs began what was to be the most long-lived and enduring man-and-animal partnership of all. The dog was the first animal that we domesticated, and today dogs possess an ability to bond with and relate to humans that no other being can match.

The belief that dogs would revert to behaving like wolves in the absence of human influence long ruled the way we trained our canine companions. Studies suggested that wolves were pack animals, with two dominant adults—one male, one female—threatening violence or expulsion to subjugate those under them. Using the argument that dogs are essentially wolves, humans were thought to have to dominate their canine pets, to prove they were the master of the pack.

In recent years much of this thinking has been turned on its head. Most studies of wolf packs were carried out in captivity, generally in zoos. Captive packs were made up of a discordant group of animals thrown together arbitrarily and with little relevance to the wild. Recent studies of wolf packs as they occur in nature prove them to be nothing more menacing than extended family units.

In nature the wolf pack usually consists of one breeding pair, plus their adolescent offspring, who help the adults bring up new cubs. The pack can turn violent, but only against another pack that tries to encroach upon its territory. Wolves, then, are naturally sociable, family-oriented animals. Within the family unit—the so-called pack—they exhibit cooperation, kindness, and care toward one another.

Likewise, most dogs simply want to feel part of the family and to enjoy family life, as others in the family unit—whether human or canine—do. Viewed in this context, training dogs by employing dominant behavior, threats, and even physical punishment is about as appropriate as doing so with a child. What dogs respond to best is love, reward, and play—and, crucially, being made to feel an integral part of the family. And luckily for Judy, she'd just fallen into the biggest, most playful and fun-loving family she ever could have wished for.

Life aboard a Yangtze gunboat was by necessity closely knit and familial. With a crew numbering in the fifties—Chinese cooks and kitchen boys not included—the *Gnat*'s company wasn't a great deal bigger than your average wolf pack. Most such packs are happy family units wherein disagreements do happen but are usually resolved harmoniously. Cooperation, not coercion, is the rule.

While Judy had yet to find her two-legged "master" aboard the *Gnat*—someone with whom to bond absolutely—within the first few days of coming aboard she was at one with the closely knit band of the ship's crew. She was at home with them all. And by the time the *Gnat* was ready to set sail, Judy of Sussex appeared to have grown well accustomed to life aboard ship. She seemed to be finding her sea legs and to be more than ready for the long voyage into the country's interior.

At 0800 hours on November 10, 1936, the *Gnat*'s crew began stowing away the last of the stores in preparation for the departure.

At 0900 hours the special sea-duty crewmen and cable parties prepared to cast off. Like all dogs, Judy had an uncanny ability to read human body language and actions. She dashed about the *Gnat*, sniffing excitedly as cables were slipped and fenders hauled aboard.

Ten minutes later the *Gnat* had slipped anchor, the throb of the twin engines beginning to shake and vibrate the deck. Twenty minutes after that the ship pulled into shore again and tied up alongside the Asiatic Petroleum Company's wharf, where 68.1 tons of fuel oil were to be pumped aboard. Judy had just endured her first short voyage "at sea," and all aboard were mightily impressed by how she had behaved. But all of this had been in the comparatively sheltered waters of the Shanghai port. The word *Shanghai* itself means "on the ocean," and the city sits at the confluence of the Yangtze River and the East China Sea.

With the fuel oil pumped aboard, the vessel did an about-face, and at 1220 hours she began to steam to a new wharf, where she would load ammunition supplies. In addition to her six Maxim machine guns mounted aft of the bridge, the *Gnat* boasted a 12-pounder anti-aircraft gun, and a pair of 6-inch Mark VII guns, which were able to fire a forty-five-kilogram shell over a ten-kilometer range. The 6-inch guns were the largest caliber of any gunboat then serving on the Yangtze, lending the Insect class boats a punch that belied their name.

Life aboard the Yangtze gunboats was colorful, but it was also fraught with danger. Hostile vessels menaced the river waters. The Yangtze was wild and unpredictable in places, and ships could easily be driven ashore or dashed to pieces on the rocky sides of the gorges through which they passed. The constant tension and danger took an inevitable toll, and young sailors needed quality downtime in which to destress and unwind. Shanghai, with its wild bars and subterranean clubs, offered them ample opportunity to do so.

But as always was the case when young sailors went partying, there were some at least who were loath to leave the joys of the shore behind them. In the past few days Captain Waldegrave had been forced to send two of the *Gnat*'s crew to the military detention quarters in Shanghai for thirty days' punishment. No doubt the sailors in question had found the beer supplies aboard the *Gnat* somewhat wanting, or perhaps they had balked at leaving a local girl behind them.

But at the same time, the captain had also found cause to issue a number of good conduct badges to his crew, and he had written up at least one for a good conduct medal. Overall, the seamen were pulling together admirably, and the captain put that down in part to the newest arrival among them. But while she'd brought them great joy and a renewed sense of purpose, Judy was about to prove that she could also bring them a great deal of trouble.

It was on the morning of November 14 when the *Gnat* finally slipped her mooring for the long voyage upriver. She steamed eastward at first, heading out to sea, before turning west into the churning maw that forms the vast expanse of the Yangtze River delta. Taking full advantage of her fourteen-knot speed and triple rudders—which gave her a tight turning circle, which was crucial for operating in the narrow confines of the river's higher reaches— the *Gnat* began to battle against the ten-knot current that was sweeping this massive expanse of fresh water out to sea.

Here, where the mighty Yangtze drains into the East China Sea, the delta is over twenty miles wide: around the same width as the English Channel at its narrowest. Gazing out over the gray November water, both man and dog would need to remind them- selves that this was a river and not an ocean. Wild eddies and cur- rents swept beneath the flat bottom of the *Gnat*'s hull; powerful waves and swells the size of ocean rollers rumbled past her sides. The cold, muddy, gray-yellow water was heavy with silt, and every now and again a swirling whirlpool spun across their path, sucking nameless debris into its depths.

As the port city faded into the distance, land was barely visible. Instead of the steady hustle and bustle of Shanghai harbor life, a new sound filled the crew's ears. It was the unearthly hollow rush- ing of the river as the *Gnat* fought her way upstream, passing over the sandbanks and mudflats that litter the Yangtze's final approach to the sea. The noise rose to a deafening roar each time the flat-bottomed vessel clawed over the narrowest of shallows, where the depth decreased to a matter of feet, then died down again as the riverbed plunged to some 100 feet or more in depth.

During the weeks that she'd spent living on the streets of Shanghai, Judy had become accustomed to the roar of the city—the ceaseless cacophony of engines, voices, industry, and human endeavor. But this was something entirely different. This was the throaty bellow of a wild waterway—the third longest river in the world—tantalizingly close and at its most awe-inspiring. This was the breathtaking power of nature distilled into a surging mass of water, and the wild, untamed strangeness of it all drew Judy to it . . . like a moth to the proverbial candle flame.

Chief Petty Officer Jefferey was the first to realize the danger. He was moving aft when he caught sight of the dog that he had half paid for nosing around by the ship's rail. As he yelled out a cry of warning, he saw her slip beneath the rail until she was poised on the polished steel plates of the outboard—the narrow outer edge of the deck. Judy gazed at the frothing water below, seemingly as unheeding of Jefferey's cries of alarm as she had been of Lee Ming's a few months earlier at the Shanghai Dog Kennels.

She danced from paw to paw, uttering excited yelps and barks at the deafening gray monster that churned and roared a few dozen feet beneath her outstretched forelegs. But a moment later Judy lost her footing completely, and with a despairing yelp she plunged out of view. Whoever said that it was curiosity that killed the cat had clearly never met the ship's dog of HMS *Gnat*!

An ashen-faced Jefferey turned and yelled to the bridge, screaming at the top of his voice in an effort to make himself heard.

"Dog overboard! Dog overboard! *DOG OVERBOARD!*"

The cry of "man overboard" is one of the last any sailor ever wants to hear at sea—but even less so on a waterway like the Yangtze. The combined speed of the river's flow and the *Gnat*'s forward progress meant that the ship's mascot was now being carried astern at something like fourteen knots, or a little over sixteen miles an hour. Jefferey's cry of "dog overboard" was equally unwelcome to those who caught it among a ship's crew who were growing to love and cherish their canine companion.

Fortunately, the captain was one of those who had heard, and he took immediate action. "Stop, and full astern! Stop, and full astern!"

Captain Waldegrave knew for certain what would happen if his ship didn't rapidly reverse its course. There wasn't the slightest chance he could turn the gunboat around in time. The climate in east-central China is similar to that in Continental Europe: it is temperate, with warm springs, hot summers, cool autumns, and bitter winters. The Yangtze in November would be icy cold, conditions that would quickly sap the reserves of even the toughest dog as she fought against the vicious currents and eddies. By the time he'd turned his ship around, Judy would have been swept far downstream in the chilly waters and lost.

She had fallen a little more than a dozen feet from the ship's rail, but even so she would have gone under, and fresh water has far less buoyancy than seawater, providing less chance of bringing a body back to the surface. All the captain could hope for was that Judy was a strong swimmer, one blessed with a gundog's natural instinct to fight for her survival—at least until they could come to her aid. Even so, he didn't rate her chances very highly. Either they got to her in the next few minutes or Judy of Sussex was going to a cold and watery grave.

By the time the captain had brought his vessel to a stop, man of action Leading Seaman Vic Oliver had readied the *Gnat*'s launch. Oliver would be on the tiller, with a colleague to operate the engine, and he had a somewhat reluctant Chinese boat boy called Wugle perched in the prow, charged with grabbing the errant dog. The diminutive craft was swung overboard and lowered over the side, but by the time she was in the water Oliver had lost all sight of the missing dog.

The last he'd seen of her was a distant black speck coursing downriver. He'd tried to fix her location in his mind so that he could steer the launch in the general direction. Unsighted as they now were, he

set off on the best bearing he could muster, the speed of the launch
combining with the current to propel the boat downriver like a cork
fired from a champagne bottle.

The little vessel slammed and bucked her way across the choppy
water, which close up appeared like a viscous orange soup as it
foamed and boiled around her prow. Oliver figured that by the time
they'd got the boat into the water Judy was maybe half a mile astern
of the *Gnat*. At the speed the launch was motoring, he reckoned
they'd overhaul her within two minutes—*if* he had them on the correct bearing.

He knew full well that if he'd gotten it wrong, they wouldn't get a
second chance. Many men had gone to their deaths in the Yangtze,
and a fall into the river this far from land very often spelled the end.
Oliver dreaded to think what the chances were for a not yet fully
grown dog.

Time dragged horribly. The boat fought its way across the river's surface for what seemed like an age. Then, quite suddenly they
crested a wave and sped past a black speck just visible off the port
side. The men in the launch had caught the flash of white forepaws
thrashing about frantically, eyes wide with fear as Judy fought to
prevent herself from being dragged under. She was keeping her
head above the turbid water, but only just.

Yelling out snatched words of encouragement, Oliver threw the
launch into a tight turn. This time they came back toward her on an
interception bearing and motoring upstream. The boat's progress
was far slower and more controlled as she fought the powerful current, and Oliver presumed that this time they had Judy within their
grasp. But as they slowed for the pickup and Wugle leaned over the
side to grab her collar, the boat pitched on a wave crest, and suddenly he was in the water too.

Boat boy and ship's dog went under, and nothing more could
be seen of them. Oliver sent the launch around in a second speeding turn. They returned to the spot, but both Wugle and Judy were
nowhere to be seen. Finally, a pair of desperate figures broke the
surface, and Oliver used the boat hook to drag them closer in. Then

all hands were reaching over the side . . . and a sodden ship's boy and a half-drowned ship's dog were dragged aboard by the scruff of their necks.

A ragged volley of cheers echoed across the water from the deck of the *Gnat*, where what seemed like the entire ship's company had gathered to watch the drama. Acknowledging them with a wave, Oliver got the launch under way once more, heading back toward the *Gnat*. Something of a natural-born showman, he gripped the tiller between his knees and sent a short message of confirmation, using the boat's semaphore—a system of flags held at arm's length in various positions, each corresponding to a letter of the alphabet—to do so.

"CHRISTENING COMPLETE" was the short but entirely appropriate message transmitted.

Bedraggled and with thick Yangtze river mud in hair, eyes, and ears, Judy and Wugle were the first to be lifted back aboard the ship. They were rushed below for a good hot bath. The scrubbing that Judy received was at the hands of Chief Petty Officer Jefferey himself, who was fast becoming one of her foremost protectors. The bath was laced with disinfectant on the orders of the ship's surgeon, for the Yangtze wasn't just laden with silt and mud—it was also thick with sewage from the many towns and cities that lined her banks.

Jefferey rubbed Judy dry with his own towel before deciding to give her a walk around the vessel, pointing out all the obvious dangers. It was like learning to ride a horse, being aboard ship: if you fell off—or overboard—you just had to get right back on again. At first Judy was noticeably scared to be out on deck. She shivered with fright and gave the ship's rails the widest berth possible. As the *Gnat* steamed ahead, she was reluctant even to take a peek at the frothing water surging past to either side of the hull.

At that Jefferey allowed himself a small smile of satisfaction. At least she seemed to have learned her lesson.

Captain Waldegrave recorded their near loss in the ship's log at 1800 hours that day: "a man accidentally overboard and retrieved by the lifeboat crew." The fact that Judy's "accident" was officially recorded as happening to a *human* crew member reflected just how those aboard the *Gnat* had begun to view their ship's dog. But while the crewmen were growing to cherish their newest shipmate, many had begun to question if she really would satisfy the third quality they had demanded of her—that of *usefulness*.

The night of the accident a shaken Judy *did* sleep in the officers' quarters, lying close by Jefferey's bunk for extra comfort. Usually in life a man will choose his dog. Just occasionally a dog gets to choose her man. After her near-death experience in the Yangtze, Judy was in need of real comfort. But she remained the kind of dog who'd make her own choice of master—or better still life companion— very much in her own good time. There were plenty of ready candidates aboard the *Gnat*: the ship's captain, CPO Jefferey, and Tankey Cooper to name but a few. Yet as far as Judy of Sussex was concerned, Mr. Right hadn't stepped onto her deck just yet.

Thankfully, tonight was a night of comparative quiet aboard the *Gnat*, devoid of the roar of tortured water rushing past the hull, or ship's screws thrashing, or engines thumping away belowdecks. As with all Yangtze gunboats, the *Gnat* steamed only during the hours of daylight, when her crew could see properly to defend themselves against the dangers that lurked along the river's length. Come nightfall, she'd either anchor in the shallows or pull into one of the many wharfs and jetties that dotted the river's course.

By any standards the Yangtze was a busy thoroughfare, and most of the local sampans and junks that plied her waters—traditional wood-hulled sailing ships—did so all hours of day and night. Few if any carried any warning lamps—customarily a red light to port and a green to starboard—as vessels are supposed to during hours of darkness. The dangers of having a collision with an unseen craft were legion.

But there were other, more malevolent forces that menaced the waters during the night hours—which was why the Yangtze gunboat captains always preferred to find a riverside dock come sundown. Even there danger still lurked. Armed bandits roamed the fertile lands of the Yangtze River delta, a vast maze of waterways, marshlands, and rice paddies that it would take the *Gnat* a week or more to navigate. Farther inland the plains, valleys, and lake lands would eventually give way to the dramatic mountains and rugged forests of the interior, all of which were plagued by warlords and the ruthless gangs under their control.

Even when moored up at night, the crew of the *Gnat* had to be ready to rouse themselves in an instant. The piercing blow of the ship's whistle and the yelled order of "Repel boarders! Repel boarders!" would mean trouble was at hand. China's nationalist government of Chiang Kai-shek was locked in a struggle with a relatively new adversary—the Soviet-backed Chinese communist revolutionaries. Parts of the country were in a state of virtual civil war, and amid the conflict and insecurity warlords and banditry thrived.

The communist rebels resented the foreign "imperialist" powers that plied the Yangtze, and they were yet another force to be reckoned with. At the order of "Repel boarders," carbines would be broken out of the ship's armory and the Maxim machine guns brought to bear as men lined whichever side of the ship the threat was coming from. But the first line of defense was to use the ship's steam hose—the scalding hot water being a nonlethal means to drive back any aggressors.

As with all British gunboats, the captain of the *Gnat* was under orders to minimize casualties wherever possible. China was a powder keg waiting to blow, and a massacre of locals could prove the spark that would light the fuse. If there was an "incident"—and there were always incidents when out on the Yangtze—Lieutenant Commander Waldegrave was to avoid deaths wherever possible unless Her Majesty's subjects or property were directly threatened.

Thankfully, the night of Judy's shock christening in the Yangtze proved entirely peaceful, which was just what she needed to aid her recovery. At the crack of dawn—the start of day two of their journey upriver—the ship's bugler blew a sharp blast to awaken the crew. It was 0600 hours and time to ready the vessel for another day's journey up the Yangtze.

In the officers' quarters, set in the bows forward of the galley and the ship's bridge, Chief Petty Officer Jefferey was woken by one of the Chinese boat boys bringing him a mug of tea. Sharing a little of the hot, sweet brew with the handsome beast curled up at his side, Jefferey wondered what the day might bring. There would, he hoped, be no further misadventures by one thoroughly irrepressible ship's dog.

As soon as he opened his cabin door a crack Judy pushed through and scampered onto the deck, head down and nose sniffing as she caught the scent of food from the galley. *Ah, eggs. Scrambled to perfection, just as I like them.*

She padded past the caged chickens, giving them a good long sniff as she went. Jefferey hoped that Judy's keen interest in the ship's poultry—taken aboard at Shanghai to provide some fresh meat for the journey—reflected the natural affinity she had for game and the performance of her duties as a gundog in the weeks ahead.

Tankey Cooper, Official Keeper of the Ship's Dog, took early morning custody of Judy so that he could serve her breakfast. Like Jefferey, Tankey was a keen huntsman, and once Judy was fed he decided to give her hunting prowess its first real test. Getting down to eye level with the lithe dog, he proceeded to explain to her in great detail and with seemingly boundless patience what was required of an English pointer when out on the hunt.

Gazing into her eyes—which under the dawn light filtering through the canvas awning seemed less coal-like and more asparkle with eager fire—he felt as if she understood his every word. With her long, floppy ears framing her face, there seemed to be something slightly mournful and intensely serious about her expression—and then she'd ruin it all by curling one lip in a lopsided smile or flopping out that long pink tongue of hers for a goofy bout of panting.

Still, she wasn't yet fully grown, and Tankey reckoned she had plenty of time to prove her worth as a gundog. Deciding a spot of practical demonstration was in order, he proceeded to "point" at the caged chickens, which were the nearest thing to game aboard the *Gnat*.

Judy stared at him for a long second, head cocked quizzically to one side. She knew from Tankey's body language that he was up to something of real import, but she couldn't for the life of her imagine what. Tankey held the pose for as long as he could—*see, like this*—before Judy gave a rigorous shake of her head, blew a snort through her nostrils seemingly in derision, and turned her nose toward the tantalizing smells wafting from the ship's galley. Her meaning was crystal clear: *message neither received nor understood!*

Undeterred, Tankey resolved to repeat the demonstration every morning after breakfast until Judy got it. But part of him wondered whether Judy hadn't been having a good laugh at his expense as he swayed about on one leg trying to show an English pointer how to point.

Once things were shipshape, the *Gnat* was untied from her mooring and she pulled into the main flow of the river. The pitch of her engines rose to their familiar throb as she got under way. Making sure to keep well back from the rail, Judy stood on the ship's raised prow, nose into the wind. They had barely made a mile's progress, but already the mascot of the *Gnat* could smell trouble on the river up ahead.

Just after midday—at 1203 hours to be precise—the *Gnat* passed by a gunboat of the Imperial Japanese Navy steaming in the opposite direction. Just an hour later, the French gunboat *Francis Garnier* followed, also bound for Shanghai. And shortly a third foreign warship, the French gunboat *Balny*, passed the *Gnat*, but this time heading upriver into the Chinese interior. No doubt about it, the Yangtze was getting busy as rival world powers vied for control over the rich trade plied along these waters.

But right now the *Gnat* was about to be menaced by another threat entirely. From her position up front Judy was first to give voice to the danger. She raised her head, took an extralong sniff, and began barking into the far distance. A vessel could just about be made out drifting lazily downriver. Twin-masted, with gray- and dun-colored square-cut sails set over a high prow, the wooden junk looked like a throwback to the Dark Ages compared with the modern steel-hulled gunboats.

This was the kind of vessel that the *Gnat*'s crew had seen hauled up the worst of the Yangtze's rapids by gangs of human coolies. Using dozens of ropes slung from the banks and attached to the hull of the ship, bare-chested men would bend to the strain as they waded through the shallows, dragging the boat behind them step by exhausting step—and all to the rhythmic cry of the gang master who hired his men out to passing vessels. The *Gnat*'s crew had grown used to such archaic scenes, but the boat ahead of them had a look that none of them liked very much.

The ancient-looking wooden vessel was lying low in the water, which meant it was laden with some seriously heavy cargo. None of the crew could be sure, but as Judy pranced about on the *Gnat*'s prow and barked excitedly, they knew something untoward was bearing down on them. Their dog had never behaved like this before, not even after tumbling into the cold and churning maw of the Yangtze. Something about that vessel had her spooked.

Straining his eyes to get a proper look at the distant ship, Captain Waldegrave turned to his chief petty officer. He had a curl to his lips that betrayed just the slightest hint of repulsion. Jefferey whipped out a pair of binoculars to take a closer look. Through the 8× magnification he could make out the distant boat in more detail. It had a dark hold lying open to the elements, and Jefferey was 90 percent certain what lay inside.

Approaching the *Gnat* was one of the dreaded "cess ships," and Judy seemed to have sensed it long before any of the crew had the slightest inkling what was coming. The ship's captain altered course, and orders were relayed from the bridge to batten down all hatches, close all portholes, and make the ship as airtight as possible—after which all crew members were to get themselves belowdecks as quickly as possible.

The Yangtze River cess ships carried human waste—invariably well decomposed and stinking to high heaven—down the great river to where it could be dumped away from the major towns and cities. More often than not it was used to fertilize the verdant green rice paddies that lay to either side of the river. The *Gnat* was approaching the riverside city of Zhanjiang, and no doubt the vessel full of rotting human ordure had emanated from there.

Thanks to Judy's barking, by the time the sickening stench was upon them most crew members were sealed inside the vessel—including one ship's dog who'd just demonstrated her unexpected usefulness. The cess ships were a constant hazard on the lower reaches of the Yangtze. If the stench got inside the vessel, it would linger in hair, clothes, and furnishings for days. Judy had just proved herself to be the *Gnat*'s onboard early-warning system.

She'd done so using her extraordinary sense of smell. A dog's world, unlike a human's, is almost entirely defined by odor. Their scent-detecting powers are so superior to our own, it's almost as if they experience an entirely different dimension—a world defined by innumerable layers of scent.

Whereas humans possess 5 million scent detectors, a gundog like Judy has something approaching 300 million. Such a dog can differentiate between over a million different aromas, as opposed to our mere thousand, and can do so at far tinier concentrations. With her wet muzzle—caused by tear ducts that ran all the way to the tip of the nose—Judy could feel the way the wind was blowing, so isolating the direction from which the smell was coming. Moisture on the nose would then dissolve the tiny scent molecules so that receptor cells could identify them.

But Judy's powers of scent detection were even more advanced than that. Because humans navigate largely by sight, we have a large element of the brain for processing visual information. In dogs, the olfactory (smell) center in the brain is forty times more developed than in humans. Scents are even picked up by a dog's whiskers, which channel them to the brain. Plus, dogs have a scent-detecting organ—the vomeronasal, situated in the roof of the mouth—that is completely lacking in humans and one that we as yet little understand.

To Judy, smell was her universe, the first sense by which she interpreted the world around her. Out here on the Yangtze, her nose was the filter through which she would sift all the scent-related information coming to her to better understand and deal with this new and exotic—and sometimes life-threatening—environment. Detecting a cess ship on the Yangtze at a mile's distance was no trouble to a dog equipped with such acute powers of smell.

This time, Judy's canine senses had saved the ship's crew from nothing more than a few hours of sickening and suffocating stench.

But the time was fast approaching when Judy would need to use her incredible canine powers to save the lives of all aboard the *Gnat*.

CHAPTER FOUR

Continuing upriver, the *Gnat* steamed past four Japanese warships, each trailing the distinctive bright-red rising-sun flag in her wake. It was ominous, the way in which Imperial Japan, China's age-old adversary, was making her presence increasingly felt this far inland. It was clear that trouble was brewing. The crew of the *Gnat* could feel it in their bones.

On November 20 the British gunboat reached Nanking, then China's sprawling capital, pausing only to pick up a sailor who was able to rejoin the ship, having been treated for an ailment in hospital in Shanghai. That done, the *Gnat* pressed onward until she reached the smaller settlement of Wuhu, where she rendezvoused with her sister ship, the *Ladybird*.

The *Gnat* pulled in to moor alongside her—the two gunboats with their tall twin funnels and long canvas awnings running from stem to stern resembling a mirror image of each other. They were also remarkably similar in another key respect: both the *Ladybird* and now the *Gnat* had dogs serving as their mascot.

Officers and men from the *Ladybird* were invited aboard the *Gnat*, and ship's rum was served and intelligence swapped between the two parties. This was an ideal opportunity for the captain of the *Gnat* to glean information about any dangers that might lie ahead, for *Ladybird* was en route to Shanghai after a long sojourn upriver.

But one member of the *Ladybird*'s crew was decidedly not welcome. Bonzo, their ship's dog, had started acting very strangely just as soon as the *Gnat* had steamed onto the horizon. A large boxer-terrier cross, Bonzo had started to dash about the deck like a crazy thing, tearing back and forth ceaselessly. With Bonzo's nose glued to the *Gnat*, it didn't take the brains of an archbishop to work out what was up. He had sensed the presence of a beautiful and glamorous young lady dog aboard their sister ship and had amorous designs upon her.

On being alerted to the threat, Captain Waldegrave ordered Tankey, as Keeper of the Ship's Dog, to maintain Judy under strict lock and key. The last thing they wanted right now was a brood of boxer–terrier–English pointer crosses. Judy of Sussex wasn't particularly happy at being so constrained. She'd always enjoyed free run of the ship, but little did she know it was being done for her own good. She remained safely locked away until the *Ladybird* departed downriver and Bonzo's dishonorable intentions toward her had been well and truly thwarted.

With Bonzo gone, Judy was free to join the *Gnat's* crew on expeditions ashore. There was a navy canteen on the Wuhu docks where—joy of joys—the beer flowed freely. For some reason the place also seemed to have an inexhaustible supply of something that Judy proved very partial to—ice cream. As soon as the ship's crew entered the canteen Judy would adopt a suitably regal pose, nose pointed directly at the trunk that contained the delicious treat.

One evening the men forgot to provide her with her customary plateful. Finally losing her patience, she sneaked behind the canteen bar, grabbed the handle of the ice cream trunk in her jaws, and dragged it out into the center of the room. She turned to the astonished drinkers, barked once in command, and demanded that her ice cream be duly served.

Above Wuhu the Yangtze narrows considerably as the flatlands of the delta give way to a series of dramatic, sweeping valleys. Three chokepoints—the Xling, Wu, and Qutang gorges—funnel the river waters through towering rock faces and knife-cut cliffs that rear up hundreds of feet to either side. Such terrain offered the perfect territory for the kind of piracy for which the Yangtze was infamous—although the *Ladybird* had been able to give no specific warnings of any such threats lying ahead.

Two days out from Wuhu the *Gnat* entered the steep-sided, echoing Xling Gorge, sparsely vegetated slopes sweeping down into the fast-flowing water. With dusk approaching the captain decided to anchor for the night. As thick smoke from the *Gnat's* funnels drifted across this valley that dwarfed the ship, he maneuvered his vessel into shallower water before ordering the anchor dropped.

With the *Gnat* safely moored Captain Waldegrave declared, "Ship secure—hands to tea." It was time for a refreshing brew after a long day's steaming on the Yangtze.

This being wilder, less-populated terrain, the crew was instinctively more alert. But as the slash of sky above them turned a velvety purple with the setting sun, there was little sign of any danger lurking out there on the darkening river. All was apparently peaceful until around 0300 hours, when Judy sat bolt upright in her box-cum-bed on the *Gnat's* bridge. Throwing aside her ship's blanket, she pricked up her ears. Moments later she'd leaped onto her four paws and made a mad dash for the open wing of the bridge.

Barely pausing to fix the direction of the approaching threat, she began to bark wildly at a point somewhere in the darkness. For a moment the officer on watch wondered whether it mightn't be another stinking cess ship that had dragged Judy out of her slumber, but it was quickly clear that her attitude and demeanor were entirely different this time. There was an aggression and ferocity in her barking the likes of which he'd never heard before.

The crew of the *Gnat* were learning by now to pay all due attention to their dog. The officer on watch took immediate action. He grabbed the nearest Aldis lamp—a powerful handheld light more normally used for signaling from ship to ship—switched it on, and turned it toward the point at which Judy was directing her fury. Immediately the reason for her behavior became apparent: two large junks were drifting silently toward the *Gnat*—though not quietly enough to have avoided detection by a dog's hypersensitive hearing.

Wasting not a second, the officer on watch drew his pistol and fired a single shot into the dark sky, the hollow crack of the low-velocity bullet reverberating around the sleeping ship and bringing the crew instantly awake. From all directions pajama-clad men tumbled out of hatches and doorways, rifles, pistols, and an assortment of other weapons held at the ready as they hurried to their predetermined stations to repel boarders.

The watch officer, meanwhile, had ordered Judy to be quiet. Now they knew what threat they faced, her early warning had given the ship's crew a perfect opportunity to get one over on their foremost adversaries—two large vessels packed full of fearsome Yangtze River pirates.

The pirates were making their attack approach in typical fashion—a pair of junks drifting silently abreast with a thick bamboo hawser slung between them. Once the rope snagged on the *Gnat's* bows it would pull the pirate ships in toward her, and upon contact the waiting men would leap aboard the still-sleeping vessel, decimate the crew, and loot to their hearts' content. At least that had been their intention until Judy had caught wind of their coming on the chill night air.

The tension aboard the *Gnat* was palpable as the seconds ticked by. Then there was a faint, barely audible thunk as the bamboo rope made contact with the *Gnat's* prow. By then Captain Waldegrave was directing operations with gusto from the bridge. As the two pirate vessels swung in toward his ship, the river gurgling under their bulging wooden hulls, he had his men positioned at the ready. One of them, a stoker, only had time to don his scarlet pajama top before grabbing a fire ax with which to set about the approaching threat.

Before the first vessel had even made contact with the *Gnat*, the captain ordered those manning the Maxim machine guns mounted on a platform to the rear of the twin funnels to open fire. They let rip with ten-second bursts, raking the flanks of the pirate vessels, splinters of wood being blasted into the river. The Maxims were mounted three to each side of the ship, chiefly for antiaircraft use, but they were also the perfect weapons with which to signal the *Gnat*'s intent.

The river pirates knew for sure now that their target was forewarned, not to mention heavily armed, but there was no stopping the drift of their vessels as the rope dragged them in. The first craft bumped alongside. Shadowy figures reared up and attempted to board the *Gnat*. But they were met with a fusillade of gunfire—plus one roaring stoker with his manhood on show swinging an ax above his head and one ship's dog barking and snarling furiously.

Battle had most surely been joined.

Two of the *Gnat*'s crewmen were stationed in the prow, and they were chopping furiously at the pirate's hawser. As the final strands of the bamboo rope were sliced through, the pair of junks were dragged free by the current and slipped into the darkness. The last of the pirates turned tail and took a leap into the void in a desperate effort to rejoin their fast-disappearing ships.

Those who failed to make that jump faced a long swim in the rough waters churning through the Xling Gorge, a christening far more fraught with risk than the one suffered by Judy of Sussex a few days previously. As the pirate junks drifted away into the gloom, triumphant cheers rang out from the deck of the *Gnat*. The feeling aboard was unanimous: it was the early warning provided by their intrepid ship's dog that had enabled them to vanquish their enemy so comprehensively.

Whether Judy would be of any use on the hunt no one yet knew, but tonight she had proved her worth ten times over—for her actions had been truly those of a lifesaver.

Prior to domestication dogs used their acute sense of hearing to track both prey and predators in the wild. They can hear a far greater range of frequencies than humans, they can do so over far greater distances, and they can pinpoint accurately the direction the sound is coming from—just as Judy had done. In fact, a dog's hearing is ten times more effective than ours: a sound a human might hear at 20 meters they can hear at 200. Had there been a mouse living aboard the *Gnat*, Judy would have been able to hear it squeak from many meters away.

Using their large, movable ears, they can pinpoint the source of a sound pretty much instantaneously—in one six-hundredth of a second—hence Judy's rapid-fire actions aboard the *Gnat*, which had allowed the ship's crew to repel the river pirates without injury or loss of life. In the fight of the Xling Gorge, Judy's canine senses truly had saved the day.

Over the coming week the diminutive British warship—the gunboats were among the smallest vessels in the Royal Navy's fleet—pushed onward through the Wu and Qutang gorges and moved into the complex system of lakes, marshes, and tributaries of the Hunan province beyond. Prior to reaching her first major stopover and possible turn-around point—the bustling treaty port of Hankow (now Wuhan), some 900 kilometers inland—the *Gnat* was set to rendezvous with the flagship of the British gunboat flotilla, the *Bee*.

Being the flagship of the fleet, the *Bee* had lost some of her main guns so that more space could be given over to officers' accommodation. In spite of this, on several patrols the illustrious *Bee* had pushed as far inland on the Yangtze as Yichang in the west and Changsha in the south, both approaching 1,500 kilometers from Shanghai and the sea. Those had been truly voyages into the wild and the unknown.

Unusually for Royal Navy ships, the Yangtze gunboats tended to sail—and to fight—as lone operators, cruising the river many days or weeks apart. Mostly, their commanders and crew had few if any senior officers watching over them. This tended to lead to a tight-knit familial atmosphere aboard ship and to a degree of independence of action rarely seen in the Royal Navy.

But without firmly enforced procedures to keep the gunboats shipshape, long weeks spent in isolation upriver could render such busy, crowded vessels decidedly unpleasant places to be. As with all gunboat commanders, Captain Waldegrave had a strict routine in place for keeping the *Gnat* spick and span. Hands were ordered daily to clean—sluicing down the decks, polishing brass, making good the paintwork, generally clearing up the decks, stowing gear, refreshing brightworks (the polished metal parts of the vessel), and servicing the Maxim machine guns.

As the captain of the *Gnat* knew well, a biannual Admiralty inspection could be sprung on any Yangtze gunboat at any time. Rear Admiral Reginald Holt, the senior naval officer (SNO) Yangtze Fleet, happened to be aboard the *Bee* when the *Gnat* docked alongside her, and he must have decided there was no time like the present to put the newly arrived gunboat through her paces. Needless to say, this would be the *Gnat*'s first such formal ship's inspection with her new crew member, Judy of Sussex, aboard.

It was the crack of dawn when the rear admiral came aboard the *Gnat*, complete with his aide, to announce the surprise inspection. The ship's officers and crew knew instantly what they were in for. The rear admiral would scour the vessel from stem to stern for the slightest infraction of ship's rules. He'd put every man and ship's department through its paces to ensure the *Gnat* was operating at peak performance and ready to wage war should such be necessary.

Or as Judy's keeper, Tankey Cooper, put it, he'd come aboard to put them through "the works!"

First off came the inspection of the crew. The men were lined up on the main deck in two ranks, at so-called divisions. The rear admiral proceeded to check over their kit and bedding, all of which was supposed to be neatly laid out, each item labeled with the owner's name. In due course he came to the newest crew member . . . Judy. She was positioned between Tankey Cooper and her ammunition box of a bed, ship's blanket neatly folded before her.

The rear admiral stared down at the seated dog with a gimlet eye. She in turn gazed up at him, tongue lolling and with the signature silly grin that she seemed to reserve for any formal occasion aboard ship. At her feet were coiled two spare leashes, plus an extra collar displaying her name clearly—"Judy." All appeared to be present and correct, so without a word or a twitch in his deadpan expression the rear admiral moved on, shadowed by his aide.

Similar inspections followed all over the ship as mess decks, storerooms, stores, engine rooms, galley, and all were given the once-over. Finally seeming to be satisfied, the rear admiral and his aide returned to where they had started—the ship's bridge. From there he began to order the men through every drill known to the Yangtze gunboat flotilla, plus some seemingly yet to be invented.

To the casual observer the ship would have appeared a mass of chaos, but to Captain Waldegrave this was strictly ordered chaos in action. Every man knew his place and his duties as block and tackle groaned and pulleys whirred and the ship was "dressed"—involving a "washing line" of brightly colored flags being raised from stem to stern—then the topmast lowered, the ship's generator stripped down and reassembled, and so on and so forth.

That done, the rear admiral gave the order to "land armed guard," and the launch was manned and lowered and it motored away from the *Gnat*. No sooner had it left than he announced a "man overboard"—which left the crew in some confusion as to how they were to rescue the fictitious victim, with the launch already halfway to storming some unseen adversary ashore.

"He'll just 'ave to swim until the ruddy boat gets back!" one of the sweating seamen muttered as he ran to a new task.

In quick succession came orders to "action stations," then "fire all guns"—with quite spectacular results—and "away kedge anchor," the kedge anchor being a light secondary anchor used to help a ship maneuver in narrow estuaries or rivers. The *Gnat*'s crew was becoming more than a little exasperated when Judy decided it was time for her to do something. As would prove to be the case many times in the future, whenever Judy sensed that her family was in distress, she'd find some means to come to their aid.

Without warning she raised her fine head to the skies above the bridge and began to bark. *Aruuf-ruuf-ruuf-ruuf-ruuf.* The barking was continuous and insistent, and the ship's crew recognized it instantly for what it was—a warning. As the barking grew to a fierce crescendo, they felt certain they were facing some kind of imminent danger—though no pirate ships were likely to attack two

British gunboats in broad daylight, and the threat appeared to be coming from the skies.

As for the rear admiral, the orders he'd been issuing had been drowned out by a madly barking dog, and he was turning a noticeable shade of puce. Just as it seemed he was about to lose control and vent his anger on Judy, the cause of her distress became clear. All of a sudden a Japanese warplane swooped out of the seemingly empty heavens and dived toward the British warships. It swooped low over the *Gnat*, flew across the *Bee* at little more than mast height, then pulled up into a steep climb and was gone.

No Japanese warplane had yet engaged a British or Allied ship on the Yangtze, but the meaning of the buzzing was all too clear. Had they wanted to, the Japanese air crew could have bombed or strafed the British gunboat pretty much at will. Japan had more or less total air superiority in the skies above China. The Chinese Air Force was pitifully ill equipped and manned, and no Allied aircraft were able to patrol this far into her territory.

Judy ceased her barking only once the Japanese plane had dwindled into an invisible speck on the horizon. Next, she did a very odd thing. She started to whirl around on the spot as if madly chasing her own tail, and once she was certain she'd completely monopolized the rear admiral's attention, she proceeded to curl up on the floor at his feet.

The rear admiral stared at her for several seconds. She was wrapped comfortably around his gleaming toe caps, seemingly sound asleep after all the barking and whirling. He glanced at the rigid face of Captain Waldegrave and raised one bristly eyebrow.

"Remarkable ship's dog you have here. Sound vibrations, presumably. That's how she did it." A weighty pause. "But the time is coming, I fear, when we all may need a dog like this stationed on the ship's bridge."

The rear admiral must have realized that he had nothing in his repertoire to compete with Judy's early-warning demonstration, and the Admiralty inspection was promptly declared over. The officers and crew of the *Gnat* had passed with flying colors—all of them, including one very remarkable ship's dog seemingly gifted with a miraculous form of canine radar.

Dogs possess eighteen separate muscles with which to raise, lower, or swivel their ears, ensuring they can pin down exactly which direction a sound is coming from. In detecting that Japanese warplane, Judy had demonstrated just how effectively those muscle-driven ears can be used to track distant sounds. But Judy's ability to detect that aircraft—and the threat it embodied—went far deeper than purely physical attributes.

Somehow, Judy had also sensed that this thunderous noise in the sky equated to danger, and since she'd yet to suffer any air attacks, there was no obvious reason for her to do so. As with the pirate ships, she seemed able to sense *danger itself*—and it was that which had so impressed itself upon the rear admiral . . . not to mention all of her fellow crewmates.

A few days after she'd passed her Admiralty inspection the *Gnat* steamed into Hankow harbor, with no more pirates, or Japanese warplanes—or even cess ships!—having menaced her onward passage up the Yangtze. Here she joined the many other British, American, French, and Japanese gunboats floating at their moorings, plus the odd Italian and German ship that also patrolled these waters.

At Hankow the captain's orders were simple. He was to show a presence and fly the flag, looking efficient and warlike to deter any trouble in this vitally important riverside city. Over the eight decades that the Yangtze had been patrolled by the foreign powers, Hankow had grown into the key treaty port and gunboat hub, largely because of its strategic location in the center of the navigable stretch of the great river. As a result, the city offered all the luxuries lacking aboard a ship like the *Gnat*.

The officers' mess on an Insect class boat was fairly well appointed for a vessel her size. The *Gnat* even had a wardroom, set in the forward part of the hull, squeezed between the captain's quarters and the oil fuel tanks. The wardroom was designed to resemble a miniature version of an English gentleman's club, complete with comfortable armchairs draped in pristine cloth, yellowing copies of *The Times* newspaper on side tables, and white-coated Chinese stewards poised to top up the pink gins when required.

But in spite of such onboard comforts, Hankow promised the officers and men of the *Gnat* an exceptionally good time ashore. Hankow resembled a classic European city of the time in terms of its grand colonial-style architecture, its layout, and its atmosphere. The fashionable Hankow Club offered excellent dining and drinking, cabaret, bridge parties, and tennis, plus good hunting in the surrounding bush. Hankow even boasted a race club, one that resembled Royal Ascot as much as ever it could here in deepest darkest China.

The Hankow Bund—the riverside harbor area where the *Gnat* was tied up—was designed to appear like a waterside promenade at any fashionable European port city. It was dominated by the Chinese customs house clock tower and the splendid white colonnades of the Hongkong and Shanghai Bank. The ground floor of the bank had been converted into a wet bar and clubroom, complete with billiard table and English-speaking Chinese bar boys.

Once a fortnight the wet room would host a navy opera, to which the assorted Royal Navy crews would invite the public for a sing-along, one that was lubricated by copious quantities of a local beer called EWO Pilsner. Produced by the EWO brewery in Shanghai, the beer seemed to give off a peculiar smell of onions, and it was unusually potent.

The wet room had been nicknamed the Strong Toppers Club after the powerful onion-scented beer quaffed in there. New members could gain access to the club only after an exacting initiation ritual. The newbie had to stand before a panel of three while undergoing the Yangtze River variation of the popular drinking game Cardinal Puff.

Holding his beer in his left hand, he'd announce a toast "to the health of Cardinal Puff," strike the table once with his right hand, stamp both feet, tap the glass on the table, then drain his beer. The sequence had to be repeated with a fresh beer, only now he had to drink to the health of "Cardinal Puff Puff" and repeat all the actions two times over. A third successful rendition—only now doing all actions three times over—and he was duly admitted to the club. But any mistake—reciting the lines wrong, getting the actions wrong, or drinking with the wrong hand—would be met with noisy jeers and jibes from the crowd. The unfortunate initiate would have failed, and he'd have to start all over again.

During the long voyage upriver Judy had grown somewhat partial to her beer. As she was by now a fully fledged member of the ship's crew—she had even had the de rigueur christening in the Yangtze—her presence was required at such convivial evenings. Hence Tankey Cooper put together his own version of the Strong Toppers Club initiation ritual especially for her. Before the assembled throng Judy had to bark once, twice, then three times in succession, each outburst of yelping punctuated by a noisy bout of lapping from someone's glass.

That completed, Judy of Sussex was declared in. She was now free to wander regally from face to familiar face, here and there taking a nibble from a handful of peanuts and a lap from a glass of onion-scented beer. Such riotous evenings ended in the traditional rendition of the Yangtze Anthem, to which Judy proved able to provide a remarkably soulful accompaniment as she threw back her head and howled along to the verses.

Strong Toppers are we
On the dirty Yangtze
"Gunboats" or "Cruisers"
We're here for a spree.

The Strong Toppers Club was largely a male environment, and Judy was one of the few ladies permitted access. And in her own peculiar way, she seemed to understand what this signified in terms of her acceptance into the bosom of the all-male family that was the crew of the *Gnat*. She'd come a long way from that lonely back alleyway behind Soo's shop on the tough streets of Shanghai, and in singing along with the ship's company in the Strong Toppers Club, Judy had truly found her tribe.

Chief Petty Officer Jefferey, by now Judy's closest companion, believed their ship's dog was developing a "human brain," or at least a means with which to view the world of the Yangtze River gunboats pretty much as the sailors did. She appeared to understand every word spoken to her and read every gesture and expression and seemed to have adapted to the nuances of gunboat life as easily as any human crew member had before her.

Early one morning Jefferey took Judy for a walk in the grounds of a smart Hankow hotel, a favorite with visiting Europeans. Man and dog strolled for a mile or so along the approach road, with dense jungle stretching away to their left. All of a sudden Judy darted off into the bush. Jefferey presumed she'd scented some game animal—most likely a deer, for he'd spotted their tracks already that morning.

Moments later he heard a yelp of alarm from somewhere within the bush. He knew instantly that it was Judy. He called her, and shortly she shot forth from the undergrowth. But she was clearly very alarmed, for she was trembling from head to toe. Jefferey had never seen her acting like this before, not even after her near-death experience in the Yangtze. He called the dog to him, but instead she bounded ahead on the road, making toward the hotel and forcing him to hurry after.

As he rushed along some sixth sense made him glance over his shoulder. There in the fringes of the bush was a large forest leopard. The thought flashed through his mind instantly—*so that's what spooked Judy*. It was only when he reached the safety of the hotel that Jefferey allowed himself to imagine another scenario—that Judy had picked up the big cat's scent and gone into the forest deliberately to distract its attention, for the leopard had in fact been stalking him!

Jefferey would never know for sure which it was. But one thing was certain—whenever she sensed that her extended family was in danger, Judy was proving herself willing to risk all to protect them.

Unperturbed by his close encounter with the leopard, Chief Petty Officer Jefferey decided to make full use of their Hankow stopover to put Judy through her paces as a supposed gundog. By now she was approaching eight months old, and she'd grown into a fine-looking animal—muscular, sleek and fit, with a glistening coat, and always ready to run around.

In fact, Hankow had offered her many a chance to hone her fitness, for the various crews were forever holding intership football, rugby, or hockey matches. With both football and rugby the ball proved a little too large for Judy to master, but she had become an absolute demon at hockey. She'd grab the ball in her mouth and streak for whichever goal was the nearest, paying little heed to whichever side she was supposedly playing for. This made for an utterly impartial player, though not one who could be counted upon to boost the *Gnat*'s score line.

With serious gundog business in mind, CPO Jefferey organized a dawn hunting expedition. After an early breakfast aboard ship the crew—consisting of Jefferey and Tankey Cooper plus four other keen hunters—set off, with Judy taking up the proud lead. Beyond Hankow in the open bush there was an abundance of king quail—a game bird in the same family as the pheasant—and that was what the hunting party was after.

At the first sign of the distinctive birds taking to the air—a flash of iridescent blue plumage above bright orange feet—the guns roared. As quail were hit and tumbled from the sky Judy looked on impassively, making no move either to point or to fetch. The men took turns using the guns while others acted as retrievers to gather up the fallen birds, and still Judy didn't seem to take the hint or make any moves to join them.

Finally, Tankey Cooper decided enough was enough. He bent to Judy's eye level and gave her a little talking to, explaining what they wanted her to do.

Then he pointed in the direction of a freshly shot bird: "Good girl! Fetch! Fetch!"

Seeming at last to understand what was expected of her, Judy gave an excited wag of her hindquarters, dropped her head, and dashed off into the bush. Now and again her long white tail popped up into view over the undergrowth or there was a flash of liver and white as she bounded over the thick scrub. For a while she seemed to be making good progress, and then all sight and sound of her was lost. The watching party waited several minutes before weapons were made safe, and Tankey volunteered to go find her.

Barely had he set off when he heard an anguished howl echo forth from the terrain up ahead. He knew instantly that it was Judy, although he'd never heard her utter anything like the tortured cries she was now making. As further heartrending yowls rent the air, he dashed forward, fearing the very worst. Was their ship's dog caught in some kind of animal trap, he wondered, or, worse still, crushed in the hungry jaws of a forest leopard?

Tankey crashed through the tall grass desperate to get to Judy, using his ears as his guide. Moments later he'd stumbled right upon her. At his feet lay some kind of pool, and somehow Judy had tumbled in. Worse still, the pond seemed to be full of a thick cloying mud from which the poor dog seemed unable to escape. As she eyed him desperately, imploring him to help, Tankey didn't for one moment hesitate—he plunged right in.

Landing on his feet, he began to wade through the waist-deep mess. It was only then and as the thick crust that covered the pond's surface was further torn asunder that his senses were hit by an unbelievable stench. As the crisp, sun-baked skin broke apart, so the ripe contents below were exposed to the air, along with their telltale odor. What Judy and now Tankey had leaped into here was an open cesspit.

Almost paralyzed from the shock and the overpowering, suffocating stench—that of human feces cooked for months under the strong Hankow sun—Tankey stood there for an instant and did as Judy was doing, howling out his distress. And then the realization hit him: whereas he was able to stand waist-deep in the sickening mess, poor Judy was having to dog-paddle—in effect, treading water in a pool full of unspeakable torment.

Forcing his brain and body to function—dragging his mind out of the horror of the moment—he grabbed Judy by her collar, threw her onto the bank, and hauled himself out behind her. There Tankey stood on the cesspit's edge, his legs, the lower half of his torso, and his arms covered in a revolting slick of ordure. The gunk was all over his hands even, from where he'd grabbed Judy's collar, plus he could feel it squelching evilly inside his boots.

But Judy was in an even worse condition: only her head had escaped immersion in the devilish pit. Using thick clumps of grass, Tankey tried as best he could to scrub off the worst of the mess. Having done what he could for himself, he turned to Judy and used the same technique to try to rub her down. But even though pointers have relatively short hair, still Judy's coat had soaked up enough of the thick black horror that it proved all but impossible to clean her.

There was nothing for it: they would have to make haste to the *Gnat*, where hot baths laced with disinfectant were very much in order. With a hangdog expression on both man's and dog's features they hurried over to the hunting party—but none of their companions would come within twenty feet of them. Too disgruntled and disgusted to care much, Tankey led Judy back toward the harbor, a thick cloud of voracious flies marking their progress through the bush.

Long before they reached the *Gnat*, Tankey heard the clanging of the ship's bell. One of those on the hunting party had clearly gotten back to their vessel before them. A voice drifted across to him as they hurried along the Hankow Bund. It was the quartermaster, calling out the sonorous chant: "Unclean! Unclean! Unclean!"

Above the ship the yellow "Q" flag had been raised—denoting quarantine—but neither man nor dog had it in them to find much to laugh at in their present predicament.

After Judy's second bath laced with disinfectant in as many months, most of the terrible smell seemed to be gone. Even so, it was several days before she was considered done with her quarantine and fit to be allowed back into the bosom of the ship's family. As for Tankey, he'd spent hours scrubbing himself lobster pink in a desperate effort to be rid of the last vestiges of the unspeakable ordure. During the process he'd made a momentous decision: there would be no more forcing Judy to be a gundog, that was for sure.

As the *Gnat's* early-warning system, Judy had proved herself to have no equal. But as far as classic pointing duties went, Tankey Cooper had concluded that she was very much a round peg in a square hole. She might have helped the *Gnat* avoid the cess ship on the Yangtze, but here in Hankow she'd led Tankey Cooper into the heart of a cesspit without rival!

The *Gnat's* crew saw out that Christmas and the New Year in Hankow, after which the *Bee* sailed into port to relieve her of her duties. So it was that in the icy months of early 1937 the *Gnat* turned her prow eastward to start the return voyage downriver to Shanghai.

Unknown to her crew, the *Gnat* was sailing into bloody trouble—as was the entire British gunboat fleet on the Yangtze. The conflict that was almost upon them would eclipse the spot of bother that the *Gnat's* crew had experienced at the hands of the Yangtze River pirates or indeed anything that had ever gone before.

Shortly, Judy of Sussex would be called upon to save their lives many times over.

CHAPTER FIVE

Late in the spring of 1937 the Japanese Imperial Armed Forces made their move. In the northeast of the country, around Peking (now Beijing), the Japanese military began maneuvers involving large numbers of ground troops. Tensions mounted inexorably as the Chinese military commanders watched what was unfolding and shadowed the Japanese soldiers' every move.

Finally, during a night exercise by Japanese forces around the strategically important Marco Polo Bridge—an ancient granite span lined with fantastic carved dragons that crosses the Yongding River, providing a crucial access point into Peking—shots were exchanged. What began as confused, sporadic exchanges of fire rapidly escalated into full-scale fighting, with soldiers hit and wounded on both sides.

This was the excuse that Imperial Japan had been waiting for. Japan demanded that all Chinese troops withdraw from the area—in effect, ordering the Chinese military to vacate its own sovereign territory. When the ultimatum wasn't met, the Japanese military launched an all-out offensive, bombarding Peking's port city of Tientsin (now Tianjin). Under fierce air and land attack both Tientsin and then Peking itself fell to Japanese forces in late June 1937.

So began what was to become known as the Second Sino-Japanese War. Age-old belligerents, the two nations had first resorted to all-out conflict in 1894. During a year of intense fighting the Japanese had scored a string of victories, and China's Qing dynasty had been forced to sue for peace. Now, barely four decades later, conflict had again engulfed these two ancient adversaries.

China's nationalist leader, Chiang Kai-shek, was quick to retaliate against the Japanese aggression. He directed the army and air force to counterattack against those Japanese forces based at the mouth of the Yangtze River in Shanghai. It was August 13, 1937, when war erupted in the port city—and the Paris of the East was engulfed in fire. Months of intense conflict lay ahead during which 200,000 Japanese troops, backed by air and sea power, would do fierce battle with the ill-equipped but spirited Chinese defenders.

If Shanghai fell, it would open up the entire length of the Yangtze to the Japanese, and the Chinese commanders knew full well what their next target would be—their capital city, Nanking, about 300 kilometers inland. Desperate to save Nanking, the Chinese strung a boom across the mighty Yangtze, one made up of what few warships they possessed interspersed with junks transformed into makeshift gunboats and with thick bamboo hawsers strung between them.

The aim of the boom was to block any Japanese warships from moving upriver, but in placing it the Chinese had unwittingly cut off thirteen British gunboats from the sea, plus six American and two French vessels. Among them was the *Gnat*, complete with her crew and ship's dog. None of the gunboats had any way of escaping the warfare that had erupted at the mouth of the great river that they had for decades patrolled with such freedom.

After weeks of bloody street-to-street fighting Shanghai fell. Though beaten back from the city, Chinese forces had won a propaganda victory of sorts. Imperial Japan had openly boasted that it could take Shanghai in three days and all of China in as many months. In reality, it had taken them three months of intense fighting—with heavy casualties on both sides—to seize the city at the mouth of the Yangtze.

As Chinese forces fell back from Shanghai, the Japanese were able to break through the boom across the Yangtze. But there was little relief for the crew of the *Gnat* or for those of the other gunboats. At a point halfway to Nanking a second boom was thrown across the river, and once more the Allied gunboats were trapped within a bloody conflict not of their making. Thus far none of the ships or their crew had fallen victim to the bloodshed, but they were hostages to fortune and few believed they could avoid its predations forever.

With the Japanese pushing inland, Rear Admiral Reginald Holt, the commander of the British gunboat fleet, tried to negotiate safe passage for his flotilla through the boom and out to sea, but to no avail. Japanese land forces were moving to encircle Nanking, and a massive aerial bombardment of the city had begun. By now it was early October 1937, and the Allied gunboats—the *Gnat* included—resorted to painting large national flags on their upper sides in an effort to avoid getting pounced upon by marauding Japanese warplanes, which daily swept the lower reaches of the Yangtze, seeking targets.

At the same time that Japanese troops closed in on the Chinese capital, reports of terrible atrocities reached the gunboats. Civilians were being tortured, raped, and massacred in the thousands. In the face of diehard Chinese resistance, the Japanese Army had been ordered to implement the "Three Alls" policy—kill all, loot all, destroy all. With the noose tightening around Nanking, the Three Alls were about to be put into practice, with terrifying consequences.

The British and Americans—the two closest of allies, united by a common language, ancestry, and culture—often performed joint patrols on the Yangtze, including antipiracy missions, bandit sweeps, and rescue operations. Increasingly, the two fleets reacted to the mounting danger by grouping river traffic into convoys, each protected by as many British and American warships as could be mustered.

In the process, the crew of the *Gnat* struck up a fine friendship with the crew of an American gunboat, the USS *Panay*. One evening during a break in the patrols, the ships' crews rendezvoused at a riverside canteen. The beer began to flow, and the sailors' voices raised the roof in song. The American sailors took a real shine to Judy, especially when she threw back her head and yowled along to their sea chanteys, making herself the center of attention.

But by the time Tankey Cooper had navigated his inebriated way back to the *Gnat*, he'd realized that Judy was no longer with him. The ship's dog being missing, he sobered up quickly enough. Sailors searched the *Gnat* from stem to stern, but there was zero sign of her. They flashed a signal from their bridge via the Aldis lamp, asking their fellows aboard the *Panay* if they had seen her. The reply that was signaled back was "Sorry, no trace of her here."

Tankey was not the only member of the ship's crew who got precious little sleep that night. He blamed himself for not keeping watch over Judy, but in truth she was the ship's dog and every man among them should have kept a proper eye out. But the following morning all seemed to be much brighter, if a little more sinister at the same time. The *Gnat*'s Chinese boat boys had heard a rumor that Judy was safe and sound—and hidden aboard the American gunboat!

"So that's how they want to play it," Tankey growled upon learning the news.

He and his fellows spent the day plotting revenge. When darkness fell that evening a sampan stole alongside the USS *Panay*. Two fleeting figures crept aboard, and when they judged the coast was clear, they seized their chance. Their business being done, they slipped back into the shadows of the sampan, and it pulled away from the American gunboat, heading for the *Gnat*.

Shortly after dawn a signal was telegraphed from the USS *Panay* to the British gunboat: "To *Gnat*: boarded at night by pirates. Ship's bell stolen."

The reply from the *Gnat* read as follows: "*Gnat* to *Panay*: we also pirated—of Judy. Will swap one bell belonging to USS *Panay* for one Lady named Judy property of officers and ship's company of HMS *Gnat*."

Within the hour Judy was back aboard the British ship, and the quarterdeck of the USS *Panay* was once again graced by the ship's bell. No one—not even the U.S. Navy—was about to part the gallant seamen of the Royal Navy from their ship's dog. But such high-spirited japes belied the extent of the threat now menacing the

Yangtze. Shortly, the gunboats were to fall victim to the rising Japanese aggression—the USS *Panay* foremost among them.

On December 11 Japanese land forces unleashed their ire against their first Allied target: the British gunboat and sister ship to the *Gnat*, HMS *Ladybird*, plus the vessels she was protecting. *Ladybird* was anchored off Wuhu, watching over several British steamships. Without the slightest warning and under zero provocation, Japanese warplanes streaked out of the skies and unleashed their bombs, returning for a second time to strafe with machine guns.

One British steamer was sunk, and another badly damaged. The radio message that *Ladybird* sent to the flagship, the *Bee*, anchored upriver near Hankow, left no doubt as to the seriousness of the situation. Immediately the *Bee* set sail to come to her aid, but she was too late to prevent the *Ladybird* from being fired upon by Japanese shore-based guns at little more than point-blank range.

HMS *Ladybird* was hit repeatedly, and the onslaught ended only when she was able to steam far enough downriver to put herself out of reach of their fire. But the damage was done. Sick Berth Attendant Terence Lonergan had been killed outright, and not an officer aboard the *Ladybird* had escaped without injury. By the time the *Bee* reached Wuhu, she too came under attack and was able to escape serious damage only by repeatedly dodging Japanese shell fire.

Meanwhile, lying off besieged Nanking, the sister gunboats HMS *Scarab* and *Cricket* were guarding a fleet of British cargo ships when yet more Japanese warplanes appeared from out of the sky toward the east. By now *Ladybird*'s timely warning had been transmitted to all British and Allied shipping on the Yangtze: The Japanese were on the warpath, and all vessels were to be on high alert for hostile acts. The British gunboats were primed and ready.

As the aircraft dived to attack, they were met by a fierce barrage of fire put up by a dozen Maxim machine guns, plus four heavier guns threading lines of vicious flak across the sky. The warplanes were forced to abort their sortie, dropping their bombs at random along the river as they raced for the safety of the clouds. But the attacks along the Yangtze were far from over, and the Japanese would turn their aggression next against their foremost future enemy—the Americans.

The crew of the gunboat USS *Panay*—Judy's erstwhile kidnappers—had just finished evacuating all remaining U.S. citizens from the besieged capital, Nanking. As a result, the little ship had become the de facto American Embassy in China: she had aboard her five officers and fifty-four crew members, plus four embassy staff and a dozen-odd related civilians. She was escorting three other ships—the Standard Oil tankers *Mei Ping, Mei An,* and *Mei Hsai*, which were in the process of evacuating Standard Oil employees from Nanking.

It was early afternoon when a flight of twelve Japanese naval aircraft swooped for a surprise attack. The carrier-based warplanes—two Nakajima A4N fighters, escorting a flight of Yokosuka B4Y bombers—dropped a total of eighteen sixty-kilogram bombs and strafed the river flotilla with 7.7-mm machine-gun fire. The *Panay* was hit by two bombs and repeatedly raked by gunfire. The gunboat sank rapidly, going down in the shallows.

As the stricken gunboat settled onto the river bottom, the three Standard Oil tankers were hit and set aflame. Many aboard were killed, and the *Panay* had herself suffered numerous casualties. Two of the *Panay*'s crew had been killed, an Italian journalist aboard was also dead, and there were forty-eight wounded and injured.

A pair of American news cameramen aboard the *Panay* had been able to film the early stages of the attack, plus the sinking of the ship once they had reached shore. When their news footage was aired around the world, the scenes of the unprovoked assault would cause widespread outrage. But for now the *Panay* was lost, and news of her sinking had yet to reach the American high command.

Admiral Yarnell, then commander in chief of the U.S. Asiatic Fleet, was the man tasked with keeping watch over the unfolding troubles facing U.S. forces along the Yangtze. Unable to raise the *Panay* by wireless, the admiral put a radio call through to the *Bee*, asking the commander of the British fleet to try to locate the missing American ship—last known location just north of Nanking.

The *Bee* was busy escorting the heavily damaged British gunboat the *Ladybird*, but she responded to the American request and steamed downriver to investigate. Rear Admiral Holt soon discovered why the USS *Panay* had fallen silent. Among the still smoldering wreckage that lined the riverbank he discovered the battered but unmistakable superstructure of the American gunboat lying proud above the waters.

The officers and crew of the *Bee* surveyed a scene of smoke-laden ruin, and at first there appeared to be no survivors. Then a pair of Americans emerged from the bush and began shouting and waving at the British warship. The remaining survivors, many seriously wounded, had been moved inland to the nearest Chinese village. The *Bee* landed a shore party of twenty-five men, and the survivors, including all the injured, were taken aboard the British warship.

When the rear admiral radioed his American colleague with news of what had transpired, it would shock the world. Reactions from the American and British governments were swift in coming. They demanded that the unprovoked attacks along the Yangtze cease forthwith, that the Japanese officer commanding the forces that had bombed the British and American warships be removed from his post, and that compensation be paid for the loss and damage caused.

The Japanese response was to claim that the attacks on the British ships, plus the sinking of the USS *Panay*, had been cases of "mistaken identity." Their pilots hadn't seen the flags painted on the vessels' superstructure and had mistaken them for Chinese warships. But they paid the compensation demanded, removed from his post the air force colonel who had overseen the attacks, and promised that there would be no further such incidents.

Just twenty-four hours after the sinking of the USS *Panay*, Nanking itself fell, and what became known as the Rape of Nanking ensued. As many as 300,000 Chinese were killed in the most horrific ways. This was still an undeclared war: Japan had yet to formally declare hostilities with China. But with news of the Nanking Massacre reaching foreign ears, strong diplomatic protests were lodged—first and foremost by the governments that still had gun-boats on the Yangtze and that were receiving eyewitness accounts of the terrible happenings.

In light of the nightmare unfolding ashore, the British and American gunboats continued with their river patrols as best they could, but always in the face of mounting Japanese aggression, par-ticularly against the locals. By March 1938 the *Gnat* found herself in Kiukiang [now Jiujiang], 400 kilometers upriver from Shanghai. She was there to find out which British residents were willing to evacuate in light of the relentless march of Japanese forces inland.

Typically, a somewhat exasperated Waldegrave reported in his March letter to Rear Admiral Holt that the British residents in Kiukiang were intending to remain where they were "throughout all hostilities." Mr. and Mrs. Porteous, Miss Rugg, and Miss Luton, all Christian missionaries of the China Inland Mission, were intent on maintaining a very British stiff upper lip in the face of the Japanese invaders.

Of course, the captain of the *Gnat* was unable to force any Brit-ish citizens to evacuate. All he could do was have a word with the local British Safety Committee—a Home Guard–like setup formed by the handful of British citizens resident in the area—in an effort to put some procedures in place should the Japanese turn against British nationals when they overran Kiukiang, as they surely would in the next few days.

The sympathies of the British gunboat crews in this unfold-ing conflict—plus their animal mascots—lay fully with the Chi-nese. They had Chinese crewmen serving on their ships, they had befriended many locals along the river during the long years spent on duty there, and there were any number of British sailors who had fallen in love with a local girl and stayed behind to raise a family with her.

In fact, the crew of the *Gnat*—Judy included—had officiated over one such marriage recently, during a stopover in Shanghai. Chief Petty Officer Charles Goodyear served on the *Bee*, but he was a close friend of both Vic Oliver, the man who had rescued Judy from the Yangtze, and of the dog herself. It was only right that both were invited to his wedding—proof of how love could flourish in the midst of war.

CPO Goodyear's chosen bride was a Russian barmaid—and widow—then serving in the Pig and Whistle bar in Shanghai. After the wedding the crew of both the *Bee* and the *Gnat* had retired to the Pig and Whistle to celebrate the nuptials. An aged Chinese soothsayer with the ability to read a person's future was persuaded to examine the palms of a number of the sailors. Of course, the groom had to be among them. But when the soothsayer had scrutinized Goodyear's palm, he'd blanched visibly and refused to say a word.

Most of those present had teased Goodyear remorselessly, but not Vic Oliver. He'd felt a strange conviction that the soothsayer *was* able to tell the future and that Goodyear and his bride would have little time together in a world about to be torn apart by war. Certainly, if their Yangtze campaign was anything to go by, the forces of Japanese aggression were going to prove nearly unstoppable.

The gunboat men were powerless to act as the Japanese drove the Chinese resistance relentlessly backward. Japanese soldiers took Kiukiang, from which the British residents had doggedly refused to evacuate. With barely a pause they pushed onward toward Hankow—the Yangtze gunboats' "home city," the headquarters of the Strong Toppers Club, and the place where only months earlier Judy had dragged the unfortunate Tankey Cooper into the cesspit.

In the face of the bloody conflict, all aboard the *Gnat* had to strive to remain neutral—including a ship's dog who had as a young puppy herself fallen victim to the cruelty of the Japanese military. Judy seemed to have been blessed with an unfailing instinct for detecting which of her two-legged fellows were dog lovers and which were inclined to view her either as a potential tasty meal or as the enemy. And it was to be in Hankow that she would next come face to face with her tormentors. But first there were old acquaintances to renew, plus some sad and heartfelt farewells to be dealt with.

It was early April 1938 when the *Gnat* found herself again based at Hankow. Hankow being her home port away from home, there was the inevitable local fixer and master of all trades there, one who had made it his business to tend to the crew's every need. In Portsmouth, the *Gnat's* British home port, there had been "Tubby" Greenburgh, a rotund and jolly naval tailor from whom the men could always borrow ten shillings on "blank" days—those immediately prior to payday—interest-free and sealed with nothing more than a handshake.

Here in Hankow, Tubby Greenburgh's equivalent was Sung. For reasons lost in the mists of time Sung was better known to all who sailed the Yangtze as Joe Binks. A huge bear of a man, Joe Binks would beam with undisguised good humor as the men poured forth from the *Gnat* intent on some quality shore time, but he reserved an especially warm welcome for the *Gnat's* ship's dog.

Joe Binks was the *Gnat's* official Hankow comprador—the man charged with supplying the ship with all the food and other stores she might require. He often brought his wife and four young children with him when doing business aboard the British gunboat, and the children in particular delighted in Judy's company. In spite of being bred for the hunt, English pointers generally display an instinctive love of children, and Judy adored being in the presence of the Sung youngsters.

Dashing about the ship, hiding in her favorite cubbyholes, and challenging the kids to find her—these were some of Judy's happiest moments amid all the tension and chaos of the war-torn lower Yangtze. Cries of delight from the children indicated that they'd discovered her, but Judy would rapidly turn the tables by dancing excitedly from paw to paw, then going rigid and seeming to point at the children's bulging pockets—for the Sung youngsters always came bearing tasty gifts for *Shudi*, the peaceful one.

Judy's next-best friend among the locals was known to all simply as Sew-sew. The reason for the nickname was self-evident: she was tasked with carrying out any sewing or other repairs required for clothing or furnishings aboard the *Gnat*. Sew-sew would spend her time perched on a stool on the open deck, needle and thread flashing in the sunlight as she attached a new white tape to the collar of a formal mess jacket, all the while talking in her soft singsong voice to her chief companion, an enraptured Judy.

But perhaps Judy's foremost family of friends among the locals was the Amah brood. Amah herself was a woman of fierce repute along the Hankow Bund. Her entire family lived in a small rattan-covered sampan that was tied up on the dockside. Contracted to the British Admiralty, Amah had fought for and won the right for her boat to be used as the British gunboats' "general use" vessel. She and her children spent their day ferrying men and matériel from ship to shore and back again, or if there was no demand for her ferry services, she'd busy herself touching up the paintwork on a gunboat's hull.

Judy had grown to adore Amah and more specifically her children. Whenever she got the chance she'd leap from the *Gnat* into the sampan, and standing proud on the bow she'd oversee operations as Amah ferried a group of sailors to shore. But by far her favorite moment was when she was able to dart beneath the boat's rattan covering, whereupon delighted squeals and shrieks would reveal that she was having a fine rough-and-tumble with Amah's children.

Such were Judy's special friends at Hankow, and via her local family she was doubtless able to get in touch with her feminine side. But on the troubled lower Yangtze in 1938 it was perhaps inevitable that few such extended families would remain intact for very long, not even those aboard the gunboats.

Inevitably, there was a churn among the British crews, as those who had completed their two and a half years of "foreign service" were rotated back to the UK. Many were reluctant returnees. Especially in the middle of a conflict like that currently unfolding, the life of a gunboat man was exciting and fraught with danger, which made it strangely compelling. By contrast, England in 1938 remained a land of stability and peace, offering none of the young sailors the buzz they could expect when patrolling the Yangtze.

But as with all good things, every crewman's gunboat posting had to come to an end. Sadly for Judy, it was now the turn of her foremost shipmates to be rotated back to England. Vic Oliver, who'd plucked her out of the Yangtze; Tankey Cooper, who'd plucked her out of the Hankow cesspit; and Chief Petty Officer Jefferey, who'd plucked her out of the Shanghai Dog Kennels and chosen her as ship's dog—all were going home. In light of the loss of so many of her close family, perhaps it was serendipitous that Judy was about to start a family of her own . . .

After heartfelt good-byes between those who were departing and the dog they were leaving behind, replacement crewmen came aboard the *Gnat*. Among them Judy seemed to take an instant liking to two very distinctive individuals. One was an easygoing giant of a man, Leading Seaman Law. The other, Able Seaman Boniface, better known to all as Bonny, was a real joker and was to become the character of the ship. It was to be Bonny and Law who'd perform the pivotal role in Judy's forthcoming motherhood.

A French gunboat, the *Francis Garnier*, had docked opposite the *Gnat*, with an American vessel, the USS *Tutuila*, pulling in alongside. At first the arrival of the two Allied gunboats was seen as being a good excuse for some fine-spirited hospitality. The crew of the USS *Tutuila* was invited aboard the British ship for *limited* use of the ship's canteen—in other words, her stock of beer. The beer was expected to last only until April 26, before rationing would again be required.

After a fine evening's Anglo-American carousing, the crew of the *Gnat* challenged their Yankee fellows to a rifle match. It was a close-run thing: the British sailors won by one point. But from the *Francis Garnier*, the *Gnat*'s crew was about to receive an altogether more unexpected challenge—and very much more than they had ever bargained for.

It was Bonny who first noticed Judy's odd behavior. He was seated in the crew's mess, in the bows of the ship, trying to concentrate on the letter he was writing to his sweetheart back in Portsmouth. But whenever he seemed to get the words he was composing in his head just about right, Judy would get to her feet, whine insistently, wander about unhappily, then flop back down again.

Finally, she padded across to the ladder leading to the main deck and fresh air and stared upward with a fixed expression on her features. Then she turned imploringly to Bonny with the most heart-melting look in her eyes that he had ever seen.

Bonny put down his pen and stared right back at her. "How d'you expect me to persuade the barmaid in the Air Balloon that it's all right for me to take her on holiday without her mom if you keep moaning and fidgeting?"

Judy flicked her gaze back to the ladder, then pinned Bonny once more with that pleading look.

Bonny got to his feet. "What's up with you? You want to go for a little walk, is that it? Go on, then—up we go!"

Judy had become a fine hand at navigating the ladder, which was set at a thirty-degree angle with wide steel rungs like steps. Bonny followed, and together man and dog hung out on deck for a good few minutes. It was then that Judy took the initiative and led them down the gangway to the *Gnat*'s mooring, which was next to an old hulk of a merchant ship with all her masts and riggings removed.

Expecting Judy to want to run around and play, Bonny was more than a little surprised when all she seemed interested in doing was parading up and down the bare deck of the hulk. Head held at a proud slant, tail up and flying like a signal flag, she sauntered back and forth in a most uncharacteristic fashion. It was odd. Very odd. Bonny was at a loss to understand what she was doing.

Then he happened to glance across to the far side of the hulk, where the *Francis Garnier* was tied up. Suddenly the penny dropped. On the French ship's bridge was a very distinctive looking four-legged crew member whose eyes were glued to Judy of Sussex's every regal move. But what struck Bonny most was this: though slightly taller and broader of chest than Judy, the *Francis Garnier*'s ship's dog could have been her brother.

He was an uncannily similar liver-and-white English pointer.

Chapter Six

Bonny stared at the *Francis Garnier*'s dog in surprise. As for Judy, she seemed to think that her work here was done. With a jaunty shake of her rear quarters she proceeded to turn tail on the French gunboat and her smitten admirer and saunter back up the gangway of the *Gnat*.

Bonny shook his head in amazement. "So that's what it's all about, then. But how like a typical female! She must have known he was there, yet she didn't so much as look at him. Just showed herself off, then disappeared!"

In no time the courtship became the stuff of legend. In contrast to Judy, Paul, the *Francis Garnier*'s dog, made no attempt to disguise the fact that he had fallen head over heels in love. Now that he knew the object of his desire lay so tantalizingly close, he was forever breaking free and careering down the French vessel's gangway, ending up spread-eagled on the hulk in his haste to get close to her.

Unperturbed, he'd bound back and forth across the open deck like a medieval knight in a heavy suit of armor, unaware that Judy would be watching in disdain with bared teeth and curled lip. Finally, in a desperate effort to gain her attention and curry her favor, Paul hammered along the entire length of the hulk at top speed, legs thrashing in a super canine show of male prowess. Unfortunately, he'd miscalculated his stopping power on the smooth deck.

With a despairing wail the French ship's dog sailed off the bow and ended up in the harbor with a loud splash. Ironically, it was now that Judy finally showed her true feelings. She sprang to the *Gnat's* rail, barking in alarm as her beau beat a path through the water toward her. Sensing that he couldn't scale the sheer side of the British gunboat, Judy raced down the gangway with Bonny close behind. With Judy peering over the edge and continuing to bark urgently, Bonny reached down, grabbed Paul's thick collar, and hauled him out of the water.

The French dog was soaked from head to toe. But his ducking and his near humiliation would prove more than worth it in the end—for in making himself a laughingstock Paul had managed to break Judy's icy English reserve. Without any further dissembling on her part she proceeded to lick his face dry, nuzzle against his wet body, and paw him all over.

Bonny stared at the two of them in amazement. From being a total no-hoper, via his exuberant misfortune Paul had gone in an instant to being the first love of Judy's life. All of a sudden this had the promise of a match made in heaven. In which case, Bonny decided, the men of the *Gnat* needed to give their ship's dog a good talking to.

By now Judy was approaching two years old, the equivalent of her early twenties in human years. Bonny figured she was as ready as she'd ever be to have a litter, and with the *Francis Garnier's* dog being on hand they had a golden opportunity both to strengthen the entente cordiale and to breed a fine line of Franco–English pointers. But that didn't mean that any nuptials could be entered into without Judy being fully acquainted with the facts of life, not to mention her responsibilities.

On the afternoon of Paul's tumble into the harbor, five chosen men of the *Gnat* sat around the mess table, on which was perched a carefully groomed Judy of Sussex dressed in her smartest collar.

Bonny eyed her with a serious expression. "We feel that the time has come when we need a proper talk. We are so to speak your legal guardians, and we naturally want to do the best for your happiness. But you'll understand that everything must be done properly and in accordance with the rules."

He paused to let his words sink in. Judy cocked her head to one side quizzically. It was as if she was saying: *come on—get on with it!* At the same time she flicked out her tongue to lick Bonny's hand as if to reassure him that she was glued to his every utterance.

Bonny nodded, happy she was paying proper attention. "Now, Paul is doubtless a very nice dog, with a pedigree too. Plus they are a very nice bunch on the *Francis Garnier*. So we've decided you can get engaged today and if all goes well you'll be married tomorrow. But only on one condition—that you name your first pup Bonny."

Judy appeared to nod her agreement, and so one of the ship's engineers proceeded to lift her left paw and slip over it an anklet designed for this very occasion.

"That," he announced, as he closed it more tightly around her ankle, "is your engagement ring."

Judy stared at the loop of silver for a long moment. She knew from the tone and demeanor of the men gathered around her that something of great import was afoot, but she perhaps didn't quite understand yet what all this signified.

The very next day Judy and Paul were to be married. They were led forth onto the center of the hulk so that both crews could watch the ceremony. Bonny officiated, together with his opposite number from the French ship. As the men of both vessels cheered and clapped enthusiastically—and a group of perplexed locals gathered to scratch and shake their heads—Bonny proceeded to pat both dogs on the head and rounded off the ceremony as appropriately as he could.

"And so, with no further ado I am pleased to pronounce you . . ." He struggled for a moment to find the right words. "Dog and bitch?" He glanced around the crowd, hoping for some inspiration. "Paul and Judy?"

Then a heavily accented voice called out from the bridge of the *Francis Garnier*. It was their first lieutenant. "One!" he cried. "Pronounce zem one!"

"Perfect—I pronounce you one!" Bonny confirmed.

And so Judy of Sussex and Paul of Paris—Paris because it sounded classy and thoroughly romantic—were duly married.

Paul was permitted onto the *Gnat*, where a special love nest had been constructed for the two dogs. After three days in doggie heaven he was returned to the *Francis Garnier* complaining loudly, but all were deaf to his protestations.

As was perhaps fitting, Judy would bring new life into the world just as death and destruction threatened to engulf all around her. During the weeks since her romantic liaison with Paul she had grown plumper and plumper, her eyes shining with anticipation of her soon to be realized responsibilities. But at the same time Japanese warplanes had started hitting the heart of the Chinese resistance hard, targeting the city of Hankow first and foremost.

As the war along the Yangtze intensified, the Japanese Imperial Air Force deployed its modern twin-engine Mitsubishi G3M medium bomber, operating from land bases in Japan. Specialist units were formed to fly missions across the East China Sea, carrying out mass bombing raids over China's key cities. The Mitsubishi G3M carried 800 kilograms of bombs—many times the payload of the carrier-based biplanes that had previously attacked the Yangtze gunboats—and boasted a 4,400-kilometer flight range.

None of these warplanes had yet targeted the gunboats tied up at the Hankow Bund. But each time they roared over the city, Judy would curl herself around her distended stomach, as if in an effort to safeguard her unborn litter, and snarl defensively at the skies. She was learning to hate these giant angry birds that pounced from the heavens, unleashing death and destruction and threatening to snuff out the lives she was carrying before they could even be realized.

But the morning duly came when—as yet another wave of Japanese bombers thundered through the skies above Hankow—there was the miracle of birth aboard the *Gnat*. A tired and unshaven Bonny (the *Gnat's* self-appointed midwife) tumbled down the steps to the mess deck.

"They're here!" he yelled triumphantly. "All thirteen of them!"

There was a rush for the ladder as the crew jostled one another to be first to see the new arrivals, not to mention their proud mother.

Sure enough, squeezed into a ship's basket that seemed barely able to contain them were thirteen tiny replicas of Judy—each liver-colored from the neck up just like their mother but with several also exhibiting their father's distinguishing white streak running from forehead to nose.

Of the thirteen pups three of the weakest quickly perished, leaving ten to grow fat on their mother's milk. Lying protectively with her brood, Judy appeared to be the perfect mom, and not even the constant stream of well-wishers who poured aboard the *Gnat* appeared able to disturb or discomfit her.

She seemed happy to show off her babies to all and sundry—Sew-sew, the Sung family, and Amah the boat lady's children included. But the one individual prevented from seeing them was the pups' father, Paul. Now that he'd done his business Judy seemed to have forgotten her French beau almost as if he'd never existed.

In no time at all, everywhere there were unsteady puppies tumbling about the *Gnat*, chubby little legs flailing as they tried to escape from the ship's crew, who were equally intent on ushering them back to their nest. They got into every conceivable corner, chewed anything even remotely chewable, and everywhere they left spreading puddles of puppy mess.

Only when they were old enough so that each could be taken on a leash for a walk did Paul finally get to see his offspring. He sniffed at them curiously, as if trying to work out if they were really his doing, before they were ushered back aboard the *Gnat*. No one wanted to be out in the open for very long. With Japanese warplanes menacing the skies, any outing around Hankow spelled danger.

One afternoon shortly after the puppies' first foray off ship, a squadron of Japanese bombers flew in to attack Hankow, using the river valley to mask their approach until the final moment. But Judy heard them coming. By now the attacks were so commonplace that she rarely had time or opportunity to issue her customary warning. Yet today she seemed to sense that this was different and that the enemy in the air was coming for her family—both her four-legged and two-legged ones.

Whining frantically, she called her pups to her, and as the bombers roared in to attack she attempted to wrap herself protectively
around them, yelping out a desperate last-minute warning to the
ship's crew. Seconds later the lead aircraft swooped over the *Gnat*,
releasing its bombs. Like evil black demons they plummeted toward
the vessel, but at the last instant their trajectory proved slightly off
and they overshot the ship.

They hit the river ahead of the *Gnat* and detonated, throwing
up huge plumes of tortured white water. The reverberations of the
explosions punched through the ship's hull as a protective mother
curled closer around her cowering brood and blasted river water
rained down all around. Taken by surprise—so far, the Japanese had
kept their promise, made after the sinking of the USS *Panay*, not to
attack any neutral ships—the crew of the *Gnat* raced for their battle
stations.

Behind the lead bomber the rest of the squadron thundered in.
But as the *Gnat*'s gunners swung the Maxim machine guns onto
their target, a new sound rent the skies above the Hankow Bund—
the howl of Pratt & Whitney Wasp radial engines. Judy couldn't
know it and her fear for her brood was doubtless redoubled under
the aerial onslaught, but a flight of ace fighters had flown to the rescue, and by the looks of things just in the nick of time.

A ragged volley of cheers went up from the deck of the ship as
the distinctive snub-nosed forms of eight Boeing P-26 Peashooters dived to attack. The P-26 was the first American all-metal
fighter aircraft ever built, and the Chinese Air Force operated several flights of the redoubtable warplane. The Japanese had already
felt the wrath of the Peashooter's Browning machine guns, with
a score of Mitsubishi G3M bombers having been shot down over
Nanking.

In an instant the bombers targeting the Hankow Bund broke formation and jettisoned their bombs in an effort to lighten their load
and escape. But some proved too slow. The Boeing P-26s were flown
by Chinese pilots aided by a handful of ace British, American, and
other volunteer airmen. They had swooped from where they'd been

flying a holding pattern at altitude, and they tore into the Japanese warplanes.

Two bombers were raked from nose to tail by the Peashooters' 7.62-mm machine guns. The Mitsubishi G3Ms shuddered under the onslaught before smoke and fire bloomed along their fuselages, and first one and then the other fell from the sky into the waiting Yangtze. The *Gnat*—and Judy and her brood with her—had been saved from what had seemed like almost certain annihilation, but the narrow escape only served to reinforce the urgent need to get the puppies out of danger.

Homes would need to be found for the ten pups, and quickly.

Unknown to any aboard the gunboat's crew, the timely appearance of those Boeing P-26 fighters wasn't quite as miraculous as it might have seemed. There was in place a secret early-warning system that signaled to the Chinese Air Force the impending arrival of enemy warplanes, and it was happening right under the very noses of the Japanese. Unwittingly, the British gunboat the *Gnat* had played a pivotal role in getting that early-warning system up and running.

Some months earlier Stanley Cotterrall, the *Gnat*'s telegraphist— her Morse code operator—had been landed at Wuhu to undergo an urgent medical operation at the American Mission Hospital. During his recuperation the hospital had needed to send a signal to the Wuhu docks to secure the help of a doctor who was serving aboard a ship moored there. Cotterrall had offered to send one using Morse code, which he duly did using a mirror from the hospital roof, employing flashes of sunlight to alert the ship.

In due course the hospital staff asked Cotterrall to teach some of them Morse so that they could do the same for themselves in the future. One or two of the Chinese staff proved to be particularly enthusiastic pupils. They very quietly went on to learn radio operation as well, and under a cloak of absolute secrecy they proceeded to install a radio on the hospital roof.

Whenever a flight of Japanese warplanes flew over Wuhu, using the Yangtze to navigate inland to their target, those Chinese medics would sneak onto the roof to send a radio warning in Morse code. Thus Hankow was forewarned, and the P-26 Peashooters were able to appear as if by magic to blast the Japanese aircraft out of the sky. Eventually the Japanese would discover that the radio messages were being sent, but they were never able to locate the transmitter hidden on the roof of the American Mission Hospital.

As far as possible, the giving away of Judy's puppies was a gradual process so as to soften the blow. First choice went naturally to the officers and men of the *Francis Garnier*. Next in line was the Hankow Race Club, which made an offer that the ship's captain felt unable to refuse: one Lewis light machine gun and four magazines of ammunition in exchange for the puppy. Further pups went to diplomatic staff based in Hankow, and one of the last was gifted to the American gunboat the USS *Guam*.

The tenth and final puppy went to a Scottish engineer who served aboard one of the steamers still operating on the Yangtze. Once more Judy was reduced to the company of her two-legged family on a diminutive British warship increasingly feeling the wrath of the Japanese. And in the coming days the steel of the gunboat crew was about to be tested as never before.

Toward the end of the summer of 1938, with Japanese troops poised to take Hankow, a Chinese customs ship, the *Chianghsing*, was out on the river moving marker buoys in an effort to make it more difficult for Japanese warships to navigate into the city's harbor. Spotted from the air, the *Chianghsing* was pounced on by Japanese aircraft and strafed and bombed.

With his ship sinking and on fire, Captain Crowley, the *Chianghsing*'s British commander, rammed her into the riverbank in an effort to allow the crew to escape. But in the process of getting his men onto land, Captain Crowley, his first officer, and his engineer were machine-gunned by the Japanese warplanes. All three were killed. Several of the crew members were wounded, and the Japanese aircraft loitered in the skies seeking out survivors.

The *Gnat* was the nearest British warship that could go to their aid. She steamed out onto the Yangtze, needing only the thick black pall of oily smoke to guide her to the crippled vessel. With her men at action stations and her guns at the ready—plus one dog barking furious warnings about the danger in the skies—she sailed under the circling warplanes and lowered both of her boats. The *Gnat*'s crewmen were able to reach the survivors and evacuate them, along with the bodies of the dead, and for whatever reason the Japanese aircraft failed to interfere.

Shortly afterward, the *Gnat* received a gift of two footballs from the Hankow Customs House. With them was a handwritten letter of thanks from those on the staff most closely connected with the sinking of the *Chianghsing*. It summed up the wonderful esprit de corps exhibited by all aboard the *Gnat*, both man and dog.

> *You British Navy men, whatever your rank, are invariably and cheerfully ready to go to the help of anyone whoever they may be. Although you regarded this trip as just part of the day's work, your attempt to pass off a very gallant act as a mere bit of routine work does not diminish in the least the feelings of respect and gratitude with which we civilians regard you.*

But no amount of such selfless gallantry could prevent the Japanese from overrunning the city of the gunboats.

With the coming of the winter monsoon, fierce winds blew the Japanese invaders into Hankow. In the final moments the Chinese resistance had decided that it was better to melt into the bush and live to fight another day than to launch a last-ditch defense of the city. As Japanese warplanes buzzed overhead and Japanese warships steamed into dock at the Hankow Bund, heavily armed Japanese sentries were posted all across this, the newest Chinese city to fall under their dominion.

Aboard the *Gnat*, moored at her customary resting place beside the hulk, the chill wind of an approaching enmity blew across the decks and along the corridors. In her ammo-box-cum-bed on the ship's bridge, Judy lifted her fine head and sensed the changed atmosphere that had descended upon her surroundings. The homely clatter and chatter of Chinese port life had been replaced by the low murmur of a people under an occupation of unprecedented savagery.

Judy's first confrontation with the invaders was not long in coming. Just a few days after the fall of Hankow, Bonny—her erstwhile midwife—and Leading Seaman Law—her giant of a protector— took her for her customary early morning walk around the Bund. The trio had completed their usual circuit without incident and were returning to the *Gnat* when trouble stepped onto the riverfront before them in the form of one of the dozens of Japanese sentries posted there.

Judy, in her customary fashion, trotted over and took a sniff of his knee-length boots. The sentry's reaction was as unexpected as it was inept and was bound to cause trouble. Within seconds his voice had risen to a screaming frenzy as he berated the ship's dog and her two fellow crew members. With flecks of spittle at his thin lips, the enraged guard gestured for the dog—and her sailor companions—to get the hell out of there.

Judy stood her ground. She raised her head from his boots, and no doubt with early memories coursing through her head of Soo, her Shanghai protector, and the beating he had endured, she curled her lips into a silent snarl. The sentry took a step backward, his face puce with rage. His hand went to his rifle, he unslung it, and the sharp *clatch-clatch* of steel on steel rang out across the largely deserted dock as he chambered a round.

The sentry went to level his gun, but this was no ordinary dog that he intended to shoot here: this was a dog of the Royal Navy, the mascot of the gunboat HMS *Gnat*, and a fully fledged veteran member of her crew. Leading Seaman Law didn't so much as hesitate. The massive form of the crewman barreled forward, shoved Judy aside, and lifted the diminutive sentry into the air, and with him screaming unintelligible abuse Law threw both man and rifle over the dockside.

There was a despairing scream truncated by a splash, and the sentry was no more. Bonny, Law, and Judy made haste for their ship. Knowing how many of the Japanese soldiers were hopeless swimmers, the trio paused only long enough to see the bedraggled sentry crawl ashore before hurrying aboard to report the incident. The first reactions from the Japanese weren't long in coming.

After an exchange of terse messages, a stiff-legged officer from the Imperial Japanese Army was piped aboard the *Gnat*, complete with a sword that threatened to trip him. Of necessity, the British gunboat captains had learned to be consummate diplomats. During the past year of hostilities superhuman efforts at diplomacy had been required to navigate the Yangtze. Accordingly, Judy had been well hidden, and by the time the Japanese visitor had departed he'd been mollified via a combination of soothing verbal exchanges and plenty of ship's rum.

There were several further such visits as the Japanese commanders tried to ascertain how and why one of the "glorious liberators" had been treated with such disrespect and who exactly was responsible for *the dog*. But the stocks of wardroom rum obviously held out, for nothing more was ever said to Bonny and Law about the incident. Yet one signal change was afoot: Judy of Sussex was henceforth confined to the ship.

Any further close encounters between Judy and the Japanese might well prove the death of her.

Chapter Seven

By the turn of the year the gunboats of the British fleet were becoming decidedly old ships. Launched in 1916, they'd first seen service during the First World War and were approaching a quarter of a century in age. For some time now the Admiralty had been intending to replace them with more capable, modern warships.

In the early months of 1939 the first of those new vessels, HMS *Scorpion, Grasshopper,* and *Dragonfly,* sailed from Britain to take over duties from the veteran gunboats HMS *Bee, Ladybird,* and *Gnat.* The first vessel, HMS *Scorpion,* the new flagship of the fleet, had been built at a cost of £168,000. She was the model design for her sister ships.

Slightly shorter and narrower in the beam than the *Bee,* HMS *Scorpion* nevertheless boasted greater speed, armaments, and protection than her predecessor, plus more powerful communications and targeting facilities. Bulletproof plating was fixed around her pair of 4-inch guns, her eight machine guns, wheelhouse, wireless office, and vulnerable machinery housings.

But ironically, these new and more potent warships would hit the waters of the Yangtze just as the rule of the gunboats was all but over.

In June 1939 the crew of the *Gnat*—ship's dog included—transferred to their gleaming new home, HMS *Grasshopper.* Much was different aboard the vessel. She came with a new captain, one Lieutenant Commander Edward Neville, which meant that by now both of those who had purchased Judy from the Shanghai Dog Kennels—Chief Petty Officer Jefferey and Lieutenant Commander Waldegrave—were no longer at her side.

HMS *Grasshopper* also had a crew of seventy-five, meaning that the atmosphere aboard ship was somewhat less tight-knit and convivial than it had been on the *Gnat*. Sadly, Judy would have to make do without even the companionship of Bonny and Law, for they were remaining with the *Gnat* as part of her skeleton crew. Yet it was now, just when all the certainties of the previous years were being taken from her, that Judy would face the greatest challenges of her life so far.

Hardly had the ship's crew gotten used to their new vessel when Britain declared war on a belligerent Germany. Japan had still to enter into the hostilities, yet few doubted upon whose side she would fight when this truly became the second conflict of the twentieth century to menace the entire world. The *Grasshopper* had barely had the chance to enjoy a few good turns of her screw up the Yangtze when she was ordered by the Admiralty to set sail for open seas.

The *Grasshopper* would accompany the *Scorpion* and the *Dragonfly* steaming via Hong Kong and Macau to the British island stronghold of Singapore. The route would take her some 3,000 kilometers, arguably in the right direction—*away from Japan*—but for Judy this would be the very first time she'd left the Yangtze River valley and headed onto the wide ocean.

Forced to leave her offspring and most of her friends, Judy planted her brave paws on the shifting deck as the *Grasshopper* pulled away from Shanghai, setting a course for the waters of the South China Sea. Behind her, the *Gnat* and many of the other gunboats were preparing to sail to Singapore with skeleton crews. The Yangtze had been the *Gnat*'s home for two and a half years and Judy's for three, but neither ship nor ship's dog would ever grace her waters again.

Designed as a river gunboat, HMS *Grasshopper* had only a six-foot six-inch draft. As a result, she rolled, slewed, and heaved her away into the ocean swell, pushing ahead at close to her maximum speed of seventeen knots. At first Judy was violently seasick. In spite of all the cajoling of those who knew her, she refused to eat or to leave her ammunition-box bed. But finally the crew got her out on deck doing regular exercise in an effort to aid her recovery. By the time the *Grasshopper* was approaching Hong Kong, Judy had found her sea legs and was eating like the proverbial horse. She would never suffer from seasickness again.

Sandwiched between modern-day Malaysia and Indonesia, Singapore was supposedly Britain's unassailable fortress in the Far East, one that would halt Japanese forces in their tracks should Japan declare war. Known as the Gibraltar of the East, this island citadel was protected by massive 15-inch guns dug into apparently impregnable coastal batteries.

Should Japan enter the war, everyone up to Winston Churchill himself expected Singapore to hold out for three months at least, buying time for reinforcements to reach the island fortress and drive back the attackers. Unfortunately, there were several flaws in this assumption. One, the Japanese had air superiority. The British warplanes based at Singapore were few and obsolete, and they were no match for a Japanese Air Force equipped with the Mitsubishi A6M2, the dreaded Zero.

Moreover, the defenders of Singapore possessed few if any tanks, and all of the coastal guns were set on the seaward side of the island. There were none positioned to defend Singapore if an invasion were to come from overland. As an added drawback, though Singapore was well garrisoned, practically none of the troops stationed there had any training in what they were about to face—jungle warfare, a discipline in which the Japanese military was to excel.

But with Japan yet to declare hostilities, the *Grasshopper* and her sister ships arrived in Singapore when it was still a place that lived up to its early wartime reputation of "business—*and pleasure*—as usual." As the conflict raged across Europe and British and Allied troops were driven out of France, Singapore remained seemingly remote and untouched by the entire conflict.

As for Judy, gradually she was settling into this strange new life aboard a warship that no longer cruised the waters of the mighty Yangtze River. Compared with the months she had spent aboard a gunboat on active duty patrolling China's waterways, Singapore proved remarkably uneventful—but it would remain that way for only so long.

Judy had made a new set of special friends aboard ship, most notably Petty Officer George White, whom she had first met in the strangest of ways. The morning Coxswain White joined the *Grass-hopper* at Singapore's Keppel Harbor he strode up the gangway to report for duty, little expecting what was coming. He stepped aboard and threw up a smart salute, only to be half knocked over by something that cannoned into his shoulders and seemed to cling there—before whipping off his sailor's cap!

Coxswain White's attacker was himself a relatively new arrival aboard the ship—Mickey the monkey. The crew of the *Grasshopper* had agreed to look after Mickey temporarily while his ship and crew were away on duties in the Persian Gulf. Judy hated the monkey, but she watched with a peculiar fascination that morning as Coxswain White was assaulted. The man proved more than a match for the monkey. Quick as a flash he grabbed Mickey before he could escape, reclaimed his cap, and dumped the little animal unceremoniously on the deck.

Screeching with rage, Mickey tried to reclaim his prize, but Coxswain White was having none of it. He replaced the cap firmly on his head, and it was then that he spied Judy. Head cocked to one side in amusement, she was sitting well out of range of Mickey, who was attached by a leash to a length of wire running the length of the ship. Coxswain White would have been struck by how beautiful she was if it hadn't been for the fact that she was watching him almost as if she'd set him up.

"She's laughing her silly head off," he muttered, suspecting that ship's dog and monkey had colluded in the attack.

Very quickly White would learn that there was no love lost between the two animals. The first time Judy had run into Mickey had been perhaps her most ignominious since her plunge into the Hankow cesspit. Unknown to her, Mickey had just been installed aboard the ship, the wire being strung up with a sliding metal ring so he could shimmy back and forth. Judy had stepped into range, unaware of the threat, and Mickey had proceeded to vault onto her back.

The entire crew appeared to be watching as Judy leaped, bucked, sprang, and cavorted like a rodeo horse, but Mickey had clung on with both hands and would not be thrown. Eventually, confused and defeated, Judy did the same thing she'd done when trapped in the Hankow cesspit—she cried out for help at the top of her lungs. Seemingly realizing the distress he was causing, Mickey had dismounted. He went to try to put a comforting arm around his steed's neck, but Judy was having none of it.

She backed away slowly, keeping her eyes on the little brute until she was able to dart down the mess steps—all to a loud round of applause from the ship's crew. From then on Judy tolerated Mickey, but that was about all. Whenever he succeeded in leaping onto her back, she'd carry him to wherever she was going, suffering in dignified silence. But she was determined to get some enjoyment out of the little devil's presence, which she'd just had in watching him ambush Coxswain White.

A second new arrival joined the gunboat flotilla that day, and like Coxswain White he was fresh out of England. Upon reporting for duty, Leading Stoker Les Searle managed to dodge the cheeky monkey, but very quickly he would be drawn to Judy—a ship's dog who had started to gain legendary status as the staunchest of defenders of the gunboats, a reputation that was about to be tested to the limit and beyond.

Driven by a hunger for natural resources—Japan possessed few of her own—and with the war going badly for Britain and her allies in Europe, Imperial Japan decided now was the time to strike. The chief aim of its carefully coordinated series of surprise attacks was to seize the rich oil and coal reserves of modern-day Malaysia,

Indonesia, Brunei, and the Philippines. With Singapore lying right in the center of the territory that it coveted, the island fortress would have to be pounded into oblivion for the Japanese plan to succeed.

Several thousand miles across the ocean in the mid-Pacific, the American base of Pearl Harbor would also have to be reduced to a burning ruin if Imperial Japan was to prevent U.S. forces from coming to the aid of their allies. American bases on the Philippines—also within easy striking distance of Malaysia and Indonesia—would also have to be bombed into submission.

So it was that at 0400 hours on the morning of December 8, 1941—although it was still December 7 across the international dateline in Hawaii—the first waves of Japanese bombers swept in to hit an unsuspecting Singapore. Simultaneously, flights of Japanese carrier-based warplanes launched a savage attack against Pearl Harbor. Striking with complete surprise, they caused considerable damage to the United States Pacific Fleet. Further Japanese air attacks struck bases in the Philippines as ships landed troops in Malaysia for the overland push on Singapore.

With waves of Japanese warplanes bombing Britain's island fortress, the British warships HMS *Repulse* and *Prince of Wales* set sail from Jamaica to come to her aid. Part of the so-called Force Z, the battleship and battle cruiser had four destroyers as escorts but no protecting shield of air cover. En route they had the misfortune of being spotted by a Japanese submarine, the I-56, which was able to vector the first of the warplanes onto them.

Successive waves of Japanese Mitsubishi G3M bombers—the same type that had bombed the gunboats along the Yangtze—hit the warships with torpedoes and bombs. At 12:35 on December 11 the *Repulse* was the first to go down, with the *Prince of Wales* sinking less than an hour later. Just four enemy warplanes had been lost.

The news that both ships had been sunk was received with utter shock in Britain. Churchill's initial response was one of disbelief. "Are you sure it's true?" he asked. It was a crushing blow for those forces tasked to defend Singapore and to halt the Japanese in their tracks.

Unbelievably, the three Yangtze River gunboats that had ended up in Singapore were now some of the largest warships available to the defenders. In the days that followed Japanese forces rolled onward, pushing ever southward through Malaya (now Malaysia) toward Singapore. The defenders fought valiantly, but they were outgunned, outmaneuvered, and menaced everywhere from the air.

The *Grasshopper* and *Dragonfly*, plus their sister ship, HMS *Scorpion*, were in action repeatedly, although they could move only at night because of the threat from the skies. They bombarded enemy forces, they lifted retreating troops out of the jungle in daring rescue operations, and everywhere they relied upon Judy's ferocious barking as an early-warning system, enabling them to hide from any marauding Japanese warplanes.

In one daring operation the three gunboats evacuated 1,500 British troops from under the very noses of the Japanese, bringing them safely to Singapore. During another mission Leading Stoker Les Searle—who'd only just recently joined the gunboats in Singapore—was put ashore as one of a party of five to try to locate and rescue Allied troops. Instead, his tiny force ran into the enemy in the darkness, and Searle was shot in the leg.

The leading stoker and his fellows made it back to their ship, and he was taken to the naval hospital in Singapore. Since the opening of hostilities Judy had made a habit of accompanying the *Grasshopper*'s sick berth attendant during his visits to sick and injured crewmen ashore. She seemed to sense that her presence among the wounded offered them great comfort.

Les Searle knew all about the *Grasshopper*'s miracle dog, but the time convalescing with his leg wound was his first real chance to get to know her. As he ran his fingers through her fine, glossy coat, his mind would drift to thoughts of home. That was the beauty of having a dog like Judy aboard ship—or visiting the sick, as she was now. It took minds away from the savagery of the war to thoughts of gentler times, ones that sadly seemed to be fading into a distant past.

There was a deep and instinctive connection between Les Searle the wounded seaman and Judy the ship's mascot. Theirs would prove to be a long-lived and life-affirming friendship in the bloody months and years that lay ahead.

It was February 11, 1942, when the fleet of little ships remaining in Singapore was finally given permission to evacuate. Over the preceding eight weeks the island fortress had been pounded into near ruin from the air. The port's huge oil storage tanks were burning fiercely, casting a thick pall of choking, toxic smoke across the harbor, which mingled with that from the fires burning all across the city.

Hoping for another Miracle of Dunkirk, many believed the flotilla would somehow evacuate all to safety—disregarding the nearly total Japanese superiority in the air and at sea. The gunboat HMS *Scorpion*, already badly damaged by Japanese bombing, was one of the first of the little ships to leave. Packed with civilians fleeing the besieged island, she reached as far as the Berhala Strait, some 300 kilometers south of Singapore, before running into the vanguard of the Japanese invasion fleet—the light cruiser *Yura* and the two destroyer escorts *Fubuki* and *Asagiri*.

Though her guns barked defiance, the diminutive gunboat stood little chance. As it was blazing from stem to stern and out of control, there were only twenty survivors by the time the ship went down, all of whom were picked up by the Japanese. One of those who perished was Chief Petty Officer Charles Goodyear, whose marriage to the Russian barmaid had been so ominously received by the Chinese soothsayer back in Shanghai. Many more of Judy's treasured friends would lose their lives before the week was out.

On February 13 the final evacuation of Singapore got under way, with some fifty little ships preparing to evacuate the besieged island city. Priority was given to women and children. As the crew of the *Grasshopper* carried frightened infants aboard and comforted bewildered mothers, they were trying to work out how on earth they were going to accommodate the hordes of extra passengers.

Judy of Sussex didn't have to worry herself with such niceties: she was everywhere that day, dashing from one new arrival to the next, tail wagging ceaselessly and nose nuzzling into the hands of those who were the most tearful and distressed. She seemed to sense somehow the gravity of the situation and to know how the presence of a dog, a symbol of normality and of home, would comfort the evacuees, many of whom had been forced to leave behind their own much-loved pets.

She was especially fantastic with the children. Judy led them around the ship, showed them the finest hiding places, and played her favorite games with those who still possessed the spirit to play. But there was precious little room for any fun, for the *Grasshopper* was becoming a very crowded ship indeed. Her normal complement of 75 had been swollen fourfold as some 200 extra bodies crowded her decks.

Petty Officer White—recently the victim of Mickey the monkey's assault—was coxswain of the ship, which meant it was his job to see to the chief needs of all evacuees. Somehow, in war-ravaged Singapore he had to find enough water and food for 200 extra souls and satisfy all their special needs, such as baby milk, soap, toilet paper, and the odd piece of chocolate for the children, if such could be found.

Since the previous September the *Grasshopper* had had a new captain. Together with his senior officers Commander Jack Hoffman was busy on the bridge studying possible escape routes, though none seemed to offer them much of a chance of making a getaway. News had just reached him that three of the little ships crammed with escapees—local vessels the *Redang, Siang Wo,* and *Giang Bee*—had been intercepted and sunk that very day.

At nine o'clock that night the *Grasshopper* threw off her moorings and headed for the open sea. She was in the company of her sister ship, the *Dragonfly*, plus a dockyard tugboat and two double-decker pleasure steamers. All five vessels were packed from stem to stern with evacuees. To the rear of the crowded *Grasshopper* Judy had found her special place. She was curled up with those who were most in need—the children who were being evacuated from the besieged island, which was being pounded into fiery oblivion even as they steamed out of Keppel Harbor.

As the *Grasshopper* headed for the comparative safety of the darkened seas, the banshee howl of diving Japanese warplanes rent the air. The spine-chilling sound was punctuated by the scream of falling bombs and the earthshaking roar as they exploded among the port facilities. The occasional searchlight punched through the smoke-laden darkness as the defenders sought to nail a Japanese bomber in its light and put up some answering fire. But to those sailing away from Singapore the fate of the island fortress was plain to see.

Come sunrise the flotilla was heading for the Berhala Strait. *Dragonfly*, under the captaincy of Commander Alfred Sprott, was leading. The sea was flat calm and the sky a cloudless blue, offering zero cover to hide from Japanese warplanes. To the south and east lay a myriad of tropical islands, and the ships' commanders were hoping to find some respite from the Japanese naval forces by hiding among them.

But the first developments that day proved darkly ominous. At around 0900 hours the distinctive form of a Japanese four-engine flying boat—a Kawanishi H8K, Allied code name Emily—appeared seemingly from out of nowhere. Powering along at her top speed of 465 kilometers per hour, the otherwise graceful warplane dived to attack the lead ship. Two bombs were dropped on *Dragonfly*, but both fell wide of the mark, after which the flying boat was driven off by machine-gun fire.

Chiefly a maritime patrol aircraft, the H8K could carry around 1,000 kilograms of bombs, so it was good to have gotten rid of it. But no one doubted what this signified.

They had to presume that their exact coordinates had been radioed through to the nearest Japanese forces, whether warships or warplanes.

CHAPTER EIGHT

Barely minutes after the flying boat had disappeared a series of deep explosions echoed across the seas as the first vessels to be attacked that morning were hit. Three little ships—*Kuala, Kung Wo,* and *Tien Kwang*—had come under attack.

A group of small islands lay between their location and that of the *Dragonfly* and *Grasshopper,* and so no one aboard the British gunboats could see exactly what was happening. But they could hear that vessels were being set upon by Japanese warplanes and that they were being bombed and strafed from the air.

Earlier that morning *Kuala, Kung Wo,* and *Tien Kwang* had pulled into the cover of the nearby Pompong Island, so luckily some of the crew had gone ashore, searching for material with which to camouflage their vessels. They at least would survive the bombing and sinking of the three ships. One of those survivors was a young Royal Air Force technician called Frank Williams. Unknown to him, his fate was tied up inextricably with a very special crew member aboard the *Grasshopper*—a ship's dog that was even now comforting the children as the terrifying sound of explosions and gunfire echoed across the early morning seas.

The *Grasshopper* and her sister ships were following a "safe channel" leading south, one that was supposed to have been swept clear of mines. That channel extended through the Berhala and Bangka straits, leading into the more open waters of the Java Sea beyond. Unfortunately, it was exactly via this route that the

Japanese invasion fleet had chosen to approach the doomed island of Singapore.

Ahead of the *Grasshopper* and *Dragonfly,* the first vessel to encounter the oncoming armada was the tiny gunboat HMS *Li Wo*, commanded by Royal Navy Lieutenant Wilkinson. The *Li Wo* found herself sandwiched between two rows of a massive Japanese naval force, each consisting of transport vessels, led by a cruiser and tailed by a destroyer.

Undaunted, the captain ordered his ship to close to within 2,000 yards of the nearest enemy transport ship and open fire. The third salvo from the *Li Wo*'s single 4-inch gun hit just below the bridge and set the enemy vessel on fire, but by now the Japanese had very much woken up to the attack.

With the damaged ship now very close at hand, Lieutenant Wilkinson ordered his vessel to ram her. This she did, hitting at top speed amidships, and the two craft became locked in their death throes. Battle commenced at close quarters. It was brutal and ferocious as each crew raked the other's vessel with machine-gun fire. The British gunners finally silenced their rivals, forcing the Japanese to abandon their ship, which was burning fiercely.

The *Li Wo* backed out of the hole she'd torn in the side of the vessel, but by now she had a Japanese cruiser in hot pursuit. Facing a barrage of fire from her 6-inch guns, the *Li Wo* kept zigzagging to avoid being hit. But after the ninth salvo had raked her with shrapnel the order was given to abandon ship. Shortly thereafter the aft magazine must have been hit, causing a cataclysmic explosion.

The *Li Wo* went down with the captain, Lieutenant Wilkinson, still on the bridge, and there would be few if any survivors. For his heroic actions in command of his tiny vessel—outnumbered and outgunned but defiant to the last—Lieutenant Wilkinson would be posthumously awarded the Victoria Cross.

Less than a mile away another of the little ships, the *Vyner Brooke*, commanded by Royal Navy Lieutenant Burton, was the next to be attacked. After two direct hits she too was sent beneath the waves. Scores of survivors, including several dozen Australian nurses, managed to reach the safety of nearby Bangka Island, only to be captured by a Japanese shore patrol. The men were marched out of sight of the nurses and bayoneted to death or beheaded in the jungle. The women were very likely raped before being driven into the sea and machine-gunned in the water.

Several dozen miles to the north of Bangka Island, the *Grasshopper* and the *Dragonfly* were heading toward this bloody, tortured patch of ocean, along with three little ships packed with civilian evacuees—the two pleasure steamers and the tugboat. And it would be Judy who would first realize that the enemy was all but upon them.

The first hint of the approaching danger came via the *Grasshopper*'s informal early-warning system. All of a sudden Judy sat bolt upright. One moment she had been playing with the children, the next her ears were pricked forward and she was frozen as only a pointer can be—limbs tense, eyes glued to the distant horizon, mind totally focused on her sense of hearing.

Seconds later she had abandoned her position and was making a mad dash for the ship's bridge. She was barking out a warning even as she flew up the iron steps, arriving at the feet of the ship's captain, Commander Hoffman, breathless and panting. The captain was about to order her below again, but he and Petty Officer White—Mickey the monkey's erstwhile nemesis—watched with a growing sense of alarm as Judy's all too familiar actions began to unfold.

She set her sleek muzzle to skies to the north and let out a long series of fierce barks, and there was zero sign of her stopping. Knowing what this must signify, the captain ordered his men to battle stations. Sure enough, as Judy's barking rose to a frenzied and staccato *ruff-ruff-ruff-ruff-ruff*, the first tiny speck appeared on the distant burning blue. It was still inaudible to the human ear; it was only the sunlight glinting off distant wings that revealed it to be not a seabird but a warplane.

This was no lone flying-boat reconnaissance aircraft. As the air armada bore down on them, those on the *Grasshopper*'s bridge counted well over 100 bombers flying in five separate formations.

During the long weeks spent under bombardment first on the Yang-tze and more recently in Singapore, the ship's crew had grown used to the sight of mass waves of enemy aircraft roaring through the skies. But to encounter them here in the open ocean, and with hundreds of civilian passengers under their protection, was an entirely more daunting proposition.

The Japanese warplanes were sleek twin-engine Mitsubishi Ki-21 heavy bombers, each carrying over 1,000 kilograms of bombs. It was approaching midday on February 14, 1942, when the first of those aircraft thundered in across the ocean to attack.

The lead bombers swooped onto the flotilla's flagship, HMS *Dragonfly*. As her machine guns and cannon sparked fiery defiance, the first of the bombs fell all around her like rain. The captain had his vessel going at full speed and circling in an avoiding action as his guns unleashed hell, and for long moments the warplanes seemed unable to hit her. But though the *Grasshopper* likewise had all guns blazing, she wasn't to be so lucky.

The first direct hit on the *Grasshopper* sent shrapnel pinging off her thick armored plating and ricocheting all around her super-structure, the explosion raking the bridge with burning hot shards of steel. Commander Hoffman was himself injured in the blast, suffering a deep gouge to his leg, and Petty Officer White's right arm and hand were peppered with flying splinters of blasted metal.

A fire had been sparked by the bomb, but the ship's crew soon managed to get it under control. Yet even as they were doing so more Ki-21s howled in, their bombs plummeting toward the ship with banshee wails that sent a shiver up the spine. Towering gouts of white were thrown up all around the *Grasshopper* as she plowed onward through the firestorm. At times the vessel was all but invisible as a result of the wall of water churned up by the explosions.

Grasshopper's guns continued to spit defiance even though the gunners were half blinded by the plumes of spray. The tug-boat and the two double-decker pleasure steamers were entirely defenseless—apart from the fire put up by the gunboats. Within minutes both pleasure steamers had come to a stop and were burning fiercely. The tugboat, which had taken a direct hit, had disappeared completely.

For several minutes the *Dragonfly* seemed to lead a charmed life as none of the bombers appeared able to score a direct hit. Then a bomb must have exploded in her aft magazine—the ammunition store, set just to the rear of the bridge—or on the depth charges stored on deck. Even from over a half a mile away, which was the distance now separating the *Dragonfly* and the *Grasshopper*, the explosion seemed devastating.

There was the blinding flash of the blast, and a roar like thunder rolled across the sea toward the *Grasshopper*. A massive plume of smoke and debris punched above the *Dragonfly* aft of the bridge. When visibility finally cleared, all that remained of the back half of the British warship was a mass of twisted and scorched metal. Any evacuees who'd been sheltering in the rear half of the vessel would have been killed instantly. The stern of the *Dragonfly* seemed to have been torn clean away, the engines had stopped, and the ship looked doomed.

As those in the *Grasshopper* watched aghast the *Dragonfly* began to sink stern first. Within a matter of minutes she was half submerged. The survivors launched a whaler, plus some circular Carley survival rafts, and the injured who could be rescued were hauled aboard. It was then that Commander Sprott gave the final order to abandon ship, and all those who were able to dived overboard and swam away from the fast-sinking vessel.

Just as she was going under, two tiny figures jumped from the bridge, ran along her side, and slid down the ship's bottom and into the sea. Commander Sprott and his first lieutenant had made it off the *Dragonfly* in the nick of time. Within seconds she was all but gone, just a few feet of her prow remaining above the waves. It was no more than five minutes since the cataclysmic explosion had torn her apart—and HMS *Dragonfly* was no more.

The few dozen survivors were clinging to Carley floats or were packed into the lone lifeboat. They were a dozen miles or more from the nearest land and crammed into hopelessly overcrowded vessels.

On the bridge of the *Grasshopper*, Commander Hoffman made the only decision that he could. He turned his vessel toward the point where the *Dragonfly* had gone down, and with the engines at full throttle he set a course for rescue. If he could also go to the aid of the survivors from the two pleasure steamers, so much the better.

But the circling warplanes were far from finished yet. As Judy pranced about barking maniacally at the thundering skies, some sixty-odd enemy aircraft turned in formation and began to bear down on the lone surviving gunboat. They separated into flights of six aircraft each and dropped down to 2,000 feet, wave after wave lining up for a low-level attack designed to finish the stubborn British gunboat once and for all.

For the umpteenth time that morning Commander Hoffman ordered his gunners to open fire, and *Grasshopper*'s six .303-inch machine guns spit defiance into the face of the attacking bombers. By now Judy had gotten used to the sound of the ship's guns. She clearly didn't like it, but as her hackles rose and she bared her fangs at the skies above the ship, it was clear that she knew from where the real danger emanated.

From the *Grasshopper*'s bridge the scene appeared almost unreal. Judy's barking mingled with the cries of the women and children crowded onto the decks, the distant jungle-clad "paradise" islands adding a surreal edge to the scene. If anything, the first few minutes of the onslaught proved even more surreal: repeated waves of Ki-21s screamed overhead as the *Grasshopper* charged onward at seventeen knots, churning up the seas in a series of tight circles, yet each time their bombs somehow seemed to miss her.

With each revolution that his ship cut through the water, Commander Hoffman was bringing her ever closer to the nearest landfall. If she was hit, as he feared she was going to be, he wanted to be close to land to have a chance of saving his crew and those civilians who were crouched in terror on his decks.

It was then that one of the Japanese warplanes must have gotten lucky. A sleek black object seemed to plummet in slow motion directly toward the bridge. At the last moment it overshot and slammed into the rear mess deck, just aft of the ship's superstructure. It exploded in the bowels of the vessel, wreaking havoc in the after mess deck, the blast shaking the ship like a dog with a bone.

The *Grasshopper* shuddered from stem to stern, but so far the damage didn't appear terminal. It was only when angry gouts of flame burst forth from the ship's hold adjacent to the rear magazine—the ship's ammunition store—that Commander Hoffman knew they were in trouble. With the fire burning furiously, the crew struggled to flood the magazine with seawater to prevent it from exploding, but it proved impossible. Word was sent to the bridge that nothing could be done to stop the flames from reaching the ammunition, which could blow at any time.

Commander Hoffman knew now that he had to get everyone off his ship and fast. If the fire reached the ammunition store, they would suffer a similar fate to that of the *Dragonfly*—the rear of their vessel would be blasted asunder. Injured though he was, Captain Hoffman was still very much in charge of his ship. With her bows pointed directly at the pristine white sands of the nearby tropical island, he demanded one final burst of power from her twin engines.

Her bow cleaving the water like a knife, *Grasshopper* made her final, desperate run. There was little time for any finesse here: with further waves of Japanese warplanes thundering in to attack, Commander Hoffman planned to ram his ship into the shallows and beach her. As the engine room began to flood, the stokers coaxed the last remaining power from her boilers. Turbines throbbed, the deck thrummed, and *Grasshopper*'s twin propellers thrashed the seas as a long plume of oily smoke streamed out into the skies behind her, acting like a marker signal to the approaching Ki-21 warplanes.

Twice more they dropped their bombs all around the stricken gunboat as she steamed hell for leather for land. Miraculously, none of those munitions found their mark. Finally, there was a tearing, shuddering impact from the bowels of the vessel, and the *Grasshopper* came to a halt, stuck fast on the bottom. The pristine white sands were barely a hundred yards distant, which should have made it easy enough to ferry the wounded and the survivors—both human and canine—to shore.

The captain gave the order to abandon ship. As the *Grasshopper*'s crew dashed about manically, launching Carley floats and lifeboats and hurrying the terrified women and children into them, the one consolation seemed to be that the skies above them had fallen mercifully silent. As quickly as it had materialized the Japanese air armada had disappeared: most likely they were all out of bombs. But even now a new and terrible drama was about to unfold around the wreckage of their sister ship, the *Dragonfly*.

The *Dragonfly*'s one lifeboat was hopelessly overcrowded—so much so that those aboard had had to refuse to take any more survivors. The Carley floats were likewise swamped, and those small groups still in the sea had no option but to start the long swim to land. But some thirty minutes after the last of the Japanese warplanes had disappeared, a new threat heaved into view. Flying in from the east and at very low level was a second wave of warplanes.

There were fewer Ki-21s this time, but there was also less work to be done. They broke into formations of three flying in line abreast and thundered in at close to zero feet above the waves. The first trio bore down on the *Dragonfly*'s single lifeboat and opened fire. Machine-gun rounds tore into the little vessel. A second and a third formation roared across the sea, likewise pounding the lifeboat mercilessly. With the tiny wooden craft having been riddled with gunfire, the Ki-21s turned their attention to those clinging to the Carley floats, plus any they could find in the water.

Having shot up the survivors from the *Dragonfly*, the warplanes turned toward their one remaining target—the *Grasshopper*. By now the wounded and the women and children had been loaded aboard the ship's lifeboat. Most of the crew was gathered around the Carley floats or had set off in groups swimming the short distance to shore. But Captain Hoffman and Petty Officer White remained on the bridge with vital work to do—directing the fire of the ship's guns.

Beached, broken, and burning she might be, but the *Grasshopper* still had fight in her. And it was vital that her six .303-inch machine guns keep firing until those making for the island had gotten into the cover of the thick jungle. With a sickening sense of anger and disgust, the crew of the *Grasshopper*, who had seen what those Japanese bombers had done to the survivors of the *Dragonfly*, was poised to meet murderous fire with fire.

Though marooned and doomed, the *Grasshopper* still made an excellent and stable fire platform—or at least she would until her aft magazine was caught by the flames and blew. Sure enough, under the protective hail of bullets thrown up from the stricken ship, the lifeboat and the Carley floats made landfall pretty much unharmed.

When the signal was finally given that all had made shore safely, the *Grasshopper*'s guns fell silent. Those few remaining aboard ship—in the gun positions and on the bridge—made a dash for the sea and the short swim to the shallows. But as Petty Officer White cast a final look around the stricken ship, he was unable to find one very special crew member—Judy. Amid the hell of battle, the *Grasshopper*'s dog and ever-faithful mascot seemed to have disappeared.

Presuming Judy must have made her own way to land, White launched himself into the sea and swam ashore.

CHAPTER NINE

Even as the last of the *Grasshopper*'s crew dived into the warm sea, the final moments of Britain's island fortress were playing out. Within hours Singapore would fall in the largest surrender of a British-led military force in history. Some 80,000 British, Australian, Indian, and other Allied service personnel would be taken as Japanese prisoners of war in what Churchill would describe as the "worst disaster" in British military history.

Just as February 15, 1942, was one of Britain's darkest hours, so too the fate of the survivors of the *Grasshopper* was proving decidedly bleak. Five of the crew members were reported dead, four were severely wounded, and there were several, both military and civilians, reported missing. Many of the survivors were in shock. Their situation on this unknown island appeared dire indeed. They had few possessions, no medical supplies, little food, and no visible sign of fresh water.

At the same time it was obvious that Japanese forces were swarming all around these islands. The first priority was to get the wounded into proper cover, where they could be hidden from view and whatever treatment possible might be given them. Commander Hoffman might have lost his ship, but he was still in charge of his crew, and he did a rapid assessment of who and what he had available to him.

In addition to some fifty-odd ship's crew, he had a handful of Australian nurses: they should prove useful caring for the wounded.

There were six Royal Marines in his company, themselves survivors of the recent sinking of the British warships *Repulse* and *Prince of Wales*. He set the marines the task most suited to them—to scour the length and breadth of the island, searching for fresh water, any local inhabitants, or survivors from the other ships.

He also had any number of women and children somehow to comfort and care for. One of the women was blind, and she was constantly being tended to by her daughter. The welfare of the civilians had to be one of his first priorities, after the wounded. Commander Hoffman set the ship's crew the task of clearing a camp where the beach met the jungle. Rough stretchers were lashed together from tree branches, and the wounded were laid in the shade on them. Next, graves were dug in the sandy soil, and the dead, such as they'd been able to bring ashore, were buried.

Later that afternoon the marines returned from their search with bleak news. As far as they could tell the island was uninhabited. They'd found little evidence of any other survivors, and worse still, there was no sign of any drinking water. This was now Commander Hoffman's chief concern. On the open beach the sun was blistering, and even under the shade of the trees it was suffocating and humid. They desperately needed water, especially if the wounded were to rehydrate after losing so much blood.

Commander Hoffman turned his gaze toward the *Grasshopper*. The tide was farther out now, leaving the beached ship lying high and at an odd angle to the sea. Smoke still roiled about her aft deck from the fire. The odd explosion echoed across the water as the flames caught on something more inflammable. There was no knowing what risks they would be exposed to if they returned to the ship, but unless they did, many of those in his company would surely die.

Hoffman glanced at a figure beside him—Petty Officer White, the *Grasshopper*'s hardy coxswain. He gave a nod toward the ship. "Cox'n, when the lifeboat returns I want you to get back aboard the *Grasshopper*. Take some hands with you and see what, if anything, can be salvaged. Priority has to be water, medical supplies, food, clothes, and some bedding."

It was White's turn to eye the ship. The lifeboat had been sent off to circumnavigate the island, doing a more thorough search for any survivors. It could be any amount of time before it returned—time that the wounded could ill afford.

"Permission to go now, sir," White volunteered. "It's only a short swim, and I can knock up a raft once aboard."

"Very well, Cox'n. As soon as you like."

The captain of the *Grasshopper* hadn't been the slightest bit surprised at Coxswain White's suggestion. He would have been more shocked if White hadn't volunteered to go. But at the same time he didn't doubt the man's bravery. In addition to the dangers of returning to the burning ship, sharks had been sighted circling the wreck, no doubt drawn to it by the bodies that had ended up in the water.

Undaunted, White strode purposefully into the sea and set out for the vessel. He was doing all he could to keep his mind focused on the task ahead of him, but his thoughts kept drifting to what might be lurking *under* the water. Did sharks always swim with their dorsal fins poking out when approaching their prey? Or might they sneak in unseen at depth and strike from below, going for the legs?

By the time he'd reached the ship, he was sure that he'd broken the world record for the fifty-yard dash! He hauled himself up one side of the vessel, which had heeled over considerably as the tide receded. His first task now was to construct a raft so he could use it to ferry any salvage to shore. Both the bridge and the wheelhouse had a deck grating—a tough wooden latticework that lay across the floor—and that should make the perfect platform for a raft.

He dragged them into the open air, lashed them together one on top of the other, then manhandled them over the ship's side. He now had a usable floating platform, which he lashed to the ship's rail with a length of rope. That done, White eased himself into what had once been the officers' quarters, set forward of the ship. This was still mostly above water and dry. He grabbed bedding, pots and pans, and as much canned food as he could lay his hands on. Each item was pushed up through the hatch and piled on the deck above. As an extra bonus he found an unbroken bottle of whiskey.

"For medicinal purposes only," he told himself as he placed it with the growing pile of salvage.

He moved farther toward the ship's main mess deck. White was careful going down the steel rungs of the ladder, for the sea had flooded into this part of the vessel and the water was soon up to his waist. He inched into the gloom, nudging his way past tables and chairs that bobbed about in the oily darkness, searching with his hands for anything that might prove useful.

The farther into the far corners he went, the darker it became, until he was finding his way about largely by feel alone. It was then that he froze. Faintly, he'd caught the most unexpected and worrying of sounds. At first White told himself that his ears had to be playing tricks on him, but as he strained to hear, he caught the noise again. From ahead of him in the eerie gloom came the distinct and uncanny suggestion of groaning.

It was such an unexpected noise to have detected down there in the bowels of a ghost ship run aground at sea. There it was again—part groan and part whine. It sounded almost like a young child crying. It sent shivers up his spine. It was almost as if someone—some being—had been left behind here in the flooded mess deck, somehow trapped and in great distress. Or was it maybe the spirits of those who had died down here come to haunt the doomed ship already.

White turned around in the sloshing water, his ears straining to track the ghostly noise. As far as he could tell it seemed to be coming from beneath an overturned set of metal lockers. Using the bulkhead as his guide, he traced his way around with his hands held out before him, his heart beating like a machine gun inside his chest. He caught himself holding his breath: *Who—or what—could it be?*

White approached the chaos of the overturned lockers, water bumping against their hollow sides as he moved closer. *Thump, thump, thump*—the water beat against the steel drawers like a drum. The whining kept growing in intensity—almost as if someone was calling to him. There was no doubt in his mind now: behind those upturned lockers was a living presence, one that was somehow still alive amid the darkness and the flooded chaos.

White felt a rush of fear mixed with adrenaline similar to that which he'd experienced as he'd made his mad dash through the shark-infested waters to get to the ship. He inched closer, his bone-white hand reaching ahead to feel behind the upturned lockers. He stretched farther into the darkness. For an instant he could feel nothing—certainly no living being—and then his fingertips made contact with . . . a clump of wet and soggy hair.

But this wasn't like any human hair he'd ever felt before. An instant later a cold and damp nose had found his hand, and White knew in a flash who he had discovered here.

"Judy! Judy!" he exclaimed joyously. "You silly bitch! Why didn't you bark for me?"

Amid all the confusion and shock of the attack and the escape, the officers and crew of the *Grasshopper* had lost track of their dog. White had presumed she was off scouring the island with the search party or maybe in the lifeboat looking farther afield. It had never occurred to him that their beloved ship's dog might be still aboard the stricken vessel and trapped. Had the captain not ordered White to search for salvage, this would surely have proved to be her watery grave.

With murmured words of comfort he lifted the first of the heavy lockers off her, and shortly Judy was free. Fearing the worst, he gathered the sodden dog in his arms and waded toward the steps, all the while muttering words of remonstration—"Why didn't you bark for us?"—plus words of reassurance in her ear. Once on the deck he laid her down carefully so he could go about assessing her injuries.

Holding her still with the one hand, he felt all along her legs and body for breakages. As he did so, Judy seemed to be giving him this look out of the corner of her eye—*Thanks for the rescue, but what on earth are you up to now?* Finally, he allowed her to go free. He watched worriedly as she climbed to her feet. He was half expecting her to stumble painfully as a broken foot or leg gave way.

Instead, Judy proceeded to shake herself from head to tail, a dog shower of seawater raining down across her rescuer. And then she took one stiff-legged leap to the left and one to the right, with her head down as if ready for play!

The next moment she had plunked herself down at White's feet and was licking his hand. He shook his head in amazement. Not knowing quite whether to laugh or to curse, he opted to do both before yelling out the good news toward the shore.

"Judy! I've found Judy! She's here on the ship!"

With Judy's help he scoured the remainder of the vessel. By the end of their search they had a large pile of all types of swag heaped up on the deck. White took several minutes loading as much as he could aboard the floating platform, and last of all he lifted the ship's dog onto the rickety craft. It proved heavy and unwieldy, and unsurprisingly it took all of his seamanship to steer the overloaded raft away from the ship.

Judy meanwhile was up on four paws, peering over the edge. Something in the water had her transfixed. Moments later she began to bark wildly, as if she were warning of a new flight of Japanese warplanes inbound—only now she had her eyes fixed on something deep below. Then, with an extra powerful yelp of warning, Judy launched herself off the raft and into the sea.

White didn't have much of a clue what she was up to, and in any case he needed all of his concentration to guide the low-lying craft toward the beach. Judy meanwhile was swimming strongly, doing laps of the raft as if she was circling it protectively. Only once strong hands had joined White in guiding the clumsy craft into the shallows did Judy stop what she was doing and haul herself onto dry land.

Then she did her second shake of the morning—head to tail and showering all her friends with seawater—before unleashing one last protective round of barks toward the sea. White hadn't liked to dwell on it too much as he'd made his way across the water, but he suspected very much that Judy's extraordinary sense for danger had detected a shark in the water. Just as she'd gone into action at Hankow to safeguard Chief Petty Officer Jefferey from a forest leopard, she'd dived into the waters off this tropical island to distract a shark from its intended human prey.

Having recruited further hands to help pilot the raft and fend off any marauding sharks, White began to ferry the rest of the salvage from ship to shore. As the pile of stores grew, the immediate issue of food had been resolved. The chief problem now remained water, for the little they'd managed to salvage off the *Grasshopper* wouldn't last long. The ship's crew had scoured the island from end to end, but not the smallest stream or spring seemed to grace this otherwise picture-perfect tropical paradise setting.

As the ship's crew continued to poke around, digging shallow holes in the dankest parts of the forest and otherwise investigating anywhere that seemed to possess even the vaguest promise of water, Judy joined them. She had a general sniff around. She trotted from figure to figure, tail wagging busily and tongue hanging out as she endeavored to cool herself in the late afternoon swelter.

But much as everyone tried to explain to her what they were doing—"We're looking for water, see"—Judy didn't quite seem to get it. She kept finding her way back to the sea, where she'd have a good splash and a roll in the surf. Like her human companions, Judy was doubtless feeling hot and bothered, not to mention thirsty, and a good dip was as good a way as any to cool off. The ship's crew kept calling her back to help in the search for water, but she seemed fixated on this one stretch of shoreline.

The rough, makeshift camp that had been hewn out of the jungle was already starting to resemble some kind of frontline field hospital. Using the medical supplies salvaged from the *Grasshopper,* the Australian nurses were tending to the wounded as best they could—bandaging up breaks, cleaning and disinfecting wounds, and doling out the precious painkillers. But without water there was a limit to what they could achieve.

Where the camp met the beach the marines were busy constructing a bush stove—one with which they would be able to cook, but without the telltale smoke that an open fire gives off. One of the marines was struck by how Judy kept returning to the exact same patch of sand, right beside the water. She'd make her way

there, whine and paw at the ground, then bark excitedly—as if trying to attract the attention of her human companions.

The marine called over to a member of the *Grasshopper*'s crew.
"What's up with your dog, chief? Can she see something down there
we can't?"

The sailor wandered over to join Judy. There was no doubt about
it—her behavior was curious. He knelt beside her, giving her a good
scratch behind the ears where he knew she liked it best.

"What's up then, old girl?"

In answer, Judy gave an eager whine, and then she began to
dig. With her forepaws flying she scooped away at the wet sand,
which went blasting out behind her. Caught up in the dog's apparent enthusiasm, the mystified sailor joined her in her excavations.
All of a sudden, there was a gurgling at the bottom of the hole and
a stream of clear water bubbled up from below.

It looked for all the world like a spring.

The sailor couldn't believe it. He bent, scooped with an eager
hand, and drank. It was fresh and sweet. He turned and yelled up
the beach.

"Water! Water! Judy's found water!"

What Judy had demonstrated here were two of the most unique
and extraordinary aspects of canine behavior. One is intelligent
disobedience—the ability to hear a human's command or request
and to ignore it because the dog knows better. Judy had heard the
Grasshopper's crew urging her to join the hunt for water in the forest, but she had other—and as it turned out better—ideas. The second is the dog's sixth sense.

So often—as Judy had just demonstrated—dogs appear able to
read our minds. They seem to have the gift of anticipating our next
move and guessing how we are feeling. In the most extreme cases,
they've been known to foresee earthquakes, the approach of a violent storm, or even the death of a human companion. The most
sensitive canine noses—like a pointer's—can detect human phero-
mones, and so they may well be able to smell our moods.

Had Judy read the body language of the ship's crew—which to her meant digging for something of vital importance—combined that with smelling their thirsty urgency, and set off to find what they were so desperately seeking? It certainly looked that way. Most likely she had heard the spring running beneath the sand or smelled the fresh water. Either way, her sixth sense had led her to understand what her human family needed and then go and find it.

With the problem of food and now—thanks to their wonder dog—water being solved, the most pressing issue had become the wounded. The lifeboat from the *Dragonfly* had reached them, guided to the makeshift camp by the burning wreck of *Grasshopper*. It was riddled with bullet holes from where the Japanese warplanes had strafed it, and few of those aboard had escaped injury. Only those seated at the very front of the vessel—the opposite end from the direction in which the aircraft had attacked—had avoided being hit.

The dead had been put overboard, for the badly holed boat had been barely able to carry those still living. Leading Stoker Les Searle—wounded already in the battle for Singapore and comforted by Judy in that island fortress's hospital—was one of the most senior surviving personnel aboard the *Dragonfly*'s lifeboat. He gave an account as best he could to Commander Hoffman of all that had happened, including that the *Dragonfly*'s captain, Commander Sprott, and his first lieutenant were most likely dead.

"We were hit by two bombs, sir, and sank almost immediately," Les Searle reported. "Most of the wounded are still on the next island, with ERA Williams in charge. No officer survived, sir. The last, Lieutenant Shellard, died there on the island."

As far as Les Searle was able to report, the highest surviving crewman from the *Dragonfly* was an engine room artificer (ERA), one Leonard Walter Williams, the senior operator of the vessel's mechanical plant. All those above him in rank—from the engineer officer all the way up to the ship's captain—had lost their lives in the sinking of the *Dragonfly* and the strafing of the survivors in the water.

"Thank you, Searle," Commander Hoffman replied. "See my cox'n and have your chaps all moved over here with us. We'll be better off together. We'll have another talk later on."

Commander Hoffman received the dire news with barely a flicker of emotion passing across his granite features. To command in a situation such as this required nerves of steel and a rock-solid demeanor to boot. The good spirits of all of those under him— servicemen, women, and civilians alike—depended upon it. But just about their biggest ever morale booster right now would prove to be Judy, their irrepressible ship's dog.

Perhaps unsurprisingly, the paradise island that they had landed upon was proving a little less than idyllic at close quarters. Defiant yelps from Judy signaled that she'd found yet another jungle creature against which to wage war. Clearing the makeshift camp had forced hordes of snakes out of hiding, not to mention gruesome spiders as big as your hand. Judy of Sussex was proving to be the critter catcher extraordinaire.

She sprang stiff-legged around an unidentified serpent that she'd managed to corner. For its part, the snake had doubtless never set eyes before on such an adversary—a liver-and-white English pointer. Judy feigned an attack, the snake darted its head forward to strike, and she sprang in the other direction, seeking the perfect time to strike. When it came, she darted in lightning fast, attacking with paws and jaws until the battle was very much won.

Then she'd grab the limp form of the serpent in her mouth and carry it proudly to the feet of the chosen one—more often than not a very fortunate Petty Officer White. But with sundown on their first day on Shipwreck Island, Petty Officer White was to have other, more urgent matters to deal with. A new and pressing drama was about to unfold on the island sands.

It was the daughter of the blind evacuee who delivered the news. There were two Dutch ladies in their party, and they were heavily pregnant. It seemed that both were about to give birth. White's first thoughts were that the Australian nurses should come to the women's aid, but they were busy tending to the *Dragonfly*'s wounded.

He could expect no help from that quarter. And so it was that the petty officer of the *Grasshopper*, aided by a tireless ship's dog, prepared to deliver two babies on an unknown tropical island in the East Java Sea.

Fortunately, White had some prior experience as a makeshift midwife. It was during the 1936–39 Spanish Civil War that he'd first lent a hand in bringing new life into the world. His then vessel, the destroyer HMS *Grenville*, had been docked in Barcelona harbor, and White had been press-ganged into acting as assistant midwife during an unexpected birth aboard ship. How much more difficult could it be, he reasoned, with two births pending and his midwifery suite to be here on Shipwreck Island?

With the blind lady's daughter helping on one side and Judy lending a sympathetic ear on the other, two baby boys were brought into the world. Around midnight White cut the umbilical cords, using what he had at hand—his seaman's knife. In due course the babies would be baptized in the sea, with Judy cavorting in the waters around them. And Petty Officer George Leonard White would glow with pride as the newborns were named George and Leonard after him.

But the hour was fast approaching when George Leonard White would leave this war-torn patch of territory, and not in the company of the dog that he had saved from the *Grasshopper*'s flooded hold—a dog that was growing to love him.

Just when Judy needed her nearest and dearest most, fate would conspire to tear them apart.

CHAPTER TEN

The five days the survivors spent on Shipwreck Island were ones of permanent battle. They waged war against the heat, mosquitoes, sand lice, and ravenous ants, plus the venomous scorpions and spiders that seemed to get everywhere they weren't wanted. With food supplies dwindling and medicines fast running out, the surprise appearance of a wooden sailing ship making directly for their position was greeted with real relief—as long as it would prove friendly.

It was clearly a local vessel. The island was part of what was then known as the Dutch East Indies (now Indonesia), at that time under the control of a Dutch colonial government, and so the ship was very likely crewed by those friendly to the Dutch, which meant on the side of the Allies. The tongkang—a traditional trading boat with twin masts, battered sails, and a "putt-putt" motor—steered part the wreckage of the *Grasshopper* into the shallows. She dropped anchor, and a party came ashore.

The local Dutch administrator—he would become known to the many Allied escapees whom he helped simply as Dutchy—had sent the ship from the nearby island of Singkep, to investigate if there were any survivors who needed rescuing. Via the tongkang the crew of the gunboats—plus the Royal Marines, the Australian nurses, the women and children, two newborn babies, the surviving wounded, and one ship's dog—were ferried across to Dutchy's headquarters in the small settlement of Dabo on Singkep.

In spite of the obvious risks—if, or more likely *when*, the Japanese caught up with him, he knew full well what his likely reward would be—Dutchy had started an escape pipeline, providing food, water, boats, and guidance to all who were passing through "his" islands. The advice he offered to Commander Hoffman was this: his party should follow the route of those who had gone before, making for the nearby landmass of Sumatra and from there by ship either west to Ceylon (now Sri Lanka), off the coast of British-held India, or south to Australia.

Singkep Island lay a little more than 100 kilometers from Sumatra's east coast. Dutchy would be able to provide a large tongkang for the voyage. The beauty of the shallow-draft wooden craft was that they were equally suited to navigating the many rivers that crisscross the islands of this region, for their onward escape route would involve journeying up one such waterway.

The intended destination, Sumatra, is the sixth largest island in the world. A landmass of 473,481 square kilometers and some 1,790 kilometers in length, it consists of dense jungle and soaring mountain ranges cut through with turbulent rivers. Dutchy's tongkang would take them first to their east coast landfall on Sumatra, from where they would need to traverse the entire breadth of the island—some 350 kilometers of river, mountain, and jungle—to reach the port city of Padang on the far side. From there Allied ships were reportedly taking off evacuees, for Sumatra had yet to fall to the Japanese.

The journey that lay before the escapees was a daunting one, to put it mildly. But the only alternative if they stayed put was to be taken prisoner by the enemy. After what the Yangtze River veterans had witnessed of Japanese atrocities in China and what all had heard and seen since during the fall of Singapore, anything was preferable to being taken captive. Most took heed of Dutchy's advice and prepared for the long journey that lay ahead.

But Petty Officer White, along with two others of the *Grasshopper*'s crew—Engineer Thompson and Able Seaman Lee—decided otherwise. White figured that with the Japanese having taken

Singapore, they would turn their attentions to the next big prize in the region: Sumatra. The massive island had stupendous reserves of natural resources, most notably rich deposits of gold, coal, and oil. In the time it would take the escapees to reach her west coast, White feared Sumatra would have been overrun by the enemy.

Though none of them could know it yet, White's suspicions were well founded. The day after the fall of Singapore the Japanese had dropped paratroopers on the strategically important city of Palembang, South Sumatra's capital. In seizing Palembang they had taken a key airport to which the RAF had withdrawn many of its aircraft just prior to the fall of Singapore. Palembang offered the Japanese a staging post from which to occupy every major town and city across Sumatra. Already Japanese troop transports had set sail for the island's coast, seeking to sweep westward and overrun the entire territory.

A seaman through and through, White argued that the only possible route to safety lay by whatever boat they could get their hands on, sailing west toward India. It was a seemingly impossible sea journey of some 2,680 miles, but better that than get cut off by the advancing Japanese forces as they took Sumatra, with nowhere left to run or to hide. Few cared to join him, and so it was that White and his two fellows parted company with the main body of survivors—Judy included.

Much that it tortured him to leave Judy, it was inconceivable that White might take her with him. The *Dragonfly* and *Grasshopper* might have been sunk and shipwrecked, their sailors left bereft of any ship, but Judy remained very much a Royal Navy ship's dog. The ship's crew remained her family, and she their mascot and guide. Judy would be going with them overland to Sumatra's west coast and, they hoped, a seagoing passage to safety.

When the moment of departure came—the Sumatra-bound party was the first to leave Singkep—White felt overwhelmed with sadness. But oddly, Judy appeared to understand all that was going on around her and didn't seem particularly troubled. She sat before White, dark head held high, nose pointed very much at his, her calm eyes locked with his gaze. She had on her face a serene and untroubled look. It was as if she had always known when their hour of parting would be at hand and why.

White had yet to find a boat with which he and his fellows might try to make good their escape. Dutchy had promised to secure one, but they were in acutely short supply. Everyone wanted an escape boat right now. For a moment he wondered whether he wouldn't be better off joining the main party, heading west to Sumatra. But he felt in his bones that journey would not go well. Somehow, he sensed that Judy knew that too but that she would go to her fate with her family regardless and loyal to the last.

With a final lick of White's hand—her signature gesture of love and now of farewell—Judy turned away to board the waiting tongkang.

During the short and largely uneventful sea voyage to Sumatra, Judy settled into the company of an old friend, Les Searle. Searle had formed the nucleus of a tight-knit group that included Jock Devani, a typically tough Glaswegian seaman who seemed to fear nothing on this earth. Jock was a scoundrel and a scrounger without rival, skills that would come to the fore in the bitter months ahead. As for Judy, she appeared like an aristocrat among their rough and ready company, but strangely she seemed to fit in well with this group of born survivors.

The tongkang on which they were embarked was under a Chinese captain and crew, so those like Judy who were veterans of the Yangtze were back with the countrymen they knew so well. The interior of the ancient ship was lit by only one lantern, which swung gently to and fro. The hold was clearly designed for carrying cargo, as opposed to human—or canine—passengers. It consisted of an empty and echoing shell that ran the entire length of the ship, but at least there was room enough on the bare wooden boards for all to lie down.

It was dark, airless, and evil-smelling, the odor of unwashed bodies and recent trauma mixing with the scent of tar and rotting timbers. Fear and shock have their own smells, ones that Judy was becoming ever more acquainted with as her family's fortunes became ever more dire. Dogs rely chiefly on the emotional part of their brains. As a result they can read human emotions extraordinarily well and probably better than we read one another. From our body language and the smells we give off, they pick up on our emotional state very quickly.

The state of mind of those crammed aboard that tongkang belowdecks—defeated, shipwrecked, shocked, and on the run—was very clear to Judy. But there was also a new scent on the dank air in that vessel's hold—one of a faint yet carefully nurtured hope. At least the escapees were on the move again, and even better, they were hidden by the ship's main deck from any marauding Japanese warplanes.

Even the giant cockroaches that scuttled across the wooden boards were preferable to the ravenous ants of Shipwreck Island or their nighttime brothers in arms, the swarms of dive-bombing mosquitoes. Hope springs eternal in the human heart and in that of our canine soul mates, and with each puff of wind in the tongkang's sails those sheltering in her hold dared to indulge a dream of escape and of home.

The tongkang reached the gaping mouth of the Indragiri River without mishap. Unlike the Yangtze, which is a vital transport artery for much of the Chinese interior, Sumatra's Indragiri River is a waterway of far lesser size or importance. Its situation is also unlike that of the temperate climes of China's mighty waterway. Lying on the very equator, which cuts Sumatra in two, the Indragiri is baking hot, sluggish, and torpid, especially on its lower reaches.

As the tongkang pushed inland, there was the flash of a white belly and a splash to left and right as huge crocodiles slid off the mudflats that litter the river and into the muddy brown waters. It would be well-nigh impossible for an inexperienced crew to navigate the Indragiri, which is plagued by shallows and strong currents. Luckily, the Chinese captain was a veteran trader, and he and his crew had sailed this way many times before.

Amid the stifling heat and the windless calm of the jungle that crowded in from either bank, the boatload of escapees chugged upriver, every turn of the ship's engine taking them closer to their end destination—the port of Padang and the Allied ships waiting to carry them to safety. To either side lay dense forest inhabited by any number of exotic species: the Sumatran tiger, Sumatran orangutan, Sumatran rhinoceros, Sumatran elephant, the Malayan sun bear, and more.

Clearly, any journey overland would present its own daunting challenges to those aboard the tongkang. The Indragiri rises into a fast-flowing and angry torrent at its source in the towering Barisan Mountains, which form the backbone of the island of Sumatra. As the tongkang hit the lower reaches of this highland waterway, navigation became ever more challenging. Eventually they reached the tiny settlement of Rengar, near where the Ombilin and Sinamar rivers converge to swell the Indragiri's waters, and from there no boat of any real size could go any farther.

Judy, Les Searle, and Jock Devani—plus other assorted gunboat men, soldiers, civilians, and the wounded who were able to travel—duly put ashore. The advice from the locals in Rengar was simple: from there on the journey west could be continued only by land. Sticking to the course of the river, the travelers should be able to make it through the mountains—which at their dizzying heights rose to 3,800-meter peaks—to a railhead that rose at Sawahluento, on the far side. From there it would be an easy 80-kilometer train ride into Padang, the port from which they hoped to sail to safety.

But the locals also had worrying news. Even as far inland as this isolated riverside settlement, one besieged by impenetrable jungle on all sides, reports of the war were filtering through. Japanese forces had landed in the south and were already marching inexorably northward. In effect, the escapees had a race on their hands to see who would be the first to reach their goal—themselves or the forces of the Japanese Imperial Army.

There was clearly no time to waste. Fashioning makeshift stretchers from branches cut from the nearest trees, the party set off north along the river, with Judy of Sussex naturally taking up the lead. In their desperation to reach Padang ahead of the enemy, few preparations could be made for the journey. As they pushed deeper into the jungle that lined the beaten track, all signs of civilization were quickly lost behind them. The forest crowded around—thick, claustrophobic, and brooding.

From the deck of the tongkang there had been something wholly exotic and noble about the dramatic jungle-clad slopes. From within and with some 200 kilometers of such terrain lying ahead of them, it was an entirely different story. Massive, wall-like roots of the tropical giants—so-called buttress roots, which anchor the tree in the thin soil—blocked their path. Stumbling into one in heavy military boots sent an eerie noise like a hollow drumbeat echoing through the dark jungle.

At the head of the ragged column of humanity Les Searle felt as if the very trees had eyes and were watching. He was more than glad to have Judy in the vanguard, ears perked up and alert for any danger. Where she led, the rest followed as she tried to pick a navigable path through the sodden terrain. The only clear route was the track running by the river, but much of the ground this close to the thundering waterway was boggy and waterlogged. Bright green vegetation gave way unexpectedly, revealing the quagmire that lurked below.

Having four paws was a massive advantage right now. The soft pads on Judy's feet helped spread her weight, and having four points of hold on the ground lent her far greater agility than her two-footed companions had. No doubt about it, in such terrain a dog made an invaluable pathfinder.

Blessed with speed, power, and a fine sense of balance, Judy could shift her body weight about rapidly to avoid being sucked under or trapped. Her powerful hindquarters, which in canines are equipped with large and long muscles, could deliver fast movement—forward jumps, springs to the side, even backward flips—almost instantly. Storing energy in muscles and tendons and with the hind knees flexed most of the time, a dog can use its limbs like springs, propelling it out of trouble.

As Judy forged a route ahead, quartering back and forth to check for any dangers, she appeared convinced that the entire party was in her care. She also seemed suffused with a sense of urgency. Every now and again she'd pause and glance back at Les Searle and Jock Devani, a look of laserlike intensity on her features, as she signaled them onward. *Come on. Hurry. The route's clear. No time to waste.*

Back at their point of disembarkation on the river, Jock Devani had somehow managed to find and liberate the distinctive gold-braided cap of an officer of the Royal Navy. He had it perched at a jaunty angle on his head, and that somewhat belied the desperate straits the party found themselves in. That distinctive golden cap acted like a visual marker for Judy whenever she got ahead of herself and felt the need to check if her two-legged fellows were still following her.

Night fell almost instantly. The sun sank into the west—the direction of their travel—but the sunset went unseen by those struggling through the ranks of towering trees. With the sun gone, little if any starlight filtered through the jungle canopy. The moon remained a fleeting sliver of brightness, glimpsed only occasionally among the skein of branches stretched high overhead. What before had been shadowed now was invisible. A thick darkness black as ink blanketed all.

The party set camp. At times they'd found themselves trudging through thick and stinking riverside mud. It had proved home to a legion of leeches. The leeches latched on to passersby, crawled up the legs, and made for the groin area. It was damp, warm, and moist in there and replete with blood. After an hour's sucking a wriggly black wormlike sack barely the width of a pencil would be swollen to more than an inch across.

The leeches weren't overly eager to abandon their human hosts. Pulling them off might leave the head embedded in the flesh, which would result in infections and horrible tropical ulcers. The only way to be rid of them safely was to burn then off with a lighted cigarette. It was also a great excuse to smoke, not that many felt they needed an excuse after the trials and tribulations of the day. And watching the horrible black balloons of blood writhe in pain under the heat of a glowing butt end proved peculiarly heartening.

The morning of the second day Judy came up against her first major obstacle on the march. It was large and obstinate, and it came equipped with an armored skin, scales, and snapping jaws. But if anything Judy was even more stubborn and unwilling to back down than the beast she faced. They came head to head at the riverside—the massive Sumatran crocodile completely blocking the way. It lay in a narrow clearing and was most likely sunning itself. Had Judy allowed it time to back away gracefully, no doubt it might have done so.

Instead, she went for it as if it were a snake on Shipwreck Island. But this was no shy and retiring serpent. Barking furiously, Judy tried the same tactics she'd used on those critters—darting from side to side, ducking low, then dancing ahead as if to strike. The croc sat there unmoving, seemingly asleep . . . but very much watching from behind slitted eyes. As Judy pranced ever closer, her confidence got the better of her, and in an instant the reptile struck.

The croc moved with lightning speed for its size. Its body jackknifed, propelling it forward, jaws opening and slashing shut, rows of knifelike teeth slicing down across one another. At the last moment Judy had sprung backward, whipping her head away. The flashing maw missed her by inches, but not the claw that the sly croc whipped around to slash her on the flank.

Judy let out a yelp of pain and staggered backward in surprise. Snake, spider, leopard, *human*—never before had any adversary managed to get the better of her. But already a row of deep slash marks was showing red and bloody high on her shoulder where the croc had mauled her.

Still she wouldn't back off. But this was crocodile territory, and no way was Mr. Smile about to run away from a fight that he'd already started to win. It was most probably the rush of human reinforcements that saved Judy. Hearing her yowl of agony, Jock Devani and Les Searle were on the scene in seconds, yelling abuse at the crocodile and with guns and sheath knives at the ready.

Sensing perhaps that discretion had become the better part of valor, the croc thrashed its tail a few times and wriggled back into the river. With a final angry and muddy plop it was gone. But the damage was done. Judy was hurt. Their pathfinder and guardian was able to put her weight on the injured shoulder only with some difficulty. More important, they'd have to properly clean and sterilize the wound, for in the intense, suffocating heat and humidity it would quickly fester.

A few miles farther on they came across an abandoned rubber factory—natural rubber is made from the sap of trees that grow in the tropics—where they could rest up and clean the wound. Oddly enough, it was the rough and ready Jock Devani who took charge, demonstrating an uncharacteristically gentle touch when tending to Judy's injuries. As for Judy she seemed to have little idea how close she'd come to losing her head in the jaws of Mr. Smile.

Once her injuries were patched up she had a good drink and a rest, after which she seemed full of energy and raring to go once more. Jock took her for a wander around the factory just to check if she really was fit and able to continue. There was another reason for having a quick nose around. Jock hoped there might be something here that they could scavenge to sustain them on their travels.

It was in a back room that he stumbled upon a most unexpected find. The first signs of the discovery were a wild Glaswegian whoop of joy and a naval officer's cap being thrown high into the air. They say you either love it or hate it, and Jock was clearly of the former opinion. Bizarrely, what he'd found in the shadowy recesses of an abandoned Sumatran rubber factory was a large stock of the British nation's favorite spread—Marmite.

They were a little short of white sliced toast to spread it over, complete with lots of butter. But while they were being careful not to rouse Mr. Smile, water was fetched from the river and boiled over an open fire. Laced with the wondrous black stuff, it made for a nourishing and refreshing hot drink.

The rest of the unopened jars were packed away carefully, fuel for the epic journey ahead.

CHAPTER ELEVEN

It took five mud-, sweat-, and blood-soaked weeks to reach their journey's end. On average, they made less than six kilometers a day. No doubt the able-bodied and their dog could have made it in a fraction of the time, but not the children and the wounded. They were everywhere hampered by the stretcher cases as they marched over streams and bogs, through savage thorn thickets, and across highlands swept by freezing tropical rainstorms seemingly without end.

Had the able-bodied forged ahead, they might well have saved themselves much of the coming years of torment, but it wasn't in the nature of the ship's company—*the family*—to so much as entertain such a thought. And so they reached their final destination, the railhead at Sawahluento, with clothes in rags, faces heavily bearded, sweat-soaked and mud-stained from head to toe but still very much two gunboats' ships' companies, plus some others.

As for Judy, she seemed to have learned her lesson well from Mr. Smile. Whenever she'd stumbled across any more of the all-powerful denizens of the jungle, she had afforded them due seniority. In the days since her close encounter, her shoulder wound had healed remarkably well. Only those who had seen her take on the croc would ever believe that at the start of their trek she had been so badly mauled.

The welcome from the Dutch running the Sawahluento railway station was heartfelt. A hot meal was served, and space was made in the rail buildings so the party could bed down for the night. A train was scheduled to leave for Padang the following morning; all was looking well. That train would be packed with those fleeing the advance of the Japanese: in addition to Judy's party, there were soldiers, sailors, and airmen hailing from across an Allied war machine then in desperate retreat, plus the civilians who accompanied them.

When that locomotive puffed into the port city of Padang the next morning, it should have felt like a triumphant entry, especially for those who had made such a seemingly impossible journey largely on foot. But oddly it did not. As this ragtag army of the dispossessed tumbled off the train, one of the first things that the Dutch officials did was to order any remaining weapons to be handed over forthwith. It was a strange way to receive what were supposedly allies retreating before a common enemy.

Those in Judy's party who still had their rifles or pistols were likewise ordered to hand them in. Exhausted from their nerve-wracking journey, weak from exertion and lack of proper food or shelter, but also elated at having made it, few saw any need to resist the order or any sense in doing so. They would come to bitterly regret that decision.

Weapons handed in, the assembled party—human and animal—had to march through the city streets under the pounding heat of the midday sun. They were making for a deserted Dutch school where they were to be billeted. It seemed odd to be making for a billet when all they wanted was to head for the docks, board a ship, and sail away to safety, but once again there seemed little sense in questioning things. After all, freedom was just one small step away.

What should have been a proud procession through the streets of Padang for those who had made it against all odds became something very different. There was an odd, frenetic, almost angry and distrustful air about the city. The battered army soon fell silent as they made their ragged way. Gradually it became clear that many of the Dutch in Sumatra blamed them, for Singapore's downfall had opened the way for the Japanese to march into Sumatra and beyond. By the time the escapees had reached their schoolhouse billet many were feeling bitter and let down. Les Searle and Jock Devani, with Judy at their side, felt as if they'd just undergone some kind of degrading funeral procession or death march, their penance for ignoble defeat at Singapore.

But there was worse—*much worse*—to come.

It was only when they reached the schoolhouse—dispossessed of their arms as they were—that the Dutch officials revealed the bitter truth to those who had spent the best part of two months fighting and then fleeing from the marauding Japanese.

They had reached Padang twenty-four hours too late.

The last ships taking escapees away from the city had sailed the day before. And though there was just the vaguest chance that another might dock at the city's port, no one really expected the British to risk sending in further vessels under the very noses of the Japanese. For that was how close the enemy was now. They were expected in Padang at any moment, at which point the Dutch administrators intended to hand the city over uncontested.

There was to be no attempt made to fight or to defend Padang, the Dutch official explained. And while the escapees weren't exactly prisoners as such, no one was allowed to leave his billet. But the very worst was this: anyone caught trying to get anywhere near the few remaining boats that were tied up at the city dock was to be shot on sight. The Dutch colonial administrators had made it forbidden on pain of death for anyone to make any further escape attempts.

After all that they had been through Les Searle and Jock Devani were in a murderous mood. They decided the Dutch administrator with his "pro-Jap" prescriptions could go to hell. *Bugger staying locked up in the schoolhouse, waiting for the enemy to ride into town.*

They made their way directly to the docks with Judy at their side, cursing with every footstep that they'd handed over their weapons so willingly. If the British seamen had still had their arms, they could have taken a boat by force if needed, and to hell with the Dutch authorities. And sure enough, the Dutch had placed armed guards all around the port area to prevent any such attempt. The Brits felt as if they had been let down, deceived, and betrayed.

In truth the Dutch alone were not to blame for the appalling state of affairs in Padang. The British authorities had to shoulder their share of responsibility. Earlier that day the British consul in Padang had heard a radio broadcast announcing the surrender of Sumatra to the Japanese and that the forces of occupation were already moving into the city. Believing it to be true, he had rushed to carry out his orders—burning all of his secret papers, including his radio code books.

The broadcast was in fact false. But by the time he had realized this, his precious code books had been reduced to a pile of ashes. Even if there were British or Allied warships steaming off the coast of Sumatra, he now had no way to make contact with them and let them know that the city was still unoccupied and that there were many hundreds who were desperately awaiting evacuation.

The full extent of his blunder was brought home when a British naval reconnaissance aircraft circled the city that afternoon. It hailed from a British warship steaming off the coast, but without the code books no communications could be made or instructions received. If contact could have been made, a rendezvous with the vessel might have been possible north of the city, away from Dutch control and the advancing Japanese. As it was, that was rendered impossible.

That evening, the enemy reached Padang. It was Judy who first alerted her fellows to their arrival. She was lying in the center of the small classroom where they were billeted. Her head was resting on her forepaws, her eyes fixed unerringly on the door. Les Searle had his gaze on Judy, but his mind was lost in angry, bitter thoughts of an escape that had been so needlessly and senselessly thwarted.

It was then that Judy rose to her feet. For a few seconds she stood there—tense, taut like a coiled spring, her senses totally focused on something outside. Just as the distant throaty roar of a motorcycle became audible to the human ear, her lips curled into a silent snarl. The tone of the engine noise changed as the rider slowed, and there was the noise of other vehicles following. They came to a halt outside the schoolhouse building.

After Judy's warning, not a man doubted what had happened: the Japanese were there.

The schoolhouse was filled with the sounds of shouted commands. Harsh orders echoed along the corridors. They were given in a high-pitched, unintelligible tongue—one that had to be Japanese. It sent a shiver down the spines of all those waiting inside.

Les Searle reached for Judy. Rarely if ever was she put on a leash. She had had the freedom of the ship's company ever since she'd first set paw among them some five years earlier. But now he reached for her and threaded a length of cloth through her collar. Keeping a firm grip on that, he held her protectively by his side.

A figure strode in, closely followed by three of his acolytes. Had the situation not been so utterly dark, it would have been a moment of great hilarity. The Japanese officer—a colonel as it transpired— was short and squat, and he stared at the thwarted escapees through thick-rimmed glasses like jam jars. Even more bizarrely, he carried an enormous sword at his side over polished jackboots, which seemed equally oversized. The sword was so obviously too big for him that each time he took a step, it half tripped him.

Face to face at last. This, then, was the victorious enemy.

The colonel ran his eyes along the line of ragged, defeated men. His pudgy face broke into a gleaming, gold-toothed smile. He barked some orders at his fellows, and they let out a chorus of brays. *Haw-haw-haw.* Dutiful laughter for their esteemed officer.

All of a sudden the colonel's flashing smile evaporated. His arm shot out, finger stabbing toward the mascot of the late lamented HMS *Grasshopper*—at Judy. A series of short, sharp sentences erupted from his lips, each ending in a peculiarly squeaky high note. His number two stood stiffly at attention, head lowered in silence and shoulders beating time to his commanding officer's utterances. The colonel's torrent rose in a final crescendo before he turned on his overlarge heel and stormed out of the room, sword clanking after him.

Judy, it seemed, had not been a hit with the Japanese colonel. His deputies followed in his wake, but not before each had thrown a disparaging look at one very distrustful ship's dog. The Japanese were gone for now, at least from the immediate environs, but no one missed the armed sentries posted at the school gates.

That night the subject of escape was on many a man's lips. It would be easy enough to scale the school wall and slip into the night, avoiding the sentries. But then what? Any escapee would be marooned on a jungle-clad island with no way off but via a journey of a thousand leagues or more at sea. The Japanese would have secured the docks by now, and the chances of grabbing a boat to make a getaway had been reduced to near zero.

Yet if escape was out of the question, then what was the alternative? All had heard the rumors. The Japanese raped and tortured the womenfolk of their vanquished enemies, and they couldn't be bothered much with keeping prisoners of war. Few slept that night. Les Searle and Jock Devani had added worries keeping them awake. Their ever-faithful dog—she who had saved the lives of the ship's crew so many times before—was clearly no favorite of the Japanese colonel, the man whom they had to presume had the power of life or death over the lot of them now.

The following morning it became clear that they weren't about to be executed, or at least not immediately. Instead, the men were separated from the women and children—which in itself was worry enough—and each party was sent to a different prisoner camp in town. The crewmen of the vanquished *Dragonfly* and *Grasshopper* were being sent to a Dutch Army barracks, and Judy—despite her being of the fairer sex—was going with them.

This march across Padang from the Dutch school to the Dutch barracks would be etched forever in the minds of those who survived the war years. It started ignominiously enough—a ragtag hodgepodge of sailors, soldiers, and airmen of various units and nationalities trudging through the early morning streets. The ground underfoot was dusty, and the locals seemed to have gathered to stare at their passing. Under escort from heavily armed Japanese soldiers, every man was aware of how dirty and unkempt he must look beside their smart, disciplined, polished conquerors.

But gradually the spirit of that procession began to change. Allied servicemen marching on foot, they began to find a collective rhythm. Their defeat and humiliation goaded many—the gunboat crews first and foremost—to lift their heads, expand their chests, and carry themselves like fighting men. Arms swinging in time to their stomping feet, the march became an opportunity to show the enemy—and the goggle-eyed locals—that their spirit was far from broken. Struggling against their pain, even the walking wounded fought to maintain their poise and their place in the line of march.

Stepping out at their side, Judy sensed the change in mood—for emotions run up leash and down again, and Les Searle still had her fastened to her makeshift leash. The English pointer—lithe, beautiful, and in tip-top condition despite her long sojourn in the jungle and her close encounter with Mr. Smile—lifted her head and scented the air. The Japanese were everywhere in this town. Judy knew them to be the enemy not only of herself but of her entire family. She could smell the aggression and enmity emanating from them, and she could read fear and defeat in the body language of her fellows.

But as the marchers swung in step through the streets of this defeated city, she also sensed something new. None of those with whom she had shared so many wild and bloody adventures had been cowed, bowed, or beaten—not yet, anyway.

The Dutch Army barracks turned out to be a benign kind of a place of incarceration, at least compared with the hellish camps that were to come. It consisted of four large one-story blocks forming a quadrangle, with a fair-sized soccer field in the center. Upon arrival the men were broken down into four groups, each of which was assigned a barracks: British, Australian, Dutch, and all officers (regardless of nationality). There were separate smaller buildings for the Japanese guards, plus a storeroom.

To the east of the camp lay a range of rugged mountains—the same that the escapees had slogged their way through for weeks on end on the journey from the Indragiri River to Padang. It served as a stark and bitter reminder of all they had suffered in the name of escape and for naught. Those thrown into this camp dreamed of an avenging army—most likely the Americans—storming across those peaks or across the Indian Ocean to liberate the many thousands taken captive.

Among the prisoners it was always the Americans who were talked about as the liberators. In those first few days it was always the hope of the avenging Yanks that crossed people's lips. Subconsciously perhaps, the British in particular had lost faith in their own countrymen. They were bruised by the shock of spectacular defeat—in particular the mass capitulation of 80,000 troops at Singapore—and it was the hope of another nation and its fighting men that buoyed their spirits.

There were many who really did believe that the Yanks were coming any day now and that the ascendancy of the Japanese would be rapidly cut short. When one officer wisely suggested that they should ask the Japanese guards for vegetable seeds and start digging a garden in order to supplement their meager rations, he was laughed at. "What's the use of digging a garden?" many asked scornfully. "We'll be out of this place before the seedlings have time to break the surface. Why, the Yanks will be coming any day now."

Such hopeful—but ultimately misguided—sentiments were soon overtaken by one overriding priority: the daily struggle to get enough nourishment to keep body and soul alive. Each prison block had its own "honcho"—a leader appointed by the Japanese to ensure their rules were adhered to. By far the greatest challenge for the honcho was to secure enough to eat for those in his domain. But for no prisoner was the food situation anything like as bad as it was for Judy.

Les Searle had done everything in his power to try to convince the Japanese camp commandant that the *Grasshopper*'s ship's dog was as much a member of the Royal Navy as any serving sailor. But his arguments had fallen upon deaf ears. Except for the odd savage kick from the guards—which Judy somehow always managed to evade at the last moment—for now at least she was largely being ignored.

But only an official prisoner with a POW number warranted a food ration, and Judy's state of nonexistence meant she got nothing.

Les Searle, Jock Devani, and the others in her immediate circle did their best for her. They each set aside a few grains of boiled rice for their beloved dog. But it was now of necessity that Judy's survival instincts would come to the fore. She stalked and killed anything that moved and was even vaguely edible: lizards, rats, snakes, and small birds; even flies caught on the wing were snapped down hungrily.

Following Jock Devani's lead, she also became a first-class scrounger from the more affluent prisoners: the Dutch, who tended to have far more material possessions than the others. Many of the Dutch hailed from Padang itself, and they had come to the camp complete with everything but the kitchen sink. Laden down with mattresses, blankets, and suitcases full of possessions salvaged from their homes—including cash—they had much with which to barter or buy extra food from the locals.

But in spite of her endeavors, Judy began to experience for the first time in her life what all the Brits and Aussies were starting to feel: a dull ache in the pit of the stomach that comes from not having had enough to eat, the perpetual pang of hunger. It drove men to steal from the camp food store such that the Japanese had to station a round-the-clock guard at the door. It was hunger that drove the British prisoners to scavenge in the trash cans that lay outside the Dutchmen's hut, seeking any edible scraps of discarded food.

It was hunger that led many to start to resent the Dutch prisoners—those who had resources and hence food for the simple reason that they had not lost everything in shipwreck and struggle or in bloody battle against the enemy. Many of the Brits and Aussies had only the clothes they stood up in. The Dutchmen were able sit on the veranda of their hut smoking cigars and supping coffee. By contrast, the British and Australian prisoners were forced to roll a smoke from the Dutchmen's butt ends in an effort to puff away the pangs of hunger.

Between supposed allies an enmity began to fester. It was born from the betrayal, as many saw it, of the would-be escapees upon their arrival in Padang, and it was nurtured by the gulf between their welfare and circumstances once they had been taken as prisoners of war. The daily ration consisted of nothing more substantial than two tiny bread buns, two bananas, and one cup of steamed rice. It was far from enough for Englishman, Australian—or Dutchman, for that matter—to subsist on, and in the former's gradual starvation an enmity of the latter was nurtured.

Those with few material possessions or little money—among whom were the shipwrecked crew of the gunboats—were forced to fall back on their wits to survive. Along with one or two other coconspirators, Les Searle, Jock Devani, and Judy formed a group of the most desperate yet resourceful. With nothing whatsoever to barter, they resorted to the time-honored tradition of expropriating whatever they could from those who were able to spare it.

Operation Snatch was their chief brainchild. On one day each week the Japanese allowed local traders to set up stalls in the camp, selling the bare necessities: chiefly food, soap, and a few scraps of bedding and clothing. Market day soon became Operation Snatch day for the team from the gunboats. Success meant relatively full bellies, but failure meant a savage beating or worse. Still, no one— Jock Devani first and foremost—balked at the risks.

Op Snatch would commence with Les Searle acting as if he had something with which to barter. With the stallholder's attention distracted, Jock Devani would nudge a few things from the stall. In an instant Judy would be there, whipping them up in her jaws and making a mad dash for safety. A fourth conspirator would be waiting in the wings somewhere unobserved so that Judy could make her way to him and deliver whatever swag she had helped pilfer, at which moment it would be swiftly hidden away.

Few stallholders were able to follow the rat runs that Judy used, or trace their wares, or catch the culprits. But by far the greatest Operation Snatch success was scored against the Japanese themselves. There were two goats kept in the camp for the purpose of supplying milk to the commandant. With banana skins used as bait, one of those goats was coaxed to the window of the British hut. As it nibbled at the fragrant skins, a noose fashioned from electrical wire was slipped around its neck, and with a savage tug the animal was hoisted off its feet and hauled through the window.

There was little sleep had in the British hut that night either by the human prisoners or by one very contented dog. Come morning, worried Japanese guards searched high and low for any sign of the missing goat. It had disappeared off the face of the earth: not a scrap of skin or hoof or horn or bone could be found. And as much as they might cast accusing glances at the bulging bellies of the British prisoners—and their accursed dog—there was zero evidence to prove what might have happened.

Of course, the forbidden fruits of the goat feast put the gnawing pangs of hunger at bay for only a few days. It was hunger that first drove Judy to leave her family's side and venture out alone in search of sustenance. During the long, dragging hours of daylight, Les Searle and the others kept her always by their side. They knew what the guards would do if they got so much as half a chance—they would shoot Judy and they would eat her. Any number had made that clear by the gestures they made whenever they laid eyes on the dog.

But at night when all were asleep Judy started to venture forth secretly in search of food. Her dark forays were discovered only when she jumped in through the half-open window of the hut and landed on the chest of a sleeping prisoner—one Petty Officer "Punch" Puncheon. He jumped out of his skin only to find a familiar figure before him—Judy, looking equally startled and with a half-eaten chicken clamped in her jaws.

Unknown to all, she had been sneaking under the wire mesh fence of the camp—rather as she had done as a little puppy in Shanghai—and heading out to scour the town for food. From then on Judy had to be tied up at night. She clearly didn't like it, but Punch Puncheon did his best to explain to her why it was so necessary.

"It's not as a punishment," he told her. "It's because we don't want *you* to get eaten!"

The days slipped by, each largely the same as the one that had gone before. There was little news of the outside world or of the fortunes of the wider war. It was almost as if they were in a world lost from time. Then rumor built upon rumor, and it became clear that the men were about to be moved from the camp. Spirits soared. Surely, anything had to be better than the perpetual dull boredom of their existence, not to mention the hunger.

In fact, Padang was a virtual paradise compared with where they were heading. Men—and dog—were hungry, certainly, but none had started to die. Yet hope springs eternal in the heart of man: many of those who heard the news of their impending departure allowed themselves to dream of a better future.

In truth, these men—and their much-loved dog—had begun a journey into a place very close to hell.

Chapter Twelve

At long last the warning to move was given. "By order of the Imperial Japanese commander," the head guard announced, speaking through an interpreter, "five hundred men will leave tomorrow for Belawan, a port on the northeast Sumatran coast. From there they will embark for an unknown destination."

Five hundred men constituted half the number currently in the camp. Les Searle, Jock Devani, Punch Puncheon, and a score of other gunboat regulars were among those listed to leave. Of course, though her name wasn't on any roster, Judy of Sussex was going with them. The prisoners boarded a convoy of waiting transport trucks. When no one was looking, Punch Puncheon lifted Judy up to the group of waiting figures, and after a few reassuring pats she was hidden from view beneath some rice sacks.

This journey was to be the first of many in which Judy's ability to understand absolutely what was required of her and why would serve to save her life. Somehow she knew that she had to lie quietly in the back of that truck for the long journey ahead so that she could materialize at their new destination seemingly miraculously and almost as if she had always been there.

As the long line of vehicles moved out of the Padang camp, there were cheerful shouts and waves from many aboard. The prisoners were ragged, somewhat emaciated, and unshaven, but at least something was happening at last. Change was afoot, and with it hopes were raised.

"We'll see you in Blighty for Christmas!" some even shouted.

It was the autumn of 1942, and none of those aboard those trucks were destined to see a Christmas at home for another three terrible years.

After a crunching of gears the convoy of twenty-odd vehicles got up speed, and the streets of Padang were left behind in a cloud of dust. From the open rear of their truck Les Searle and his fellows could see just what kind of terrain lay to the north of the city. If anything it was even more remote and rugged than that which they had passed through on foot some six months earlier. The road to Belawan ran 500 kilometers or more northward, threading its way along the spine of the dramatic Barisan mountain range.

The road had been carved out of dense jungle, plunging crevasses, and towering rock faces, forming a series of crazy hairpin bends around which the convoy flew at speed. But despite the questionable driving skills of the Japanese soldiers at the wheel, the men's spirits rose. They had the wind in their faces, and they were speeding through breathtaking scenery. When you weren't tasked to march through them on foot, the Sumatran highlands were stunningly beautiful.

On the afternoon of the fourth day the convoy reached the high plateau around Lake Toba, a place of unique loveliness that had long been a hill station and a holiday destination for the Dutch residents of Sumatra. The Japanese guards decided this was a good place to stop the vehicles. An early lunch—the same scanty rice ration as always—was served by the roadside, from where all could admire the view over the shimmering expanse of water and into the majestic pine-clad hills beyond.

Lake Toba was magical and uplifting. No one could fail to be stirred. Even the Japanese guards seemed moved to soften their attitude. With apparently reassuring smiles and gestures they handed around bunches of bananas, but in retrospect, this would only serve to exaggerate the contrast between the beauty of this place and the darkness and drudgery that were to follow.

The final destination of the convoy was the village of Gloegoer, a clutch of native houses clustered around a street lined with Chinese shops. Along a side road lay a former Dutch Army barracks, with beyond that a lunatic asylum. These were to become known as Gloegoer One and Gloegoer Two, respectively, and they were to be forced-labor camps for Imperial Japan's prisoners of war.

The men were herded off the trucks and into Gloegoer One, the former barracks. Hopes that had been buoyed by the long and invigorating journey were ebbing fast. Gloegoer One was far smaller and more dismal than their former camp had been. One thousand men were herded together in an area not much larger than a football field. It consisted of a serried rank of long barrack blocks separated by thin stretches of grass.

Once again the men were divided by nationality, with one hut reserved for the officers. Accommodation was basic. Wooden boards had been laid across steel girders to form shelves running along either wall of the huts—the prisoners' sleeping platforms. Between them ran a central gangway about eight feet wide—a bare concrete floor. Above, the tiled roof was infested with ferocious banana-eating rats.

There were unglazed windows lining the walls, complete with steel bars and wooden shutters. Each prisoner was allocated a slot on a sleeping platform around two and a half feet wide and six long. This tiny space constituted his home. There he would eat, sleep, and pass the dragging hours, and it would be his sick bay when he fell ill with malaria or the numerous other debilitating diseases that would plague Gloegoer One. Here there was to be no privacy for any man but in his own thoughts.

That Gloegoer One would prove a sorry sequel to Padang was confirmed when the first food rations were handed out. The camp's central kitchen served two meals a day. It would rarely if ever vary: a cup of watery rice known as "pap"; a thin, tasteless soup with a few leaves floating around in it; and an unidentifiable gooey mess that was actually flour boiled into a stodgy porridge. If at Padang they had been on hunger rations, Gloegoer One's looked set to starve them.

At first the men were kept locked in the barracks all day long. There was no relief from the stultifying boredom and inactivity, not to mention the airless heat. Many wished they were back in the relative liberty and luxury of Padang. Some drifted into hopelessness and apathy. But after three weeks of enforced captivity, Colonel Banno, the Japanese camp commandant, announced that the prisoners had now completed their "punishment for fighting the Imperial Japanese Forces" and from now on would be treated "properly" as prisoners of war.

Colonel Banno was an enigmatic figure: a tall, somewhat distinguished-looking former farmer, on first impression he gave the appearance of being a relatively reasonable, fair-minded Japanese officer. But beneath his apparently benevolent air there lurked a darker heart—one that viewed enforced imprisonment for weeks on end as being perfectly reasonable retribution against those who had dared stand against Imperial Japan.

None of the prisoners had had the slightest idea that they were being punished by being locked up, but just to be allowed out of the huts during daylight felt like blessed release. Further changes were afoot, Colonel Banno announced. Work parties were to be sent out of the camp so that the prisoners could labor on various projects that the Japanese had initiated in the area. Local traders were also going to be allowed to set up stalls twice weekly, selling such "luxuries" as fruit, eggs, tobacco, soap, and even pencils and paper.

With news of such improvements morale lifted a little at Gloegoer, but only for so long. It was via the presence of the local traders around the camp that the prisoners were first to witness the unspeakable savagery that the Japanese were wont to unleash on anyone who dared cross them.

Gloegoer One was staffed by both Japanese guards and their Korean underlings. The Koreans wore Japanese Army uniforms but were seen as being inferior by the Japanese. There was a rigid pecking order. The Japanese officers looked down upon and regularly abused and beat their own troops. The regular soldiers looked down upon and abused and beat the Korean guards. The Korean guards in turn would take it out on anyone under them—chiefly the locals and, in time, the POWs.

The first sign of the savagery this system engendered came when a local trader was caught trying to smuggle some money into camp. One of the POWs must have offered something to sell—a watch maybe, or perhaps a precious gold ring. But such barter was forbidden under the camp rules—POWs could only exchange money for goods with the locals.

First, the POW was beaten unconscious by the guard commander himself, the most senior officer having the honor of delivering the first blows. After that, the entire guard force was free to set upon the unconscious figure. Each tried to outdo the other in the enthusiasm with which he rained down blows from rifle butt or boot upon the prostrate form. Finally the victim was revived by having a bucket of cold water thrown over him, after which he was lashed to the flagpole by his hands and left there to hang under a burning sun.

But if anything the punishment meted out to a Chinese trader—the Chinese being Imperial Japan's age-old enemy—was even worse. Accused of theft, he was strung up with a notice hung above his head on which was written the one word "THIEF." A noose was slung around his neck, attached to a large canvas bag. All passersby—POWs included—were encouraged to place a stone in the bag so that the noose would slowly tighten with the weight . . . and strangle him.

Those who witnessed these sadistic acts were sickened, but they also saw in these very public punishments a warning as to what would befall any POWs who fell afoul of the camp rules. And in Gloegoer the rules were sacrosanct. First and foremost, all POWs had to bow whenever they were in the presence of a Japanese or Korean guard. They had to do so from the waist, leaning as far forward as possible, preferably to touch their toes. The lower the kowtow, the less likely it was to trigger a vicious beating for not showing "proper respect" to the victors.

Learning when to kowtow wasn't easy but most prisoners of necessity learned fast. Even if a Japanese or Korean guard was barely within sight he had to be bowed to. Failure to spot the guard was no excuse not to have bowed, and it was sure to unleash a paroxysm of verbal abuse and violence, whereupon the culprit had to stand at attention while the guard rained punches on his chin and kicked his shins. It was crucial to stand and take the punishment and not go down, for then the guard would put the boot in and literally kick the victim's head in.

Les Searle, Jock Devani, Punch Puncheon, and the others in "Judy's gang" watched such acts of casual savagery with deep revulsion and concern—as much for their dog as for themselves. In her own way Judy seemed to have learned to kowtow. She slunk around the Gloegoer camp with her eyes downcast and her head low and doing her utmost to avoid the guards. But she couldn't hide her hatred of them completely. Whenever one was nearby, her lips would curl into a silent snarl. More than once she went for one of the worst of the guards, and she seemed to be the only prisoner incapable of not speaking her mind.

Such obvious hostility from a lowly dog put Judy's life in constant danger. This was especially so with the Korean guards, who were very partial to eating dog, as were the locals. In this part of Sumatra any dogs that weren't strictly under someone's protection were hunted, shot, and placed in the pot. And in Korea dog meat was viewed as a particular delicacy. There were any number in and around Gloegoer who wanted to get their teeth into the Royal Navy's mascot.

With camp rations in Gloegoer being so meager and with Judy's protectors having little or nothing to trade with the locals, there just wasn't enough food to go around. Once again Judy started to sneak out of camp in search of food. She'd return with a snake or a chicken clutched in her jaws, darting past the angry gate guards and making a mad dash for the British hut and her family.

Not once did she release her hold on her prize until she'd found them and was able to drop it triumphantly at their feet. In time Judy would return from one of her expeditions outside the wire having gotten much more than she had bargained for—but for now it was worry enough that she was running the gauntlet of getting seen, shot, and eaten.

With the lockdown being over in the camp, the forced labor began. Groups of men were formed into "work parties" and marched out daily to their allotted tasks. One of the earliest for Les Searle, Judy, and their fellows was to fetch sand from the nearby river for construction work at the Medan airfield. The Japanese were intent on lengthening the runway so that it could host their heavy bomber squadrons. Digging out and carrying the sand in wicker baskets was hot and exhausting work, and it was only the opportunity to cool off in the river that made it half bearable for man and dog alike.

Knowing the capability of America's long-range Liberator bombers to strike even this far afield, the Japanese ordered tracks to be cleared into the jungle so that concealed fuel and ammo dumps could be built. This was hard, intensely physical labor, but it offered its own compensations to those for whom hunger had become a constant companion.

Felling the massive tropical giants with hand axes took considerable skill—even more so to get one to crash down in the direction of the Japanese or Korean guards, forcing them to flee in headlong panic. At the yell of "Timber!" the tree—which could be over 100 feet in height—would fall, dragging other, smaller boughs and branches with it.

The second the tangle of vegetation hit the floor, scores of figures dressed in rags would swarm across it, searching for their quarry. The jungle was full of wildlife, and much of it—snakes, birds, lizards, small mammals—proved edible to those who were as desperate as the inmates of Gloegoer One. And there was never a prisoner that was quicker off the mark in seizing her prey than Judy of Sussex.

The forced-labor projects began to multiply as the Japanese set about industrializing their rape of Sumatra's natural resources. Ships docked at the nearby port of Balawan carrying cement, barbed wire, and ammunition, all of which needed unloading by the POWs. Among the supplies were drums of oil and gas, which needed loading onto waiting railway trucks. With their will and their spirit of resistance far from broken, the human pack animals—Les Searle and Jock Devani among them—saw an opportunity here for a little sabotage.

They stacked the drums on the flatbed carriages with their bungs facing downward. The bungs were loosened when the guard's back was turned. The hope was that the bumpy ride inland would shake the bungs free so that the drums would empty themselves of their contents along the way. But more often than not the attempted sabotage was discovered, whereupon the guards would fly into a volcanic rage, seizing the first prisoner they could lay hands upon.

After the compulsory savage beating, a new and unspeakable punishment was instituted for any prisoner who had the temerity to try anything so audacious as sabotage. It was Colonel Banno, the camp commandant, who instigated the dreaded solitary confinement cell. At Gloegoer One there was a tiny dark hovel of a hut, one that had once been used to store animal manure. The place still reeked to high heaven.

The only light or air came via the one door, which had thick wooden bars. It had a movable section at the bottom that could be slid aside to allow a prisoner to be shoved and kicked inside. On the colonel's orders any would-be saboteur would be thrown inside the hovel for a period of punishment lasting days, weeks, or even months at a time.

But it wasn't the cell itself that betrayed the colonel's full sadistic bent—it was the accompanying torture. For the long hours of daylight the prisoner wasn't allowed either to sit or to lean against the cell walls. The agony of having to stand for twelve or thirteen hours without a rest was unbearable. But if the man broke and slumped against the walls, he'd get a savage beating from the watching guards. He was allowed nothing to sleep on but the hard stone of the floor, not even a blanket with which to try to fend off the swarms of mosquitoes. And in Gloegoer, the nights were thick with clouds of such blood-sucking, disease-ridden pests.

No sentence in the cell came without starvation—most usually one sparse meal every third day. The only relief from the gnawing hunger and the ache of limbs locked into one position in an effort to remain standing was to gaze through the wooden bars. But even that brought its own kind of torture. The kitchen lay to one side of the cell, and at mealtimes the work parties would pass close by carrying the cauldrons of rice and soup en route to the barrack blocks.

The punishment cell reduced some to tears, others to sheer madness. Occasionally it moved the Japanese sentry placed on guard to pity, and he'd slip a banana or a piece of Japanese chocolate through the bars. Those who did so revealed their human side. They weren't all monsters. They were also taking a massive risk, for if a superior saw one of his men showing pity to a prisoner—especially one singled out by Colonel Banno for punishment—he would be in real trouble.

But in spite of such horrors there were still moments of lightness in Gloegoer One, at least in the early months. That July a rumor circulated around the camp that the Solomon Islands had been retaken by the Allies. The Japanese had seized the Solomons—a chain of islands lying far to the east of Sumatra—during the first half of 1942 in an effort to cut supply lines between Australia and New Zealand and the United States. The Allies had counterattacked with the landings at Guadalcanal and neighboring islands, initiating a series of savage battles fought by land, at sea and in the air.

The news that Allied counteroffensives had begun proved a massive morale booster for the Gloegoer One prisoners. They celebrated as only they could—by holding a special race in the British barrack block. The hut was around 100 yards long, and makeshift hurdles had been put up using empty kerosene cans. Judy was tasked to race up and down the length of the block, leaping the hurdles at each end, ears flapping crazily and tail streaming out behind her, as the prisoners roared and cheered. As everyone agreed, Judy of Sussex was quite the character at Gloegoer One and an incredible boost to their collective morale.

They would defend her with their lives, as Judy would on pain of death defend theirs.

Chapter Thirteen

For Judy the main struggle was to keep out of the guards' clutches while still getting her paws on enough food. In this she was to be aided by a fellow prisoner, one of the first brought into her family of friends from outside of the gunboat crews. Private Cousens of the 18th Infantry Division was one of the many British foot soldiers captured after the fall of Singapore. Cousens had fought alongside Indian and Australian forces in Malaya in an effort to halt the advancing Japanese, most notably in the Battle of Muar.

But after the mass surrender at Singapore, Cousens had ended up as a Japanese POW. Even once he'd been sent to Gloegoer One, Cousens remained a happy-spirited young man, with a cheeky grin and a ready wisecrack for his fellow prisoners. Cousens had a special skill that proved both a blessing and a curse in the camp: he was an accomplished maker and repairer of shoes. On learning this Colonel Banno had set him up as the official Gloegoer One cobbler—but not for the prisoners, of course.

After months of fighting, fleeing, trekking the jungle, and now laboring as POWs, few prisoners had any proper footwear. Instead, they'd fashioned crude wooden sandals, which were fastened to the foot by a length of rag or a scrap of wire flex or whatever else could be found. Real leather boots were the luxury of the victors, which meant for now the Japanese. The upside for Cousens was that it got him out of the more strenuous work parties. The downside was that he was forced to have regular contact with the Japanese, which was always a hit and miss affair.

Cousens was forever having to visit the Japanese officers' quarters to measure one or another who fancied a new pair of knee-high jackboots. Cousens would take with him a large burlap sack stuffed with half-finished boots for try-ons, strips of leather, knives, hammers and nails, and all the rest of his shoemaking equipment. The visits were invariably fraught with danger. Close contact with the officers was best avoided, in particular Colonel Banno but worse still his second in command, Lieutenant Matsuoka.

An exceptionally ugly man, Lieutenant Matsuoka was better known to all as Piggyeyes. He was feared and hated by his own men as well as the prisoners. The next senior in rank was the so-called camp doctor, a man whose giant two-handled sword was so large that it seemed almost taller than he was. The Japanese guards knew their doctor to be so incompetent and careless that they would quietly consult the British or Dutch medics if ever they were ill.

Below the doctor came the camp interpreter, who on the face of it appeared rather like Colonel Banno, a kindly, almost distinguished-looking old man. But looks can be deceptive. Many thought the interpreter to be just that—a harmless, friendly sort—until the day he was spotted smashing a Dutchman's head against a concrete block wall, and for no other reason than that the prisoner was tied up in the punishment block and hence made an easy target.

The most junior officer was Takahashi, and he was the exception that proved the rule. Takahashi either was quietly pro-British or he'd realized that Imperial Japan was unlikely to win this war and was cleverly hedging his bets. He was supersmart, an archdisciplinarian, and one whom many Allied soldiers would have considered to be a good officer. He was scrupulously fair to all prisoners regardless of rank or nationality.

On one occasion, Takahashi came to the British hut late one night and passed a brown paper bag to the hut honcho—its leader. "Keep well hidden," he whispered before leaving. The bag contained a photograph of Winston Churchill beneath which was the caption

"The man of the hour." At other times he'd notice a prisoner turn his face skyward as an aircraft flew overhead, scrutinizing it for Allied markings. When invariably it turned out to be Japanese, he'd shake his head and remark, "Never mind. Better luck next time."

More was the pity when Takahashi was transferred to Changi, an infamous POW camp in Singapore. With Takahashi gone, Cousens was left having to deal with the old guard, who were unrelentingly unpredictable and capable of fits of savage violence, seemingly without provocation. Yet Cousens proved himself willing to risk all in the cause of keeping Judy alive, and in doing so he exemplified a simple truth about her existence in Gloegoer. In this awful place, Judy had gone from being a ship's mascot to being the mascot of an entire community of prisoners of war. She had become the talisman of the Gloegoer One camp.

In her dogged survival and her unfailing humor and her sense of occasion, Judy embodied the spirit of the thousand-odd prisoners who inhabited this place. They had come to see her as a symbol of their resistance, and her renown had spread far and wide. As she had become Gloegoer's mascot, so in a sense the thousand prisoners had become her wider family. But Cousens, through his cobbling and his brave generosity, would enter into the first tier of her companions.

Cousens had gotten into the habit of sitting in the shade of an overhanging roof, where he could work on his shoes and boots in the open air. The Japanese provided him with the leather to do so, and like everything that was in very short supply, its use was carefully monitored. But as he cut the leather to craft a new pair of boots, he would hack off a piece especially for Judy, who was very often to be found lying at his side. It was tough and only just bordering on the palatable, but it was after all animal skin, and it never proved too unpalatable for a half-starved dog.

Over the days and weeks Cousens the cobbler grew to care about Judy deeply, especially her welfare. He knew full well that she couldn't survive on the odd scrap of tough leather. As with the rest of the prisoners, the weight was slowly dropping off her. Her flanks showed sharp and bony through her coat, which was losing the last of its shine. What they all needed—man and dog alike—was food in bulk, and the only way to get that would be to steal it off those who had it—the Japanese.

Since he was part of Judy's core of diehard companions, it was only natural that Cousens would recruit Les Searle to be his partner in crime in his harebrained yet audacious scheme. Cousens waited until he had a large and heavy sack of boots to deliver to the camp officers, whereupon he enlisted Les Searle as his fellow sack carrier. When he explained his intentions, Les balked at what Cousens was planning. The irrepressible cobbler intended to use the boot delivery as an excuse to steal a bulk consignment of rice from right under the noses of the Japanese officers.

The two men crossed the camp compound, heavy sack held between them, with Les Searle feeling like a fly walking into a very hungry and venomous spider's web. Having delivered the boots to the officers' quarters, they now had an empty sack into which they managed to manhandle their intended loot—a sack stuffed full of rice set aside for the officers' consumption. With the booty hoisted between them, they hurried back to the British hut, fearing every moment to be discovered. As luck would have it, the theft went without a hitch. It was the aftermath that neither man had anticipated or prepared for.

The next day a pair of Japanese guards entered the British hut and announced a surprise inspection. No one doubted they were searching for a large sack of rice that had mysteriously gone missing. Les Searle and Cobbler Cousens had hidden the purloined rice rolled up in a blanket and stuffed beneath one of the sleeping platforms. But one thrust from a guard's bayonet would soon uncover the theft.

As the guards moved systematically down the length of the hut, both men felt the fear rising in their guts. You could cut the atmosphere with a knife as bit by bit the guards neared the hiding place.

Ever since meeting her, Les Searle reckoned that Judy could sense just about every human emotion there was. Fear, happiness, sorrow, loss, dread—somehow she was able to pick up on them all. Right then, she must have sensed the utter terror that seemed to have gripped the hut or at least held two of her closest companions—the rice thieves—in its thrall. She could feel that the air was replete with mortal danger, for the guards would happily decapitate a prisoner with a savage swipe of a shovel or bayonet him to death for a far lesser misdemeanor than this.

Just as the nearest guard seemed poised to reach beneath the sleeping platform and thrust his bayonet into the forbidden bundle, Judy came tearing into the hut with something gripped between her jaws. Upon spying her, the guard closest to the hidden rice sack froze. An expression approaching fear spread across his features as Judy charged down the length of the hut, her ears flying, her eyes glowing red and crazed, and her jaws wide with the macabre object that she had grasped between them.

In her mouth was a gleaming human skull.

She tore past the guards, leaping any obstacle in her path, reached the far end, and in a rerun of the recent hut hurdling races, she turned and started back on her second lightning-fast lap. The guards began to scream crazily at the dog and yell at each other in alarm. As every prisoner knew, the Japanese guards coupled their predilection for savagery with a seemingly unreasoning fear of anything to do with death. Skeletons, bones, graves, skulls—all of it had them utterly spooked.

As Judy raced past them for a second time, skull gripped tightly in her mouth, their cries rose to ones of sheer panic. Cobbler Cousens and Les Searle were expecting at any moment to hear a shot as one or another of the guards leveled his rifle and fired upon the camp's beloved mascot. Judy must have sensed it too. With a final mad dash between the two guards, she turned and sprinted from the hut, skull still grasped firmly in her yawning jaws.

No one had a clue where Judy had gotten the skull. Presumably, she must have dug it up from the camp graveyard. But of one thing Les Searle and Cobbler Cousens were certain: she'd done what she had in the full knowledge of the grave danger two of her closest family were in and of the impact her actions would have upon their would-be aggressors.

Few in the hut who were aware of the rice theft doubted that Judy knew what she was up to. Hers had been a mission of trickery and deception. She'd sought to trick the guards into believing she was some kind of a hellhound—a devil dog possessed by the spirits of the dead. In that she had succeeded spectacularly.

The guards were utterly spooked. Ashen-faced and babbling away to each other, their voices unusually high-pitched and squeaky with fright, they turned after Judy and hurried out of the hut. With that the impromptu inspection was over, the purloined sack of rice lying miraculously undiscovered.

As December 1942 approached and with it the dire prospect of their first Christmas as POWs, the men were to receive a morale boost as fantastic as it was unexpected. In the officers' hut they had managed to cobble together a clandestine radio. Its very existence was a closely guarded secret. Only a handful of officers were in on it, and for very good reasons. Were the radio to be discovered, the men of Gloegoer One would lose a very fragile link with the outside world, quite apart from the terrible consequences facing those who had been operating it.

News was disseminated from the radio in dribs and drabs and only as the operators saw fit so as not to raise the suspicions of the camp guards. More often than not it was released long after the event had taken place, when the officers perceived a real need to boost camp morale. Perhaps that was why in the run-up to that first Christmas in captivity the news of the heroic raid on Saint-Nazaire was made known.

Earlier that year British commandos had launched one of the first—and among the most daring and successful—cross-Channel raids on occupied France. An ancient British destroyer, HMS *Campbeltown*, was packed full of explosives and rammed into the vitally important dry dock at the French port of Saint-Nazaire. The charge was hidden inside a sarcophagus of concrete and steel secreted in her bows, and it was fitted with delayed-action fuses. By the time it exploded, the dry dock was destroyed and the commandos had gotten ashore to sabotage the dock machinery.

Five Victoria Crosses would be awarded for the raid, in which 169 were killed and 215 were captured, mostly commandos who had fought until they were surrounded and all out of ammunition. When news of this stunning operation—which became known as the Greatest Raid of All—was circulated around Gloegoer, the men jumped to the conclusion that the long-awaited liberation of Europe had finally begun. Finally, the English lion had found her roar, and those who had for so long felt utterly defeated—including one doggedly defiant English pointer—began to hope and to believe once more.

As they headed out of Gloegoer's gates on their work parties, Les Searle and others began to take up the words of a poem written in Judy's honor. It had become like a sacred chant, embodying the spirit of those who found hope where there was precious little to find, embodied in the mascot of Gloegoer One. They would sing it as they marched to bolster flagging spirits.

They would stagger to their workplace
Though they really ought to die,
And would mutter in their beards,
If that bitch can, so can I . . .

In light of the Saint-Nazaire raid, the POWs started to examine the possibility of escape with newfound vigor. It had been discussed endlessly during the long months of captivity, but it had always been viewed as nearly impossible. Getting out of camp would be easy enough, but then what? A white man couldn't exactly blend in with the local population. Plus it wasn't as if this was a German POW camp in Europe, where the escapee could head for the nearest border with a neutral or friendly country.

The only escape route lay hundreds of miles across the India Ocean. An escapee would need to lay his hands on an oceangoing vessel, and to get one he would need serious money, which few if any had anymore. But most of all he'd need the help of the locals, and they were fully in the thrall of the Japanese. Moreover, Colonel Banno, the camp commandant, had warned that anyone caught trying to escape would be tortured and then shot, as would all the men in his hut who had helped him make his getaway.

In spite of this, every soldier knew that it was his duty as an Allied prisoner of war to try to make a bid for freedom—regardless of how impossible it might seem—and news of the Saint-Nazaire raid had quickened that sense of duty. But it was now that the Japanese chose to strike a blow that would dash utterly their newfound spirit of resistance.

Only the Japanese could have dreamed up such an idea: a contract that every single Allied POW had to sign, binding him under "law" never to try to escape. This was simply a case of the conquerors lording it over the vanquished, and it felt like it too. But to sign such an agreement ran against every tenet of international law, and all in the camp were agreed—they could not and would not sign.

It was late in 1942 when Colonel Banno had the prisoners stand on parade so he could storm about in front of them, raging and issuing dire threats. Not a man stepped forward to sign. Colonel Banno ordered that the guard numbers be doubled. A vicious-looking machine gun was set up, covering the entire parade ground—but still the prisoners stood firm in their decision not to sign away a precious liberty. Of course, with Judy not being on the official camp roster her paw print wasn't required, but she sure as hell wasn't volunteering it, either!

Finally, on Colonel Banno's orders the British prisoners were herded into the Dutch barracks, together with the Dutch POWs, whereupon the doors were locked on the overcrowded hut. Moments later the wooden shutters were slammed closed, after which the hammering began. The Japanese guards were nailing the shutters tight. To those inside it felt like being sealed inside a gigantic coffin.

The rest of that day and night was spent in increasing torment as the air became fouler and the heat grew to intolerable levels. No food was provided, and there wasn't even enough space to lie down and sleep. The siege continued all through the burning heat of the following day. In the rancid, saunalike conditions of the hut's interior men were going down with malaria and dysentery. Nothing could be done to help them. Some urged the hut leaders to give in. Others were equally determined to hold out.

A second day and night passed in such hellish conditions. It was clear that the camp commandant wasn't going to buckle, yet neither were the prisoners. But how far would the Japanese go?

Was Colonel Banno really prepared to let every prisoner—dog included—die?

CHAPTER FOURTEEN

Two things combined to break the impasse in that accursed hut. The first was an ultimatum given to Sergeant Major Dobson, the man in charge of the British contingent of nonofficers: either he and his men would sign or they would be starved to death and even denied water. The second was the advice of the British and Dutch doctors who urged that sense prevail. Much more of this and there would be an epidemic of dysentery and deadly typhoid, with horrific consequences.

It was late that afternoon when a message was finally sent to Colonel Banno, accepting capitulation. A small table was set up on the parade ground. One by one the prisoners stumbled out to sign. The officers held out for a while longer before they too were forced to capitulate. But a signature obtained under threat of death had no standing in law, as all the prisoners were told. For those who had resisted for so long, a victory of sorts had been won.

As for Judy, she went delirious with delight when finally she was released from the barrack-prison and could tear around the camp, relishing the taste of relative freedom once again. Spirits rose still further that late November when some extraordinary news reached the camp: a vessel had docked in Balawan's harbor carrying Red Cross parcels for the prisoners. Every man was dreaming about what impossible luxuries that mercy ship might hold.

The air was electric with anticipation as a work party was sent out to unload the unexpected bounty. The first trucks arrived around dusk, and it was as if Christmas had come early. There were cans of bully beef and condensed milk; cases of canned fruit; sacks of sugar, beans, and cocoa; and boxes of chocolate and cigarettes; plus there was the old faithful from the Indragiri River trek—*Marmite!*

For half-starved prisoners this was booty beyond their wildest dreams. The consignment had been put together by the British Red Cross and shipped out from East Africa and was intended for British POWs only. Some who remembered how the Dutch had done so little to help their fellow prisoners back in Padang wanted nothing to go to the Dutch hut. But that wasn't the spirit that prevailed. Many of the Dutchmen had the added burden of knowing that their wives and children were incarcerated in the nearby "family camp" in Medan, and most Gloegoer One inmates—regardless of their nationality—pitied them for it.

The food was distributed to all, with a good deal being set aside to send to the family camp. Each man at Gloegoer One got a dozen cans of bully beef, several cans of condensed milk, fruit, and other delicacies. Soon, the interior of the huts looked more like your average corner shop than the prison cells they were. With Christmas just a few weeks away, men deliberated on what to do with such plenty. Some would be eaten in a celebratory feast right away. Some would be saved for Christmas festivities. And a proportion would be kept in reserve for emergencies and barter.

With the unexpected provisions now on hand, Les Searle, Jock Devani, Punch Puncheon, and Cobbler Cousens were able to prepare a feast fit for a queen—for Judy. But the unexpected bounty was also the cause of a rare spot of trouble between some of Judy's gang. Unsurprisingly for men who had suffered such interminable hunger, the hoarding of the food stocks became something of an obsession.

One evening the workers arrived back at camp after a long day's toil, only for Jock Devani to become convinced that someone had stolen one of his cans of bully beef. He eyed Les Searle's neat stack angrily. In an accusing tone he announced that he was going to count them all. He stretched out his hand to do so, but equally forcefully

Les Searle pushed it away. In the struggle that followed, Jock's false teeth were knocked to the ground and Les accidentally trod on them. There was a sharp crack as the denture snapped in two.

The argument over food was instantly forgotten. Jock bent to retrieve his precious teeth, cursing Les for having trodden on them. He made a beeline for the Australian hut, where it was reckoned they could fix just about anything. Jock returned a while later, grinning broadly and with the denture back in place. It had been patched up using a length of sticky tape.

In the spirit of reconciliation Jock brewed some coffee from his Red Cross supplies, and the two men drank to their mutual good health. Trouble was, for Jock the toast ended in a strangled gasp. He went puce in the face, grasped his throat, and choked as if he was going to die. Under the influence of hot coffee the sticky tape had lost its stickiness and gotten stuck halfway down Jock's throat when he swallowed.

Once his throat was finally free of sticky tape, Jock's spirits were revived in part by the wheeling and dealing he was able to embark upon, courtesy of the Red Cross. He now had goods with which to barter. In theory, bartering was punishable by a savage beating or even death—depending on the mood of the guards. But the British block had developed a covert means by which it might flourish in relative safety. The hut still had its shower room and toilets, which flushed via narrow chutes leading to the outside. It was through these that the barter in secret was effected.

The system required absolute trust between prisoner and local, for more often than not the two parties to a deal never got to set eyes on each other. But amazingly, promises were kept and deals completed without anyone ever cheating. The main danger in these transactions remained the guards, and so a strict watch had to be maintained. It was organized on two levels. The first set of eyes and ears were Judy's, for she could always be relied upon to issue a warning bark if ever a guard was inbound toward the hut.

The second watcher was a human lookout. Whenever Judy yelped in alarm, the lookout would call out a coded warning—"Red lamp." With the Red Cross parcels having enabled a resurgence in barter, the camp guards must have grown accustomed to their every arrival being greeted by a loud cry of "Red lamp!" One of the friendlier among them even took to calling out proudly "Red lamp" whenever he was approaching, to preannounce his own arrival.

With December 25, 1942, all but upon them, the men of Gloegoer One were facing their first Christmas in captivity. Those who'd cried out "See you in Blighty for Christmas" when leaving Padang had been sorely mistaken. Fevered preparations got under way for the festivities—and the feast, made possible largely thanks to the Red Cross. Grudgingly, Colonel Banno agreed to recognize such a "heathen festival" by allowing a day off for the work parties, and from somewhere he even secured a barrel of captured port for the coming occasion.

Christmas morning was spent singing carols, the British, Dutch, and Aussies joining one another in belting out one another's favorite hymns. Courtesy of the Red Cross, the cooks had managed to cobble together a fantastic feast, as opposed to the usual slop of rice. Steak, new potatoes, kidney beans, and brown gravy were served to all. And in spite of her not being on the Gloegoer One official camp register, Judy of Sussex was invited to sit down with the rest and enjoy her plateful.

After the feast came the pantomime, a takeoff of Snow White and the Seven Dwarfs that was a skit on prison life. The Japanese officers and guards formed part of the audience, and they joined in the uproarious laughter—though thankfully they didn't seem to understand that the joke was largely on them. During the raucous and bawdy panto songs, Judy was seen to lift her fine head and howl along an accompaniment, just as any camp mascot should do—and just as she had done in the Strong Toppers Club back in the heady days of gunboat diplomacy on the Yangtze.

But when all was said and done, the Christmas merrymaking at Gloegoer One was forced. Refusing to be cowed, the prisoners were making the best of a bad job. The sense of awfulness, the separation from family and loved ones, the homesickness—none of that could be banished by one good meal and a jolly sing-along. All in Gloegoer longed for 1942 to end, ushering in a New Year that they hoped would bring a turnaround in the fortunes of the war and see the Allies victorious, a New Year that would see their dream of liberation from the prison camps become reality.

In truth, 1943 would be the year in which the chill wind of death would be felt, even among Judy's gang of fellows. The Japanese decided to launch the New Year with a massive new labor project, one that would become known as the White Man's Mountain. Little would better demonstrate Imperial Japan's bloated sense of destiny—her belief that this one small nation alone could conquer China, India, Southeast Asia, and the United States—than the temple mount that the Gloegoer prisoners were ordered to build.

The work began with the clearing of an overgrown tobacco plantation, after which the laborers were given the Herculean task of piling up a man-made mountain. It took fifty men weeks of sweat-soaked toil, using billhooks and parangs—locally made hoes and machetes—to hack away the vegetation. With the blistering sun beating down, dark swarms of mosquitoes, giant stinging ants, and other savage insects took full advantage of bare, unprotected bodies to bite, sting, and feast to their heart's content.

But among the dangers there were also opportunities abounding in the thick bush: notably, the sudden appearance of a Sumatran water monitor—a giant lizard. As big as a crocodile, they looked to those who had never laid eyes on one like a mythical Chinese dragon. And although Judy had never seen one either, it didn't stop her from barking furiously, spooking one that was in hiding and sending it tearing across the cleared ground in search of safety.

For their size and ungainly appearance, these giant lizards can move incredibly swiftly—but not as fast as Gloegoer One's dog could. With Judy snapping at the tail of the spitting and hissing creature, a giant lizard hunt could be strung out for a good hour or more, in large part to avoid the grinding monotony of the work. In spite of their gnarly, prehistoric appearance, the monitor lizards made for fine eating, the flesh tasting like chicken but with a faint hint of fish.

Once the vegetation had been scoured away, it was burned, after which the soil had to be sifted by hand for any tiny scrap of root, seed, or vegetation. The work went on relentlessly, the guards driving the prisoners like slaves, until the area resembled a badly plowed field. Next came the grueling job of leveling the earth, after which the only way was up. Building the temple mount proved the most exhausting task both physically and mentally that the prisoners had yet been given. Tons of earth had to be shifted onto the growing mountain, and the only way to move it was by using a pair of wicker baskets slung on either end of a pole.

With the men staggering under the weight, the pole balanced across emaciated, bony shoulders, the work became an agony of endurance as the guards aimed blows from rifle butt or boot at any who faltered. They insisted the baskets always be filled to the brim, disregarding the fact that the thin scarecrows before them could barely lift their load off the ground, let alone stagger to the far side to dump the contents on the cursed hill. The higher it rose, the more the hillside became a slurry of mud up which the prisoners had somehow to haul their burden.

By the time the White Man's Mountain was nearing completion, conditions in Gloegoer were worsening daily. Even as the wooden temple itself was erected atop the hill—ornately carved dragons writhing above the doors to a house in which the souls of the ancestors could dwell—the brutal working conditions and the lack of sustenance were claiming their first victims.

As the temple mountain had risen from the earth, the food ration at Gloegoer—chiefly the rice slop—had shrunk in size almost as if the two were inversely linked. And even that pathetic amount of sustenance wasn't guaranteed to all. Those who formed the work parties got their daily share. Those who were too weak and were confined to "light duties" were placed on half rations. And those too ill to work at all received practically nothing to eat—meaning that men already sick were further weakened by starvation.

It reached the stage where the daily slop of rice simply *had* to be supplemented by extra food or the prisoners—especially those forced to labor so mercilessly on the White Man's Mountain—would die. But at the same time the Japanese currency—on seizing Sumatra the Japanese had replaced the Dutch-issued coinage with an occupation tender, the Sumatran or Nippon dollar—had plummeted in value.

The prisoners were paid a few cents a day for their labor, a pittance that might buy them a few eggs or vegetables at best. But as Imperial Japan's fortunes in the war began gradually to worsen, her legal tender became increasingly worthless. By the time of the temple mount's near completion, two weeks' wages was needed to purchase a single egg. It was the cruelest of blows, coming on top of a constellation of circumstances that seemed designed to sicken and to kill.

Weakened by hunger, Private Cousens was struck down by disease. The ever-cheerful cobbler—he who had fed Judy surreptitiously from the scraps of leather reserved for the Japanese officers' boots—was carted off to the hospital hut. There, with an ever-faithful four-legged companion more often than not at his side, Cousens sickened further and died.

On more than one occasion the soldier-cobbler had risked his life for the Gloegoer One mascot, and they had grown close. After his shock disappearance, Judy would be found lying under the overhanging roof where he used to work, still and silent and with her head resting on her outstretched paws. There was a deep sadness in her eyes as yet another of her special protectors had been taken from her at just the time when she was most in need.

Perhaps it was this resounding sense of loss that would send Judy in search of a new companion, or perhaps it was the cumulative effect of being repeatedly parted from so many of those who had grown to love her. For whatever reason, it was now that Judy opted to seek out and choose her "master."

Shipwrecked in the Berhala Strait just hours prior to the *Dragonfly* and the *Grasshopper*'s sinking, Leading Aircraftman Frank

George Williams had found his way to Gloegoer One by a similar route to that of Judy and her fellows. From the tropical island where he'd found himself marooned, Williams had traveled by tongkang, launch, truck, RAF warplane, and other means in an effort to escape the encircling Japanese but had nonetheless ended up in Gloegoer after a short stay in Padang.

Williams was a tall, softly spoken individual blessed with a ready wit and a boyish appearance that belied his apparent wisdom and maturity. One of six siblings, he'd lost his father when he was nine years of age, and life after that had been hard. He'd had to save up for two years to buy his first bicycle, perseverance becoming something of a Williams family trait. Age sixteen, he'd joined the merchant navy, which was a tough and challenging career but one that offered the considerable benefit of travel to the four corners of the world.

Hailing from Portsmouth in Hampshire, he'd only just turned twenty when war broke out. He had enlisted in the Royal Air Force, service number 751930, joining the RIMU—the RAF's Radio Installation Maintenance Unit. He was duly posted to Singapore, joining the ground crew that supported those gallant RAF airmen flying sorties against the Japanese. Outnumbered and outgunned by the far superior Japanese warplanes, the RAF crews had battled to the very last, but with the fall of Singapore many had been taken captive, Frank Williams among them.

With his kindly face beneath dark, wavy hair, Frank Williams wasn't the toughest or roughest of the POWs in Gloegoer One, and he certainly wasn't the most outspoken. But he was a lover of animals almost without equal, with a correspondingly big-hearted loyalty to boot. Perhaps it was for this reason that Judy was to discover her master in Frank Williams—although "life companion" would be a far better description for the extraordinary relationship that they would forge.

Frank was squatting in his hut, gazing into the can containing his meager rice ration, when he felt a pair of eyes upon him. He glanced up to find that a striking-looking dog was staring at him intently. The two eyed each other for a long moment before Judy began to advance. She seemed slow and uncertain in her movements, as if unsure of the reaction she might receive from a stranger—especially at feeding time. But still there was the faintest suggestion of a wag in her slender tail and just a hint of the love that was to be forged between them in her intelligent, somber eyes.

Frank could see how thin she was and how hungry she had to be, but even so she remained a strikingly beautiful English pointer. He eyed the gooey mess in his can once more. It looked and smelled as revolting as ever, but every prisoner faced the same unpalatable choice at mealtimes: eat or die, eat or die. Everyone received the same ration, so it was his alone to consume—and most felt they had only themselves to look out for whenever the slop was doled out.

He hesitated for just a moment before tipping a dollop into the palm of his hand. He held it out to Judy. Her eyes flicked to the proffered food, but still she wouldn't move. She let out a low, plaintive whine but stayed where she was, eyes flicking from rice slop to Frank and back again. It was obvious she needed some sort of reassurance, some sign from Frank that his was an entirely friendly, selfless gesture and that he was not trying to trick her somehow.

Over the year or more that she'd spent in the camps, Judy had learned to be suspicious and guarded until someone proved himself worthy. Frank understood. Placing the can of precious food on the ground, he reached forward and fondled her behind the ears.

"It's okay. It's okay," he murmured softly. "Make yourself at home."

Only then did Judy seem to relax. She took the food that he'd offered, lapped it up, then settled contentedly at his feet. Frank was by no means the first to share his ration with her, but he was one of the first strangers to do so—someone who lay well outside of Judy's normal fellowship. Neither quite knew it yet, but each had found in the other a companion for life.

From the very first Frank Williams seemed to have a nearly magical way with Judy. In short order she appeared to learn many a whispered instruction from the young RAF man, almost as if she understood his every word. He even had a command that he'd give when he wanted her to go and lift some of the fresh fruit that the Japanese guards would lay on the graves of their dead, their cemetery lying just outside the camp boundary.

The Japanese practice two forms of religion that run side by side: one is Shinto, an ancient animistic or nature-based worship, the other the more modern form of faith, Buddhism. The wooden spirit house built on the newly completed White Man's Mountain would be a Shinto or Buddhist shrine—they would often be placed side by side. But for prisoners dying of starvation, fresh fruit was far better in their bellies than being left to rot above the bodies of the dead, or so Frank and his fellows reasoned.

As the food situation worsened, such risky forays by Judy became ever more vital to keeping both man and dog alive. But each time she ventured forth she risked being nabbed by the camp guards, whose own rations were often not a great deal better than those given to the prisoners. Very soon now, Judy would find that one of her daring expeditions outside the wire would put her life in mortal danger.

But it would do so in the most unexpected of ways.

Chapter Fifteen

For those of Judy's companions who had always believed that sex was the prime human motivator, Gloegoer One had soon taught them otherwise. Les Searle, Jock Devani, Punch Puncheon—and now Frank Williams—had found that food had long become the foremost inspiration for both waking dreams and sleeping nightmares.

Not for months had any of the prisoners talked about women or told the usual soldiers' smutty stories. Talk about the fairer sex had given way to endless discussion about food. Sometimes it was the wonderful meals they used to eat at home. At other times it was the wonderful meals they would eat when they got home. Even the scant news cobbled together from the secret radio eventually got boiled down to food: when they might get out of there and get to a place where they might enjoy all the wonderful meals they had planned.

Judy's fellows had presumed that sex was very much off her menu as well. How wrong they were. Not long after finding Frank Williams, Judy returned from one of her nightly forays with more than a little extra food: *she was pregnant.* At first no one could quite believe it. How could it have happened? Every dog in the area seemed to have been shot and eaten long ago. The men joked among themselves that maybe she would give birth to a litter of tiger cubs or maybe even goats!

But beneath the humor there was real jeopardy. The larger Judy became, the more sustenance she needed—for she had a hungry litter of young ones now growing inside her. For Frank and his fellow Judy protectors, the daily struggle to find enough to eat for themselves was challenge enough: now they had Judy and her unborn offspring to fend for as well. Their greatest worry was this: the fatter the expectant mother became, the more she appeared like a feast fit for a Japanese or a Korean guard, not to mention a local Sumatran family.

Judy's protectors banned her from leaving the camp unless she was in the company of a work party so she could be better protected. Every now and again a precious can of food from a dwindling Red Cross hoard was volunteered for her. Daily she grew plumper, until the puppies were about due. And perversely, it was in their impending birth that Frank Williams saw an opportunity finally to secure for the Gloegoer One mascot the protection that she was due.

Under the care of Dr. Kirkwood, Gloegoer One's British medical officer and himself a POW, plus a team of Dutch POW medical staff, Judy gave birth to nine puppies. It was four fewer than she'd managed aboard the *Gnat*, and these certainly weren't pedigree English pointers. But under the circumstances, she had done incredibly well. As she licked them clean and nuzzled them onto her teats, four were clearly too weak to suckle and survive. They were passed to one of the men for proper disposal, leaving her with five healthy pups.

So, amid the misery of Gloegoer One, Judy became the proud mother of those five mischievous balls of blind fluff and hunger. Even if it was half the number of pups she had managed aboard the *Gnat*, in its own way it was even more of a miracle. On a diet of bully beef and condensed milk—courtesy of the Red Cross food parcels—Judy's puppies grew fat, healthy, and strong. Five balls of boundless energy started to totter around the British hut, causing amusement, havoc, and chaos in equal measure wherever they ventured.

Once they were as chubby and irresistible as ever they were going to be, Frank put his plan into action. Judy never had been able to hide the loathing she felt for the Korean and Japanese camp guards. Indeed, only recently she'd gone for one of them whom she'd sensed he was threatening one of her pups. But for some unknown reason she just about tolerated Colonel Banno. In fact, over time the Gloegoer One mascot and the Gloegoer One camp commandant had developed a kind of playful antagonism, which Frank hoped betrayed an unexpected softness on the colonel's part—that he was secretly a dog lover.

The colonel loved nothing more than to draw his sword and pretend to threaten Judy with it, seemingly with the aim of making her growl and snarl, at which he'd burst into laughter. He seemed to find it great sport. Frank also knew that the colonel had a special friend in Gloegoer—a young and beautiful local lady. He'd also noticed how Colonel Banno's lady friend always made a real fuss over Judy. Whenever she was around, she'd sing out "Judy—come!"—which were about the only words that she knew in English.

One evening when he was sure that Colonel Banno was drinking alone, Frank took Kish, one of the most irresistible of the pups, and made his way to the colonel's quarters. Any prisoner approaching the Japanese officers' part of camp did so with utter trepidation. A story had gone the rounds recently of how sickeningly and inhumanely Colonel Banno and his fellow officers had treated one of their own soldiers.

A while back the colonel had ordered tea for himself and his officers. A soft-footed orderly had entered, tea tray perched in one hand, and he had succeeded in bowing so low that his head almost touched the carpet, all without spilling the tea. Unbelievably, the man had a white gauze mask over his nose and mouth to prevent him from breathing any of his lowly germs over his superiors. The orderly had finished serving tea when he turned to leave and happened to stumble over a polished boot of one of the officers.

Before he even had the chance to utter an apology, the boot had slammed into his groin area. The orderly collapsed in silent, writhing agony. The rest of the officers grinned and nodded their satisfaction as the assaulting officer got to his feet and proceeded to kick the orderly unconscious. Colonel Banno smiled his approval once the job was done and promptly rang for another orderly, whose job it was to drag the bloodied and unconscious figure away from their esteemed presence.

That was the kind of environment that Frank Williams, a mere prisoner, was voluntarily heading into now. He didn't underestimate the dangers. More often than not, a prisoner who had the effrontery to approach the camp commandant's quarters without being summoned faced a long stretch in the solitary cell or even summary execution.

Fortunately for Frank, Kish proved to be an instant success with the quick-tempered, irascible colonel. Frank placed the tiny puppy on the desk before him, and the colonel seemed to find the scene of her wandering her wobbly way toward him almost as funny as he did her mother snarling at his swordplay. But what really seemed to do it for him was when Kish stopped, flicked out a tiny pink tongue, and had a few licks of the colonel's sword hand.

Trying to keep the tremor out of his voice—he knew just how much he was walking on eggshells here—Frank explained to the colonel that Kish was a gift for his esteemed lady friend. The colonel nodded and chortled his enthusiasm. This was a very fine idea indeed, very fine. Seizing his chance, Frank asked whether perhaps the pup's mother might be rewarded by being made an official Japanese prisoner of war. She was after all a Royal Navy mascot and a serving member of His Majesty's Armed Forces, so it was perhaps the least she deserved.

The colonel appeared to weigh the suggestion for a long moment. His face darkened. Much that he regretted having to refuse, he could see no way in which he could explain a sudden new addition to the camp roster to his superiors. It was then that Frank truly risked all. He had a suggestion to make, he ventured. If the suffix "A" was added to his own prisoner number—Hachi-ju-ichi; 81—then Judy could become Prisoner 81A. That way, everyone would be happy. Kish's mother would be happy, the colonel would be happy, and most important, his lady friend, Kish's new owner, would be happy.

The colonel rolled the puppy backward and forward a few times, his hand buried in her pudgy tummy. He was clearly enjoying the play. He reached across his desk with the other hand for his official writing pad. There and then he began to scrawl out an order making it so. Judy was being given the Japanese prisoner of war number 81A-Medan, just as Frank had requested.

But as Colonel Banno scrawled out the precious missive, Frank felt his heart sink to his boots. Beneath Kish's bottom a puddle had started to spread across the colonel's polished desk. Frank had to hope and pray it didn't reach the writing pad before he was done scribbling. Barely had Colonel Banno handed him the precious slip of paper and dismissed him than Frank practically ran from the room.

As no insanely angry voice yelled expletives after him in Japanese, Frank figured he must have gotten away from the officers' quarters before the puddle was discovered. By the next morning Judy was sporting a new metal tag on her collar, one fashioned by her protection committee using the flattened piece of a tin can. On it was etched in fine lettering: "POW 81A-Medan."

The news of Judy's promotion in status spread far and wide, just as would word of the exploits of the four remaining pups. With Kish gone, Rojok, Sheikje, Blackie, and Punch proved bundles of maverick-spirited foolishness, and they got themselves into all sorts of trouble. They were too much for their mother to keep a watchful eye over. Fortunately, claims were about to be made on them. The women in the family camp—Gloegoer Two—had heard about the puppies. They sent word with a local fruit seller that consisted of a scribbled message hidden in her basket:

"Please, can we have one of your puppies?"

None could refuse such a request, especially as the men of Gloegoer One dreaded to think what life must be like for the Dutch women and children in their camp. Les Searle argued that Sheikje was the most beautiful of the four pups, which made her the most fitting to send. When the fruit lady again visited, a space was made at the bottom of her basket. Sheikje was put to sleep by a tiny dose of chloroform administered by Dr. Kirkwood, wrapped in a cloth, and covered over with some bananas before being whisked out of the camp in the basket balanced upon the woman's head. Risking all kinds of reprisals from the camp guards, the fruit seller smuggled Sheikje out of Gloegoer One and into the family camp. And once she'd woken from her chemical-induced sleep and settled into her new home, Sheikje did no end of good in raising the morale of the women and child prisoners.

As the three remaining pups grew bigger and stronger, feeding them and controlling them became ever more of a challenge. The next to go was Rojok. He was passed through a hole in the camp fence to be given to a Swedish Red Cross official who was based in Medan as a long overdue thank you for the food parcels.

But a horrific fate awaited one of the remaining pups: Blackie, perhaps the most curious and nosy—a trait inherited no doubt from his mother. One dark night Blackie ventured out of the hut on some whim or fancy. Sadly, he ran into a drunken Korean guard, who proceeded to beat the puppy to death. The Koreans in particular were like spoiled children, and they could fly into a savage rage for no apparent reason. They were even worse whenever they had been drinking.

Poor Blackie had found himself in the wrong place at the wrong time.

There was no doubt about it—in recent months the disposition of the guards had been worsening. Many put it down to the fact that things weren't going all Imperial Japan's way in the war. For months now the guards had been boasting about the Japanese Army's invasion of India. A huge map of India had been displayed in a prominent window, with arrows indicating the line of the Japanese march. But for several weeks now that line had remained static at a hill station called Kohima, on the Imphal-to-Kohima road on India's eastern border.

The Battle for Kohima would become known as the Stalingrad of the East. From April 3 to April 16, 1944, the Japanese attempted to storm the Kohima ridge, which dominated the road by which the British and Indian troops at Imphal were supplied. The tiny force at

Kohima held out against all odds, and by mid-April the siege was broken. British and Indian troops then counterattacked, forcing the Japanese to abandon the positions they had captured, driving them off the road and away from Imphal completely.

Imphal had been marked on the map at Gloegoer One with a prominent Japanese flag, as had the next several objectives in line all the way to Delhi itself, the Indian capital. But after weeks during which the flags had remained firmly fixed, the map was quietly taken down. It was never to reappear.

The prisoners at Gloegoer couldn't know it yet, but Imphal marked a decisive defeat for the Japanese. From there on General Bill Slim's magnificent 14th Army—the so-called forgotten army, a polyglot force of dozens of nationalities speaking numerous different languages but united in their fight against the Japanese—would drive the Japanese Imperial Army back into Burma and beyond.

But with the turning of their fortunes in the war, the spirit of those guarding the Sumatran POW camps would turn darker still.

It was the second week of June 1944 when Colonel Banno left Gloegoer, to be replaced as camp commandant by one Captain Nissi. The moment of the captain's arrival was a dark day for all. At the crack of dawn on his first morning as commandant, Captain Nissi ordered all prisoners to appear on parade. And when he said "all" he meant all—no matter how sick or injured anyone might be.

Those who were unable to stand were supported by their fellows. Those who couldn't walk were carried. Even the stretcher cases had to be formed up in one rank of the sick, the lame, and those close to death's door. Captain Nissi stood in the center of the parade ground, lord of all that he surveyed. His cane slapped against his long leather jackboots as he gazed over the pathetic stream of humanity that had stumbled and crawled and been carried forth from the huts.

But as he ran his gimlet eye down the emaciated figures, his cane stopped slapping quite suddenly. He had spotted Frank Williams with a distinctive four-legged figure at his side. Captain Nissi had gone quite rigid. His eyes bulged in disbelief at spying the English pointer sitting to attention as if she were one of his prisoners. A dog? *A dog!* What was a dog doing on his parade?

Captain Nissi moved toward man and dog at a slow, predatory pace, his face dark as thunder. His sword hand crept toward the hilt of his weapon. Frank Williams watched the captain's approach with a quaking heart. At his side was a thin and worn Judy, who was still recovering her strength after raising her brood. Her body was trembling slightly at the new commandant's approach, and her lip had curled into a barely audible snarl.

Captain Nissi came to a halt.

The atmosphere was fraught with tension.

Not a man spoke—neither prisoner nor guard.

Frank knew this was balanced on a knife edge now. If the captain was allowed to bark out an instruction for something unspeakable to be done to Judy, then the guards would be duty bound to execute it. He had to strike the first blow, and before the captain started yelling orders.

With a shaking hand he delved into the pocket of his ragged shorts. He pulled out the piece of paper that Colonel Banno had penned for him—Judy's "official" POW permit. Gesturing with one hand at his dog, he held out the permit in the other, Colonel Banno's swirl of a signature prominently displayed. The captain stared at that dog-eared scrap of paper for a long second before snatching it away.

As he read it incredulously, his cronies gathered around, nattering away and gesticulating at both the note and the dog. Finally, there was a series of head scratchings and blank-faced stares between the captain and his fellow officers. However implausible it might seem, this note about the dog seemed to come from Colonel Banno himself, a superior-ranking officer to Captain Nissi. The colonel appeared to have conferred upon Judy official POW status, and in the rank-obsessed Japanese Army no one ever went against the decision of a superior officer.

For now at least Judy was no longer a legitimate target of Captain Nissi's ire. Instead, he turned his attention to the men. Everyone but the wakeful dead was sent out on forced-labor parties. The guards had clearly been given orders to up the work rate or face the consequences. Captain Nissi seemed determined to drive the men to exhaustion and death in record time, and the prisoners were soon dropping like flies.

Day two was even worse, and if this was kept up the hospital hut would soon be filled to overflowing. But on day three came a reprieve of sorts. Mustered again at dawn on the parade ground, the men listened to Captain Nissi as he barked out a new order.

"All prisoners are to be shipped forthwith to Singapore."

The news came as a total surprise, but it was greeted with barely disguised elation among the men. *Singapore.* It was a bustling metropolis compared to Sumatra, this jungle island where the prisoners had labored for so long in forgotten isolation. *Singapore.* It was sure to offer news of the outside world and perhaps a sense of how the war was going in Europe. *Singapore.* Surely there might be better treatment there—*and more food*—and perhaps even letters from home.

If nothing else, the urge to leave Gloegoer was so strong and surely anywhere had to be better than this. Les Searle used a rag to wipe the perspiration from one of the stretcher cases laid next to him on the parade ground.

"Cheer up, mate," he whispered, "you'll soon be out of this."

That evening the huts were a scene of frantic activity as men packed and repacked their meager belongings in preparation for departure. Each hut received a visit from the guards, warning all to be ready to set off at first light the next morning.

For Frank Williams, there was to be a different kind of a visit. Captain Nissi himself came to have words with Judy's chief protector. The commandant delivered a curt directive. He wished to make himself clear: the dog would not be going to Singapore. As Judy was Gloegoer One's mascot, at Gloegoer One she would have to stay.

Once Captain Nissi was gone Frank took a few quiet moments to try to digest the news. But he felt truly shaken. He sat in one corner of the hut with Judy clasped between his knees, and he tried to think up a plan—a plan to thwart the cruel camp commandant and keep Judy with her fellows, her natural family. He knew he could rely on Les Searle, Jock Devani, and the others to help him, but the main risk in all of this would have to be his own.

He eyed Judy for a moment. He couldn't expect any of the others to sacrifice their lives for her—and certainly, disobeying Captain Nissi's order would be life-threatening in the extreme. The Japanese—and especially ones like the new camp commandant—were incapable of dealing with loss of face. If the plan now forming in Frank's mind was successful, when Judy was discovered gone, everyone would know that the captain's order had been disobeyed, and by a lowly POW. The loss of face that entailed was incalculable, as would be the punishment that would inevitably follow.

But Frank was absolutely determined: where he was going his bitch was going too. No matter who might be issuing the orders, they would not be parted. Man and dog hardly slept that night. They were up for many an hour as Frank went about teaching Judy a new trick—a variation on the fetch-the-fresh-fruit-from-the-Japanese-grave game.

The prisoners were going to be shipped to Singapore aboard an old freighter. Frank spent those few quiet hours before dawn—when the hut was filled with the groans and snuffles of hungry and exhausted men lost in the uncertain release of troubled sleep—teaching Judy to run to a burlap sack that he was holding, at his signal. When she seemed to have grasped that much, he taught her to jump in and out of the sack at a quiet click of his fingers.

Regardless of their breed, dogs respond best to training when the reward offered is play or praise. Frank had little else to offer Judy but play and praise in abundance.

As the first rays of dawn broke across the roofs of the Gloegoer One huts, Judy seemed to have mastered her new trick perfectly. She didn't quite grasp what it was for yet, but she trusted her teacher implicitly.

Little did she know it, but her life was hanging by a slender thread.

All they could do was to wait and hope.

CHAPTER SIXTEEN

At dawn the prisoners were ordered to muster for their final parade. But one, prisoner 81A-Medan, was left tied to a post in the British hut. Thanks to his days serving in the merchant navy, Frank knew just about every seaman's knot there is to tie. He'd used a slipknot to fasten Judy, one that would come loose under moderate pressure. Knot tied, he'd ordered her to stay and left to join those lining up in the dim light outside.

After less than a week of Captain Nissi's brutal rule there were now two rows of stretcher cases. God only knows how the prisoners would have fared had they been forced to endure his murderous rule for any longer. Les Searle, Jock Devani, and the other old faithfuls were in on Frank's Judy-rescue plan, and each had his part to play. They waited tensely as the guards counted and recounted the POW numbers and checked and rechecked their bags of pitiful possessions.

It was crucial to Frank's plan that he was seen to be carrying a bulging sack, although in truth he possessed little of anything that was worth taking with him. He'd stuffed his sack with an old blanket so that it appeared bulging fat and full to those who might scrutinize it. At last the guards seemed satisfied with their inspections, and they reported to Captain Nissi that all were present and correct.

The captain gave the order to move out.

For the last time—at least for these prisoners—the camp gates were swung open. The first to move off were those removed from the hospital hut, borne on hastily improvised stretchers. As the stretcher carriers passed through the gates of Gloegoer One bearing their living skeletons, it was as if the tombs of the dead had opened. These were once men, but through a combination of brutal forced labor, tropical disease, and starvation they had been reduced to wraiths.

Those who were still fit—though that term in Gloegoer One had a very different meaning from the norm—watched this ghostly procession of the barely living in stunned silence. While busy on the work gangs, few had had the energy, the want, or the need to venture into the hospital hut. Under Captain Nissi's orders that hut had been forced to disgorge its secrets. Many a man felt himself biting his lip or driving his nails into his hands as he struggled to master the hatred he felt for those who had done this and to resist the urge to strike back. Anyone who did so would end up either dead or in the hands of the dreaded Kempeitai, which was a fate worse than death.

The Kempeitai was the Japanese equivalent of the Gestapo, Nazi Germany's secret police. Among this procession of the walking dead were those who had had cause to fall into their clutches. Mostly they were Dutch officers who'd been interrogated and tortured in unspeakable ways as the Kempeitai had sought intelligence on the territory that they had overrun. They had returned to Gloegoer broken men: it wasn't so much their bodies that were finished as their minds. They stumbled along like zombies, lost in a world to which their tortured psyches had, in desperation, retreated.

Frank lingered at the rear of the line of those deemed fit, waiting his turn to move. As the column began to snake ahead, he joined the very end so he would be last out. The moment he was through the gates he gave a faint whistle, the call that Judy would recognize as the signal for her to come. But as he followed the last in line toward the nearby railway siding—they were catching a train from the camp to the docks, the first leg of the coming journey— there was no sign of his beloved Judy anywhere.

Frank was worried sick that he'd tied the knot too tightly. But what could he do? He could hardly turn back for her. He was bound to be spotted, the questions would begin, and Judy would quickly be discovered. So he did the only thing he could do, moving along those lining up to board the train, his eyes searching everywhere for any sign of his dog.

It was then that he saw it—a dark and moist nose and a pair of shining eyes, half hidden in the shadows beneath a railway truck. He went down on one knee, and a screen of bodies formed around him— Les Searle and Jock Devani herding others in closer to hide what was about to happen. Once he was completely surrounded, Frank whipped the blanket out and clicked his fingers, and Judy darted out from her place of hiding and leaped inside the empty sack.

With the blanket packed down on top to better hide her, Frank hoisted the heavy sack on his shoulders and climbed aboard a waiting railway carriage. With Judy thus hidden, the journey to the dockside proved a bittersweet affair. Even though the future was uncertain, the British and Australian prisoners were mostly relieved to be getting out of Gloegoer One. But for the Dutch prisoners there were distant and anxious farewells to be said as they streamed past the family camp and desperate rags and handkerchiefs were waved out of the carriage windows.

On reaching the harbor, the carriages shuddered and squealed as the brakes were applied. Now came the real test of Frank's plan. He released Judy from the sack, and she darted from the open door to her hiding place beneath the wagons, almost before the train had come to a stop.

Again the men were formed up in ranks as the Japanese did the second head count and baggage inspection of the day just to ensure no one had made a break for it during the train journey or was carrying any hidden contraband. The prisoners eyed the ship that lay before them with some concern. The ship's name—the SS *Van Waerwyjck*—had been painted over with a Japanese one, the *Harukiku Maru*, and the tall gray-painted hull was streaked with rust and dirt.

The SS *Van Waerwyjck* was a Dutch vessel captured and pressed into military service by the Japanese. She had been built in 1910 as a passenger steamer, and the Royal Dutch Navy had commandeered her at the outbreak of the war and then scuttled her at the entrance to Tanjung Priok harbor in Java, the island lying to the south of Sumatra, in an effort to prevent a Japanese invasion by sea. But once the Japanese had been victorious across the region they had refloated the ship, repaired her, and pressed her into service as a transport vessel. She was the biggest ship that any of the prisoners had ever seen in the port of Balawan.

The head count seemed to go on forever, as did the inspection of the prisoners' possessions. Once his sack had been searched and the coast seemed clear Frank gave another whistle. Word ran down the line of waiting men, whispered from mouth to mouth, that Judy was coming. Having made as much progress as she could crawling beneath the train, she popped out and weaved her way between the ranks of prisoners, making directly for Frank's position.

Not a man among them so much as glanced down as she passed by. Seizing his moment, Frank bent again and whisked her into the sack, and moments later he had her hoisted onto his shoulders. So far, so good. The waiting men began to shuffle their way up the gangways leading onto the *Van Waerwyjck*'s main deck. The prisoners were divided into two parties: officers and wounded for the front hold, all others for the rear.

There were some seven hundred prisoners gathered on the quay-side, and it was taking an age to get them loaded, especially the wounded. The midday sun beat down mercilessly from a cloudless Sumatran sky. Sweat poured off the men standing unmoving in their ranks. Frank felt his limbs weakening with exhaustion, but he was determined not to buckle under the heavy weight slung across his shoulder.

He sensed the tall Australian beside him lean across and place something on his head. It was a wide-brimmed Aussie bush hat.

"If I fall down, someone'll pick me up," he muttered cheerfully. "But if you fall down, mate, you've had it—you and your dog."

Quite suddenly, Captain Nissi materialized right before Frank. For a second or so he scrutinized the wide-brimmed hat perched

atop the prisoner's head. Frank could see the captain's mind working away feverishly behind brutish eyes. Captain Nissi had seen
Judy tied to a post back in the hut in Medan. He'd seen Frank's sack
inspected once back at the camp and once here. Presumably, the
dog had been left behind, as ordered.

"*Ino wa arimasen deshita?*"—"The dog's not come?"—he
demanded menacingly.

"*Ino wa arimasen deshita . . .*" Frank confirmed unhappily.

He did his best to look utterly crestfallen at the loss of his faithful friend, eyes cast at the ground, but at the same time the heavy
sack was biting deeper into his bony shoulder. If Judy so much as
breathed right now, the captain would be bound to notice.

"*Ino wa arimasen deshita!*" Captain Nissi affirmed, a triumphant
smile spreading across his features.

With a curt nod he moved on.

His knees shaking, Frank made it to the top of the gangplank,
the contents of his precious sack still undiscovered. Rough hands
grabbed him and shoved him toward a series of steep iron ladders
leading down into the forward hold. No life jackets were issued to
any of the prisoners. They remained locked in the wooden cupboards on the upper deck, adjacent to the ship's lifeboats.

With the sack slung over his shoulder, Frank was all but thrown
down the steps, joining the mass of bodies in the darkness below.
At the bottom of the stairway he found that the ship's hold had been
converted into a prison ship. Rough wooden platforms ran along
either side of the interior, dividing it into two floors. Those first
down the ladder had been herded into the all but total darkness of
the lower level.

Conditions were abominable. With only four feet of headroom,
those on the lower level couldn't stand, and they were packed so
tight that there was no room to lie down. Instead, they squatted,
row upon row upon row. Frank found himself a place on the upper
floor. It was little better except that there were portholes, which at
least held out the promise that when the ship began to move there
might be a little air.

Frank settled down with Les Searle, Jock Devani, and the others, his back to a steel bulkhead. The heat was already intense. The entry hatch to the hold appeared like a small square of daylight above them, a shaft of sunlight streaming through it and piercing the thick darkness. But shortly, even the hatch was slammed shut, sealing the men inside a giant metal oven. In no time the prisoners were sitting in pools of their own sweat.

With the hatch locked shut Frank felt he could finally risk releasing Judy. She poked her head out of the sack, tongue lolling and panting heavily as she gazed around at her new surroundings. An instant later Frank had her out and she was lapping thirstily at the water that he'd brought with him from the camp. That done, they settled down to endure as best they could the sea voyage to Singapore.

It was midafternoon when the SS *Van Waerwijck* slipped her moorings and steamed out of the harbor. Once she hit the open sea, she formed up in a convoy with two oil tankers, another cargo ship, and a pair of Japanese Navy corvettes for protection. She steamed onward, keeping close to the Sumatran coastline, the rhythmic slap of the waves beneath the hull lulling many into an exhausted sleep. But it was fitful and uneasy. With limbs entwined there was little room to lie down and less still to move around.

Les Searle found himself desperate to stretch his legs. He was curled up tight against the bulkhead, with another prisoner lying in his path. As for Judy, in spite of the terribly cramped conditions she seemed happy enough. She was with Frank and her wider family—her fellow conspirators—and for now at least she had escaped whatever fate had awaited her at Captain Nissi's hands.

With dusk the ship came to a halt and dropped anchor. The engines were shut down, but still the oppressive heat in the cramped hold lasted long into the night. With dawn the *Van Waerwijck* was quickly under way again. It was June 26, 1944, a day that would be burned forever in the minds of those aboard that ill-fated ship.

After repeated complaints to the Japanese guards, some respite from the terrible conditions below deck was granted. In small batches, prisoners were allowed up into the fresh air twenty minutes at a time. But of course, prisoner 81A-Medan was going nowhere. Judy the stowaway would have to remain ensconced in the darkest recesses of the hold or she risked getting discovered.

A constant stream of buckets of hot water was lowered so the men could brew tea. But the more quickly they drank, the more quickly the sweat seemed to pour from their bodies. By midday the fierce heat was reaching its zenith. From stem to stern a deathly quiet gripped the vessel. The prisoners suffered in numbed silence, the ovenlike conditions seeming to roast their very brains. It was only the malaria and dysentery patients who kept disturbing the mute stillness, the eerie moans and cries of their fevered delirium echoing back and forth.

Tucked away in her corner, Judy sat so still and so statuesque that it was almost as if she knew that she was a stowaway and what the costs of discovery might be. Once again, just her presence among the prisoners proved a massive morale booster. The very fact that she was still there showed how they had put one over on the Japanese. She was a symbol of their stoic resistance and their survival— survival that in her case had been achieved against all the odds.

Across the hold from Judy sat a young British Army sergeant called Peter Hartley. Hartley had distinguished himself during the battle for Singapore by being one of those who had refused to surrender when the order was given to do so by his commanding officer. Instead, he had stolen a boat from Singapore harbor, and via the Indragiri River he had embarked upon a journey to Padang that was almost a carbon copy of that undertaken by the gunboat crews—both man and dog.

He'd reached the besieged city at the same moment as Judy and her fellows, so missing the final ships sailing to safety, and he had likewise ended up in Gloegoer One. There a strange series of events had unfolded. Being a particularly religious man—he was a strong Christian even before the outbreak of the war—Hartley had been recruited by the camp's British padre to assist in his services and especially to help officiate at burials. But before the padre had been able to instruct Hartley very much, he had himself sickened and died.

Hartley—not properly trained and certainly not ordained—had become by default the padre of the British at Gloegoer One, and in that he had done a sterling job. Ensconced in the hold of the SS *Van Waerwijck*, he gazed at the large liver-and-white dog across the way from him, marveling at the incredible life she had led. All in Gloegoer had heard of their mascot's string of wild adventures—on the gunboats, in Singapore, and during her long flight to the POW camps—and it strengthened their determination to have her remain one of their number.

Now here she was again—smuggled aboard and miraculously still with them. Hartley thanked God that she had not been discovered. Having her there on that hellish ship was oddly comforting. Hartley watched the Gloegoer One mascot lay her fine head between her forepaws, as if to rest. Gradually, he felt his own eyes closing, the stultifying heat and the motion of the vessel lulling him to sleep.

Neither man nor dog would rest for long.

In the seas off eastern Sumatra, June 26 was a calm and sunny day. The *Van Waerwijck* steamed onward toward Singapore, her captain and crew remaining blissfully unaware that a British submarine had spotted her.

The first sign that Commander Robert Alexander, the captain of HMS *Truculent*, had detected of the small convoy was a plume of smoke on the distant horizon. Minutes later he'd spotted an aircraft circling overhead, forming some kind of an escort. He'd closed to within 3,500 yards, a range from which he could study the vessels properly.

As he hunched over his periscope, gazing intently at the enemy ships, the British commander realized he'd stumbled upon a small Japanese convoy. After he scanned the cluster of vessels from end to end, one—a twin-masted steamer with a single funnel churning out a dark plume of smoke—clearly presented the largest and most juicy target. Unaware that she was carrying hundreds of British and Allied POWs, Commander Alexander unleashed four torpedoes, then dived, settling upon the bottom at 58 feet depth.

Onboard the *Van Waerwijck* Les Searle had just been called onto the open deck. It was a chance to grab a little fresh air. The sense of relief after the punishing conditions below was unbelievable— even though he'd been summoned to help with a decidedly unpleasant task, that of cleaning the ship's latrines. Midway through the work some sixth sense made him glance out to sea. He froze. Just below the surface were the unmistakable tracks of white turbulence formed by torpedoes. Four of them, and bearing down on them fast!

Les felt overcome with shock and disbelief, yet still he managed to yell out a warning. "Torpedoes! Torpedoes off the port side!"

His cry came too late for the ship to take any kind of evasive action. Moments later the first torpedo struck the SS *Van Waerwijck*, throwing up a geyser of white water high into the air. It tore into the ship's hull just to the rear of the forward hold and adjacent to the coal bunker. Those who were on deck knew instantly what had happened, and several threw themselves into the sea. But those packed into the rear hold had heard only a deafening thud reverberating through the vessel, and they couldn't know what calamity had befallen the ship.

As Les raced across deck to warn them, the second torpedo was ahead of him. The blunt-nosed projectile tore into the rear hold, where several hundred prisoners and one dog were packed like sardines. The explosion proved so violent that it buckled the deck, blasting several Japanese guards high into the air. Seawater began pouring into the ruptured hull.

The *Van Waerwijck* let out a tortured groan and started listing badly to port. In the forward hold the bulkhead that had separated the prisoners from the engine room collapsed. Blasted coal dust turned the air black as night as ghostly, soot-covered figures fought one another for a place on the ladder and the chance to climb to safety. On the deck above a chaplain was crying out Hail Marys and Our Fathers at the top of his voice as he wrestled open the cupboards holding the life jackets and handed them around to those fighting to get clear of the sinking ship.

Drums, chests, and falling planks of wood crashed about the badly listing deck, trapping those who were struggling to get free. The ship was sinking stern first, and the water was already claiming its first victims. In the rear hold it was utter chaos. Figures clambered over each other to get access to the stairwell. As the ship heeled over still farther the wooden platforms disintegrated into heavy planking, massive splinters crashing down on top of bodies and trapping many. The huge covers for the hatches had been blown inward by the force of the explosion, crushing those below.

As the ship heeled over still farther, the packing cases that constituted the deck cargo broke free and crashed into the hold. Seawater swirled and gurgled as bodies fought to make their escape. Les Searle peered in through the open hatch, searching amid the mass of twisted metal, wood, and seawater for Jock Devani, Frank, Judy, and the others. He leaned into the darkness and hauled figures upward as he joined those trying to drag as many as possible out of that giant steel coffin.

But Jock, Frank, and Judy were nowhere to be seen.

When the first torpedo struck, Peter Hartley, Gloegoer's makeshift padre, had woken with a start. He'd gotten to his feet, a sense of panic sweeping through the hold, only to be blasted down again by torpedo number two. Moments later sounds began to filter into his numbed brain: rushing water, splintering wood, the agonized screams of those who were trapped. The harsh wail of the ship's siren rent the gloom while the floor beneath him rocked and shook as if an earthquake were tearing through the ship.

High above him he saw a square of daylight—the hatch—with figures clustered desperately around it. The ladder was besieged. There was no way he could make it out by that route. Instead, he began to climb up the jagged mountain of packing cases that had tumbled into the hold. If he could make the high point, he might just be able to attempt a leap for the open hatch.

For an instant he glanced across at where Judy had been sleeping, her head resting on her paws. The most amazing sight met his eyes. Frank Williams had hoisted Judy up and was trying to squeeze her out through a porthole. When the torpedoes had struck, Judy had been nestled comfortably between his knees. He'd known that there was no way he could carry her through the mass of men who had began to fight for the one escape route—the ladder leading out of the hold. Instead, he'd turned to the nearest porthole, wrenched it fully open, and lifted Judy toward it.

Trusting to the last, she'd allowed him to ease her head and forelegs through the opening even as the ship had begun her final death throes. She'd turned her head toward the stricken vessel, eyes searching for Frank, as if she'd expected him to be following after her.

Instead, he'd uttered a few encouraging words. "Out you go, old girl! Swim for it!"

With that he'd given a final push on her hindquarters, and Judy of Sussex had tumbled into the sea.

CHAPTER SEVENTEEN

It was four minutes past two in the afternoon when the SS *Van Waerwijck* gave up the ghost and was claimed by the waves. It had taken just twelve short minutes for her to go down. But not all of the ship had disappeared. The stern was stuck in the mud, and the bow section remained likewise just above the waters. She'd broken in two, but she hadn't been lost from the survivors' view completely: there were hundreds in the water all around her, fighting for their lives.

Meanwhile, her nemesis, HMS *Truculent,* was doing her best to make her escape as the Japanese corvettes came hunting. A pattern of six depth charges was dropped, massive eruptions showing where they'd exploded deep beneath the waves. This first salvo hit wide of the mark, so the corvettes swung around to release a second, this one falling much closer to the British submarine. A third attacking run sent more depth charges churning up the waters around their target, the shock waves pounding out a deathly rhythm against the British submarine's hull.

But by now Commander Alexander had gotten his vessel under way, and he managed to creep away silently and make good the *Truculent*'s escape. The British submarine left behind her a sea that was littered with debris and flotsam, plus hundreds of men struggling for their lives.

The *Van Waerwijck* had been sunk in the Malacca Strait some 500 kilometers north of Singapore. The shore was several miles distant, and there were few who were able to swim for it. Instead, figures clutched on to just about anything that might provide some form of buoyancy—broken wooden beams, life rafts, scattered life vests. Amid the thick, oily scum that covered the water, crates of live chickens bobbed about, their worried clucking adding a surreal touch to the ghostly scene.

A flight of Japanese bombers with fighter escorts appeared overhead, searching for the British submarine, but to no avail. HMS *Truculent* had slipped into deeper waters just as stealthily as she had appeared. With the threat gone, the Japanese tanker ships steamed back into view, having moved closer to the shore in an effort to hide. Lifeboats were lowered, but the crew had strict orders to prioritize the rescue of their fellow Japanese and Koreans. The British, Dutch, and Australian prisoners would have to wait their turn.

Among the first POWs finally to be plucked from the sea would be Frank Williams. He'd been in the water for a good two hours, clinging to a lump of wreckage. For all of that time he'd kept his eyes peeled for a familiar figure, one that he was so desperate to spot—a liver-and-white English pointer dog-paddling through the oily swell.

When Frank was finally able to clamber up one of the nets thrown over the tanker's sides he was exhausted from the time he'd spent in the water, his eyes showing as white circles in his otherwise oil-blackened features. With a last despairing glance over the ship's rail, he allowed himself to be led aft to the galley. As he did so, he consoled himself with the thought that he had done all he could to save Judy.

It was in the lap of the gods whether she lived or died, though he very much doubted whether the Japanese would make much of an effort to save a dog, especially one that was a forbidden stowaway. His biggest worry was that she might have gone back aboard the stricken ship to search for him and had failed to get out before the vessel went down. After all, she'd gotten herself trapped aboard the *Grasshopper*, and only the spirited action of Petty Officer White had saved her.

Along with the rest of the rescued prisoners, Frank was given a ball of sticky rice to stuff into his mouth with his oil-smeared hands, plus a mug of tea. As more and more soot-blackened figures joined them, the deck became horribly crowded. There was only the open steel above the oil tanks for the survivors to squat on, and the afternoon sun was heating it up like a furnace. Soon it was impossible to so much as step on the deck without burning the soles of the feet. All the men could do was squat under the burning sun and suffer in a shocked and stunned silence as the search for more lives to save went on and on.

Unknown to those rescued prisoners, the greatest ever four-legged lifesaver was hard at work out there on the water. Les Searle had managed to escape from the stricken *Van Waerwijck*, whereupon he'd set out to swim for the nearest Japanese tanker. As he was stroking his way through the wreckage-strewn seas, he came across the most incredible sight of all. A finely shaped dark head was arrowing through the water, powerful forepaws thrashing at the surface. There was a figure at Judy's side, and he had one arm thrown across her shoulders as she pulled him toward safety.

Les could barely believe it. Why didn't the poor bitch shake him off? he wondered. Surely, under the dead weight of a fully grown man she'd drown.

But Judy made it to the nearest rescue boat—a local tongkang that had arrived on the scene—after which her shipwreck victim was hauled aboard. Yet still she wasn't done. With cheers of encouragement ringing in her ears she turned around and set off to find others. She helped bring in a good half dozen survivors before she became too exhausted to drag any more to safety, at which point she resorted to pushing lengths of driftwood toward those who were the most in need.

Eventually, she allowed herself to be hauled aboard the tongkang. Bedraggled and smeared in oil, Judy was more dead than alive. She was totally exhausted, her ribs showed sharp and angular through her emaciated sodden flanks, and her eyes were red-rimmed and smarting, but she was still very much the heroine of the hour.

Sadly, there was little opportunity to treat her as the champion lifesaver that she was. Instead, she had to be hustled under a length of canvas that had been used to cover the bodies of some of her most hated human oppressors: a pair of Korean guards who had drowned during the ship's sinking. Judy would have to keep those corpses company for the remainder of the voyage to Singapore— otherwise the guards might discover her presence and, remembering Captain Nissi's orders, unleash savage retribution.

One of the last men to be plucked out of the sea was a Captain Gordon of the Royal Artillery. He'd managed to swim to a native fishing trap set offshore and cling to it for several hours. From there he was picked up by one of the Japanese corvettes. Having thanked the ship's captain for rescuing him and many others, Captain Gordon asked the Japanese commander if he would be willing to make one last search of all the wreckage. He agreed, and by four-thirty that afternoon all the survivors had been plucked from the sea.

The convoy formed up and got under way once more, steaming south for Singapore. But with sundown the decks that had been boiling hot during the day were transformed into a freezing cold, icy bed for the night. Without any blankets and with many even lacking clothes—they'd lost them during the shipwreck—the survivors huddled as close together as they could, trying to share some body warmth. As a chill wind whipped across the exposed deck, the curses and shivers of the survivors mingled with the hollow, despairing cries of the wounded.

Among those who had escaped from the *Van Waerwijck* sinking were Les Searle, Jock Devani, Frank Williams, and Judy of Sussex, plus Gloegoer One's makeshift padre, Peter Hartley—but they were spread across various vessels. Ahead of them lay a journey during which they would be frozen at night, baked under the burning sun by day, and forced to bury at sea many of their comrades—the worst wounded, who would not survive.

By the time the battered convoy sailed into Singapore, most were too numb with shock and exhaustion to register anything other than a dumb recognition that they had arrived.

Over two years had passed since Frank Williams had served with his RAF unit here in Singapore, or since Les Searle, Jock Devani, and Judy had striven valiantly aboard the gunboats to escape the encircling Japanese, or since Peter Hartley had refused the order to surrender and made his desperate escape bid. The vessels that were carrying them chugged by the sunken forms of the wrecks that still littered the harbor before passing the sleek gray forms of a pair of German U-boats emblazoned with huge red-and-white swastikas.

The first ships pulled alongside an empty wharf. The reality of what had happened started to sink in for the shipwreck survivors crouched like naked scarecrows on the decks. Naked and smeared with oil they might be, but somehow five hundred of the *Van Waerwijck*'s contingent of seven hundred POWs had survived. Dirty, bloodied, and bare they might be, but few felt ashamed now they were back in civilization.

Instead, they gave thanks for being alive.

But for one prisoner, 81A-Medan, the most life-threatening moment of this nightmare journey was still to come. The tongkang carrying Judy pulled into dock where there was a convoy of waiting Japanese Army trucks. A distinctive figure stood among the gray vehicles, looming head and shoulders above his fellow officers—Colonel Banno. After the horrors of Captain Nissi's rule, some of the prisoners—Les Searle and Peter the padre Hartley among them—almost felt glad to lay eyes on Gloegoer One's former commandant once more.

At first the colonel greeted their arrival with a smile. But it soon gave way to a look of horror as he surveyed the human skeletons clustered along the deck and the awfulness of what must have happened hit home. He was as changeable as ever, and the sight seemed to move him to a rare show of pity. He turned to his guards and began issuing orders, gesticulating wildly with his hands at the figures on the vessel.

The tongkang scraped its way along the concrete dockside and came to a halt. The gangplank went down, and volunteers were called forth to carry the wounded, including those Korean guards who had jumped from the ship in the first seconds after she was hit, only to be caught by the shock waves of the second torpedo and suffering horrific internal injuries as a result. Then there were the prisoners from the rear hold, who had been injured in the explosion caused by the second torpedo. A few Japanese guards had jumped into the sea with a supposed ready-made life raft gripped between their legs—a length of wooden planking from the ship, perhaps—only for its impact to cause serious injuries.

With the wounded unloaded, the order was given for the able-bodied men to disembark. As Les Searle coaxed Judy out of hiding, he had no sack in which to hide her or any means to click his fingers and get her to dart inside. He had no choice but to lead her down the gangplank in full view. Together with Padre Peter Hartley he and Judy half stumbled the short distance, for they were in a terrible way. Hartley's legs and arms were cut to shreds from all the splintered wood that he'd had to fight his way through, and neither Les Searle nor Judy was in very much better condition.

But as soon as the three survivors made the quayside the Gloegoer One guards noticed Judy. The atmosphere surrounding the disembarkation changed completely. Two of the guards stormed forward, mouths spouting invective and arms jerking maniacally at the dog, at Les Searle, and then at the sea. The meaning was clear: they were threatening to throw Judy into the harbor and very possibly her human companions with her. Les Searle doubted whether he could survive another immersion, and as for Judy, even she was looking half beaten.

As the guards went to snatch the errant dog, a powerful cry rang out. Hands froze in midaction. It was the voice of Colonel Banno. Having seen what was happening, the colonel had barked out some form of counterorder. The guards jerked stiffly to attention and then bowed before the colonel before stepping away from the dog.

Colonel Banno strode forward. The guards bobbed their heads in cringing subservience as he tore into them. Then, rather than drawing his sword to bait Judy, he bent down to pat her oil-stained ears, clearly signaling that she had won her reprieve. In the eyes of many of the prisoners, in that one moment Colonel Banno had atoned for many of the past cruelties that he'd visited upon them at Gloegoer One.

The POWs were formed up in ragged ranks. Many were completely naked, their only covering being a thick layer of greasy soot and oil. More trucks pulled up at the quayside. Head count completed, the men—plus one dog who'd won an eleventh-hour reprieve—were ordered to board the waiting vehicles. But beside one of the newly arrived trucks stood another familiar figure, and this one was far less welcome.

It was the dreaded Captain Nissi, fresh onto the scene. As Les Searle went to hoist Judy into the rear of one of the trucks, the captain let out a strangled scream of rage. A torrent of abuse shot forth from his lips. A pair of soldiers stepped forward, rifles at the ready.

In her appearance Judy was very different from her heyday on the Yangtze gunboats. She was painfully thin, her white coat was stained black with oil from repeated forays into the sea, her teeth were yellow beneath snarling lips, and her red eyes burned with hatred for those about to seize her. Yet just at the moment when they were about to strike, an older, more commanding voice rang out. It was Colonel Banno once more, and this time he was countermanding Captain Nissi's orders: prisoner 81A-Medan was not to be harmed.

Much as he hated having to do so, Captain Nissi was forced to give way. Before there could be any further attempts to do her harm, Les Searle bundled Judy into the truck and vaulted after her. Shortly they were off jolting along the harbor road, every man lost in a dark corner of the vehicle and entombed in his own thoughts. Not even the fact that they'd succeeded in frustrating Captain Nissi's murderous intentions could lift the men's sagging spirits.

The convoy roared through the streets of what had once been Britain's island fortress but had been transformed into a stronghold of the hated enemy. Just a short drive across the city, the trucks pulled to a halt. The prisoners were ordered out. They had been brought to a new camp—or at least it was new to them—but a more dilapidated and dispiriting place they'd yet to imagine.

The huts were made of rough-hewn wooden frames, supposedly topped off with atap—rough thatch harvested from the jungle. But with many the roofing had blown away or rotted through completely. This accursed place was called the River Valley Road Camp, presumably because there was a garbage-choked drain running through the center of it.

The first survivors from the SS *Van Waerwijck* marched into the camp, passing through a group of huts that were already occupied by Allied POWs. They were forbidden from stopping or talking to anyone. They were herded across the stream-cum-sewer, through a barbed-wire gate guarded by sentries, and into what appeared to be the most godforsaken corner of the entire godforsaken place.

This end of the camp was strewn with garbage and filth. On the far side was a rank of bare huts, each equipped with wooden sleeping platforms. For now, this was home.

These men had lost everything when the SS *Van Waerwijck* went down. What few possessions they'd taken with them from Gloegoer One had gone to the bottom of the Malacca Strait. Reduced to numbed, naked animals, suffering from shock and exposure, their hair matted and oily and their faces covered in filthy stubble, most were almost as crazed as they looked—for right now the survivors of the *Van Waerwijck* sinking were close to being an army of the insane and the damned.

Landfills were ransacked for empty cans to use as mugs or bits of sacking from which to improvise clothing. A meal was served. It was rice and dried, salted fish. The men were forced to eat with their hands, using leaves cut from the trees as their plates. Harsh unsweetened black tea was sipped from rusty, dirt-encrusted cans. But the ration drove some even closer to the brink, for it wasn't enough even to begin to satiate their gnawing hunger. There had been little to eat after the sinking of their ship, for the tongkang's crew hadn't expected to need to cater for dozens of Allied POWs.

And now this—*starvation rations*.

When Les Searle retired to his hut to rest his aching limbs, his shrunken stomach grumbling painfully, he expected Judy to come with him. But oddly, she refused. Instead she went from hut to hut, checking each in turn. That done, she proceeded to crisscross the entire length and breadth of the camp. By now Les had an inkling what she might be up to: she had to be searching for their missing friend—for Frank Williams. But he could think of little to say or do to comfort her.

It was as much as he had been able to manage to save Judy from Captain Nissi's ire—with Colonel Banno's help. He had no idea if Frank Williams had survived the shipwreck. They'd all heard the story of Frank pushing Judy through the porthole, but after that, who knew? Yet Judy was not to be deterred from her quest. Once she was certain that Frank wasn't anywhere in the camp, she settled down at the gate, her head resting on her forepaws and her somber eyes fixed in the direction from which she hoped her master would miraculously reappear.

For two days she kept her lonely vigil. Judy's was a watch that would not be broken. Too often in life she'd been parted from her greatest protectors—Petty Officer Jefferey and Tankey Cooper of the *Gnat*, Petty Officer George White of the *Grasshopper*, plus Private Cousens the Gloegoer One shoemaker, to name but a few. Losing Frank Williams was something that Judy simply refused to accept, as if by force of will alone she might bring him to her alive.

And so she waited patiently for a reunion that she felt certain was coming.

Some forty-eight hours after the first arrivals had reached the River Valley Road Camp, Frank Williams made it there too. Weakened by exposure, physically and mentally exhausted from the shipwreck, he was doubly traumatized by what he believed to be the loss of his beloved dog. Bit by bit, he seemed to be losing his will to live.

He clambered down from the truck, every movement causing him agony, and stumbled into the dreadful camp. He was blind to much of what was around him and lost in a dark world of his own.

So cut off was he from his surroundings that when he felt the first blow to his shoulders as he staggered through the barbed-wire gate, he shrugged it off as just another exhausted prisoner stumbling into him.

The second blow had the power to send him sprawling facedown in the dirt, so weakened was his physical condition. He lay there feeling little but dull incomprehension as someone or something scrabbled anxiously at his head and shoulders as if desperate to attract his attention.

And then he heard it. At first he couldn't—*wouldn't*—believe his ears. A low, insistent whine had reached him, cutting through the hunger, the trauma, and the crushing exhaustion that had so befuddled his mind. As if to confirm his impossible hopes, he felt something cold and wet nuzzling into his face—and now the whining was right in his ear.

His hearing wasn't playing tricks on him! *It was her! It was Judy!* Somehow the dog he thought had perished in the seas around the stricken *Van Waerwijck*—the dog he'd pushed through the ship's porthole in an effort to save her—had come back from the dead!

Sensing that he recognized her at last, Judy flung herself upon Frank's prostrate form in a wild frenzy of delight. Managing to roll over, he clasped his arms around her and gazed into her suffering but ever-hopeful eyes. He felt the thick crust of oil and soot that matted her fur. He felt how dreadfully bony were her ribs and her haunches. He sensed too how desperate she'd been to find him.

They embraced for a while, miraculously reunited and with nothing needing to be said between them. It was one of the sweetest of moments. Frank felt as if his heart would break with sheer unadulterated joy. As for Judy, her long wait had been rewarded. And in this one moment Frank seemed to have found the will to live again. He clambered to his feet, and summoning up his newly found reserves of strength, he scooped up his dog in his arms.

"Come on, old girl," he told her with tears in his eyes, "and stop acting so daft."

Together, man and dog moved into their new quarters.

That first night Judy lay stretched out at Frank's feet. In spite of her recent ordeal, she remained ever watchful over the one she loved the most. At any movement from across the slumbering camp she'd open one eye, sniff the air, and flick her ears forward, checking for the barest hint of any danger. Judy was determined not to lose her best friend ever again.

Only when she was certain that nothing wicked was approaching did she close her eyes and drift into an aching, exhausted sleep.

The next few days were spent in rest and recuperation—not that the camp provided much of the means for either. It—and Singapore in general—offered none of the luxuries that these desperate men had so longed for. There would be no mail from home and little news of the fortunes of the wider war, their rations were worse than they had been at Gloegoer One, and the camp itself was a shabby, leaking, windswept ruin of a place when compared with their solidly built barracks on Sumatra.

The daily ration of rice and dried fish lacked the essential green vegetables or fruit needed to stave off beriberi, a debilitating disease caused by acute vitamin deficiencies. Already, every green and edible leaf had been stripped from the trees around camp. Occasionally, a dollop of dried seaweed accompanied the daily ration, but it looked and tasted like salty old rope. The Dutch and British doctors were forecasting dire consequences should the rations not be improved in both quality and quantity.

But nothing changed.

The Japanese issued new clothes to replace those lost in the shipwreck—yet these were mostly patched and repatched Japanese Army uniforms, ones that looked as if they had been removed from the bodies of the dead. A few battered British Army boots were handed out, but there were nowhere near enough to go around. For the first time since they had been taken prisoner, a blanket was issued to each man. They were sorely needed, for the huts leaked like sieves. Time was spent trying to sleep and recover or manufacturing crude spoons and plates from old cans and makeshift toothbrushes from tree branches.

On the first Sunday after their arrival Peter Hartley—Gloegoer One's make-do padre—cobbled together a makeshift service. He had no Bible, having lost everything when the *Van Waerwijck* sank. He managed to beg and borrow some scraps of paper and a pencil, and he scribbled down as much as he could remember of four hymns, filling in forgotten lines with the help of other prisoners. The service was held in one of the skeletal huts. The singing would have raised the roof had it not been so rotten, as those who had survived the worst mourned friends gone but not forgotten and offered thanks for their own deliverance.

But in truth, that deliverance was a mirage. Their stay here would last only four weeks—the time that the Japanese reckoned the POWs needed to recover from their ordeal. This was but a transit camp, and in the last week of July 1944 the announcement was made that the Gloegoer One POWs were moving on. In Gloegoer—and now here in River Valley Road Camp—these men had thought themselves in a place very close to the underworld. But where man and dog were headed next would take them into the very jaws of hell itself.

They were returning to Sumatra to work as slave labor on the hell railroad.

CHAPTER EIGHTEEN

It was in the late 1800s that the Dutch had first considered driving a railroad through Sumatra's seemingly impenetrable central highlands. The terrain was impossible. It consisted of rugged peaks wreathed in mist and cloud, their perilous slopes cloaked in a carpet of dense jungle, one crisscrossed with fast-flowing rivers and deep gorges and undercut by a labyrinthine network of caves and tunnels. But the prize was also potentially stupendous: *black gold.* The Sumatran mountains harbored some of the richest coal reserves on earth.

The route that the Dutch railway engineers had first explored was only a little different from that taken by Judy and her fellows in the spring of 1942 as they traveled up the Indragiri River, trying to escape from the encircling Japanese. Much of it followed a knife-cut gorge where the Kuantan River—a tributary of the Indragiri—carved its way between jagged-toothed ridges. The sides of the gorge were nearly vertical slabs of rock, and where massive boulders had tumbled into the river its flow was rendered into a series of tortured rapids white with foam.

At places the river appeared almost to disappear entirely into the earth, only to gush forth again like a giant geyser farther downstream. At one stage a dark, bat-infested cave led off from the river valley some four kilometers into the stony heart of the mountains. At first it seemingly offered the Dutch engineers the promise of a route to push the railway through the worst of the terrain, only for all further progress to be blocked by a massive underground lake.

W. Ijzerman, the Dutch engineer leading the perilous expedition, never had a chance to see the fruits of his labors realized. He was standing in shallow water in the Kuantan with his measuring instrument in hand, when all of a sudden the sand beneath his feet gave way and he was sucked into a swirling subterranean abyss. His body was never found.

Subsequent surveys confirmed that the route Ijzerman had pioneered—from the riverside town of Pakan Baroe southwest to Moera via the Kuantan gorge—did offer the possibility of driving a railway through this daunting terrain. But still the Dutch government balked at the prospect: it would prove staggeringly expensive, there was no guarantee of success, and the railway would have to penetrate an area largely uninhabited by man but rife with wild animals and diseases like malaria and typhoid. Such an undertaking would very likely prove costly in human lives, and so the project was abandoned before it ever really got up a head of steam.

For the Japanese in 1944, however, there were to be no such limitations, blessed as they were with thousands of Allied POWs making up a free—and wholly dispensable—labor force. As the fortunes of the war began to turn inexorably against Imperial Japan, she was in ever more desperate need of natural resources. In particular, the Japanese motherland was bereft of reserves of raw energy, and many of the older ships feeding her war machine were coal-fired.

The untapped coalfields of the central Sumatran highlands were capable of producing 500,000 tons of the finest black gold a year. So it was that the Japanese, in extremis, resurrected the long-abandoned colonial Dutch railway project. Their aim was to open up a rail and river route into the Sumatran highlands so the rich coal reserves could be dug out of the ground and shipped east to fuel their ships, first in Singapore and then to all corners of the Japanese conquests.

By far the largest contingent of forced—slave—labor earmarked for the railroad were locals, the so-called romushas. *Romusha* is the Japanese word for "laborer," and tens of thousands were forced to work on the railway at the end of the barrel of a gun. But on

Friday May 19, 1944, the first contingent of Allied POWs arrived in Pakan Baroe to join the romushas driving the iron rails into the jungle. Frank Williams, Les Searle, Jock Devani, Judy of Sussex, and their fellows from the SS *Van Waerwijck* shipwreck were only a few weeks behind them.

The SS *Van Waerwijck* survivors reentered Sumatra on July 27, 1944, following a route that all but mirrored many of the prisoners' first forays into this harsh but beautiful land. The main difference was this: now their journey's end would be the remote settlement of Pakan Baroe, surrounded on all sides by a seemingly endless expanse of swampy, malaria-infested jungle—as opposed to potential escape via an Allied ship from the port city of Padang on the coast.

Upon arrival at Pakan Baroe, the *Van Waerwijck* survivors were met by the Japanese camp commandant, Lieutenant Miura, who informed them of their fate. To that point they'd been led to believe they were being sent to work on a fruit plantation. Lieutenant Miura rapidly dispelled all such misapprehensions. The prisoners were to have the "honor" of building a railway line for the emperor of Japan. When finished, they would all receive a medal from the emperor for their efforts.

From the muttered comments of those gathered to hear the lieutenant speak, it was clear where they felt the emperor could stick his medal. Luckily, neither Lieutenant Miura nor his fellow officers understood enough English to catch the under-the-breath remarks. The Japanese—and Koreans—in charge of the railway construction were experienced in such work, most coming directly from the infamous Thai–Burma railroad. They'd grown accustomed to seeing thousands of Allied POWs worked to their graves.

Peter Hartley had made it to Pakan Baroe, and before leaving River Valley Road Camp the Japanese guards had procured for him an English Bible. It was darkly fortuitous, for now more than ever before the make-do padre would need it, as he was called upon to officiate over the burial of the dead in droves.

The *Van Waerwijck* survivors were placed temporarily in Camp 2, about five kilometers along the route of the proposed railroad. Camp 2 was supposedly the hospital camp, but it would soon become known as the Death Camp. There they fell under the leadership of Wing Commander Patrick Slaney Davis, himself only recently arrived in Sumatra from the prison camps of neighboring Java.

The Japanese had appointed Wing Commander Davis as the Allied commander responsible for all POWs laboring on the railway. Tall, emaciated, and with dark rings around his sunken eyes, he would forge for himself a somewhat conflicted reputation. While some of the POWs saw him as distant and aloof, he would earn unsurpassed renown for his fearlessness in the face of Japanese brutality and for his courageous and wily negotiations to manipulate and compel the enemy on behalf of his human charges.

But the task facing this twenty-eight-year-old RAF officer was a nearly impossible one. Wing Commander Davis would have thousands of Allied POWs under his purview, spread across a 220-kilometer stretch of railway traversing horrendous terrain that was served by as many as seventeen separate camps along its length. Out in the far jungle, where the word of the sadistic and brutal guards would be law, there was precious little the wing commander could do to protect his POWs.

After resting up in Camp 2 for just long enough to prove they were—in the eyes of the camp guards—fit, the shipwreck survivors were sent down the line into the jungle. Their destination was Camp 4, at Tera Takboeloeh, some twenty-five kilometers along the route of the still barely nascent railway.

The Japanese had fitted an old diesel truck with steel railway wheels for shuttling prisoners to and from the camps. As the truck chugged its way along a perilously thin knife cut slashed through the jungle, towing two railcars in its wake, the atmosphere among the prisoners was at its darkest. Like many of his fellows, Les Searle sensed that their fortunes had reached their very nadir.

All had heard stories of the terrible privations and degradations of the Thai–Burma railroad. There was every reason to fear that this would be as bad and possibly worse. Les Searle was sure that ahead of them, to paraphrase Churchill, lay only blood, sweat, and tears, but here they would be shed not to defend Britain from Nazi domination but to further the war effort of the hated Japanese. To be used as slave labor of the most expendable kind and all to fuel the enemy war machine—what fate could be less enticing?

As the converted truck motored down the line, Judy and her fellows felt utterly forgotten—lost men in a lost world. Most had accepted that their chances of survival were at best slim. Perhaps the most awful thing of all was that to the outside world they were already dead. They'd received not a postcard or letter from Britain, and the few official cards that the Japanese had handed out for them to write home had been burned on the camp fire. As they were sucked into this wilderness without end, a place utterly lost in time, the sense of being dead to the world was all-consuming.

Yet in the midst of this truckload of the damned sat an emblematic figure—the erect and apparently undaunted figure of Judy. Dogs have long been bred to embody particular traits, one of the most important of which is to be man's best friend. Their faithful companionship is a quality that we value in them possibly above all others. Over the millennia they have become extraordinarily well attuned to human emotions. In that cursed rail truck rumbling through the wet, rotting heat and the suffocating riot of vegetation, Judy's companions could sense that she knew how they were feeling.

Her gaze fell upon them, and it was full of a gentle warmth and empathy. One look from her long-suffering but caring eyes spoke volumes. It spoke of compassion and understanding. More than that, there was something in her panting, open-mouthed smile that was utterly maternal and reassuring. It was if she was saying, *I know how you're feeling, but trust me—we're going to be fine.* Judy's very presence among them, plus her indomitable spirit, gave these men the strength to face whatever lay ahead with shoulders just a little more squared.

Of course, Judy would be sharing the same fate as they, and indeed her chances of survival were arguably less than those of her fellow human prisoners. In the eyes of the railway guards she was a much-loathed but entirely edible dog. And as unspeakable brutality was unleashed upon her fellow companions she would feel compelled more than ever to protect them, which in turn would incur the guards' savagery and ire as never before.

That first night in Camp 4 provided a searing indication of things to come. Les Searle, Frank Williams, Jock Devani, Peter Hartley: each was allotted a slice of hard wooden shelf eighteen inches wide as his new home. POW 81A-Medan got nothing, but she was happy enough to curl up at Frank's feet, content in the knowledge that she was still—miraculously—with the one she loved the most, plus their fellows. By the crude light of a homemade lantern—a scrap of rag floating in a can of coconut oil—the appalling state of the hut in which they were billeted was clear to see.

Wall and roof were made of nothing more substantial than palm leaves bound to rough bamboo poles. Under the sleeping platforms tropical weeds reached out their hungry fingers, and the interior of the hut was thick with the voracious insect life that infested the jungle. A swarm of biting, bloodsucking flying things circled around the light, unidentified critters peeling off to left and right to attack one or another of the hut's human occupants. And from the jungle on every side the rhythmic *preep-preep-preep* of the insect chorus rang out deafeningly. Who could ever manage to sleep through all of this?

The air in the hut was thick with the stench of damp, waterlogged wood and rotting vegetation, to which was soon added the stink of unwashed sweat and sleepless fear. Bullfrogs took up a chorus of damp, throaty croaks, calling to one another across the darkened jungle. Howls and shrieks of unknown beasts sent eerie echoes rebounding back and forth through the trees like crazed laughter. At times they sounded spitting-distance close. It was mind-bending.

A warm bath, the feel of a clean towel, the caress of a loved one, the comfort of a home-cooked meal—all the norms of life seemed so impossibly distant.

On that first night the men felt as if they had been asleep only for a matter of seconds when the harsh call of a bugle tore through the fetid hut. It was pitch-dark still, but no doubt this was their wake-up call. Life began at seven o'clock on the railway, but that was seven o'clock *Tokyo time*. Here in Sumatra it was four-thirty in the morning, the depths of the night. No matter: in the minds of their Japanese taskmasters everything from Imperial Japan was superior, and that included even time itself.

Responding to the blare of the bugle, figures stumbled about in the dark trying to find the hut doorway and get out on parade. There was a brutish simplicity to life here that reflected how low these men had fallen: there was no need to change into day clothes, for there were none; no need to pull on shoes, for most had none; no need to scrape a blade across angular features, for their thick, matted beards would have defeated all but the sharpest cutthroat razors and few had any shaving kit, less still the facilities with which to wash or to shave.

Under the ghostly light of the moon the prisoners lined up for parade, plus the obligatory head count. Before them in the shadowy half-light lay the smoking silhouettes of oil drums with fires burning beneath them, signifying that breakfast was served. The first light of dawn was filtering into camp by the time each man received his one ladleful of gray-brown slop in a battered can or bowl. This was the entirety of breakfast—so-called ongle-ongle, a sludge of tapioca flour boiled in water that set like tadpole jelly as it cooled.

Tapioca is made from the pounded root of the cassava plant, a kind of tropical potato. Devoid of sugar or salt, ongle-ongle was entirely tasteless and completely lacking in vitamins or sustenance other than a small dose of carbohydrates. Yet this was the ration upon which these men were supposed to embark upon a full day's— invariably more than a full day's—hard labor on the railway.

The work gangs were divided by task. One group of men was sent deep into the jungle in front of the railhead to build successive camps for the main body of laborers to follow. A second, larger body of men was tasked to raise the embankment for the railway itself—digging out sand or mud by hand and carrying it in woven baskets to the rail route. This was some of the toughest work of all, and it was mostly given to the romushas—the local slave laborers, most of whom hailed from the neighboring island of Java—the living dead of the railroad.

Further gangs cut wood from the forest for the railway construction, or loaded sleepers and iron rails onto the rail truck for movement forward, or planted those sleepers on the raised embankment, or laid the rails on top of them, with a final gang bringing up the rear to hammer the rails in and fix them to the sleepers.

At Camp 4 the SS *Van Waerwijck* survivors were allotted their tasks as the Japanese corporal in charge saw fit. Les Searle was one of the lucky ones: he joined a party of thirty-odd men being sent forward of the railhead to build a new jungle camp. Frank Williams—and Judy with him—got the grim task of unloading the iron rails from the rail truck, carrying them up the line, and laying them on the sleepers.

From the very first the casual brutality and the apparent cheapness of life here were shocking. For Les Searle's party work was announced with the screamed command of *"Kura! Kura! Kura!"* Few knew exactly how that word translated into English, but all understood its meaning: "Oi!" Here on the hell railway it meant "get to the storehouse now and grab your tools, or else!"

For the new camp the Japanese engineers had chosen a site near a stream so that it would be close to water. The first task was to clear the area of vegetation, after which piles of bamboo had to be cut and split battering-ram fashion by lashing an ax head to a tree and running the bamboo into it. This bamboo was as thick as a man's forearm, and it grew to sixty or more feet in height.

Lashed together with jungle vines, the bamboo lengths formed the frame upon which all huts were constructed, after which they were thatched with vegetation cut from the jungle. All of this required orders to be both issued by the guards and understood by the prisoners, and in a language that one side barely understood.

Invariably, the prisoner who failed to catch on faced an outpouring of savagery.

Les Searle was sickened to witness one such prisoner get beaten to death with a shovel simply because he didn't understand Japanese. It was such a senseless way to die. Certainly, there had been beatings before now and terrible abuses—like the punishment cell back at Gloegoer One. But the casual and sadistic violence here would come to be a daily occurrence, one seemingly designed to snuff out the prisoners' lives as quickly as possible. It constituted an inhuman and murderous cruelty that many would never get inured to.

Being a sergeant, Peter Hartley the makeshift padre was appointed the honcho—head—of one of the labor gangs. The honcho had less work to do, but he was directly responsible to the guards for ensuring that those under him did whatever was required and exactly as instructed. As such, the role was to be avoided at all costs, for the wrath of the guards more often fell upon the honcho's shoulders when anything was misunderstood or went wrong.

One morning Hartley saw a Japanese guard set about one of his men for no apparent reason. The guard swung a heavy shovel edge, aimed at the man's head. It was a blow designed to maim terribly, if not to kill. The guard missed by a hair's breadth, but he recovered his balance and went for a second swing. Acting on instinct, Hartley reached out and grabbed the guard's arm, preventing the shovel from hitting home. After that he had no memory of how he got back to the camp—only that he woke later heavily bandaged and scarred for life himself from a shovel's blade.

But conditions were the very worst for those tasked to labor at the railhead itself. At least Les Searle and his gang were able to work mostly in the shade of the deep jungle, but out on the open railway prisoners were exposed to the merciless sun. Just south of Camp 4 the projected route would cross the equator. Once the early morning mist had burned off the jungle, the temperature there was unbearable, especially for seminaked men forced to work without a break for every hour of available daylight.

Frank Williams made up one in an eight-man rail-portage gang. First, the men had to line up in descending order of body height to keep the crushing weight of the iron rail evenly distributed across their bony shoulders. On command, the rail was hoisted into the air. Moving with 300 kilograms of iron slung between two lines of starving, emaciated, seminaked men, most of whom possessed no shoes, would be a perilous activity at the best of times. Doing so along a slimy, steaming uneven rail embankment in the burning heat of the day was sheer murder.

The two lines of men had to march in sync in an effort to prevent the load from becoming unbalanced, falling, and crushing someone's feet. But newcomers to the rail gangs—like Frank and his fellows—had yet to learn the tricks of the trade. Under the relentless sun the iron rails heated up to searing temperatures, and unless a pad of protective cloth was placed on the shoulder, the bare metal would burn and scorch itself into bare skin. And always the work had to be done at the double, any slacking being punished by kicks or blows from rifle butts.

A guard waited at the delivery end, where the rails were to be set into place on the sleepers in line with the ones behind. On a shouted word of command the dead weight would be lifted off shoulders and held in position before being carefully lowered. The sleepers weren't anchored to the ground yet, and if they hadn't been laid true, they could flip up with the weight of the rail, injuring the nearest prisoners.

Each time a rail was successfully positioned, a stick was handed out to that gang's honcho. When the team had accumulated a dozen such sticks, they were permitted to go for a cup of tea—swamp water boiled in an old oil drum at the side of the railhead and with a bare sprinkling of black tea leaves. No dawdling during the tea breaks was allowed, for a guard was always on hand to kick the team back to work.

At the approach of midday the sun hung directly overhead, huge and blindingly bright. It had become the rail layers' single greatest enemy. The earthen embankment shimmered in the heat haze. It threw back the glare, dazzling unshielded eyes. The air itself seemed to be on fire, each breath dragged into heaving lungs in a painful inrush of burning. The merciless heat of the sun sucked moisture from unprotected skin and burned into bare heads and shoulders.

The midday meal offered a few precious minutes of relief. But all it consisted of was a single cup of boiled rice, leveled with a stick by the server, plus a watery soup made of cassava leaves. No sooner had the lunchtime ration been wolfed down than the work began again, and minds began to wander to the evening, when ravenous bodies might again be able to rest and eat. As they lifted the heavy rails Frank and his fellows found themselves calling out time to the men opposite.

"Left, right, left, right, left, right . . ." they cried as they marched under the crushing load.

If their movements were not completely synchronized, one bony shoulder would be going up as the rail came whipping down, with agonizing consequences.

As for Judy, she would be harrying back and forth just ahead of them, snuffling for anything of interest in the jungle to either side of the tracks. Every now and again she'd turn to check on the rail-carrying party and to make sure the guards weren't causing any trouble. In spite of the bad company they were forced to keep, Judy loved being out in the jungle. There were all sorts of weird and wonderful creatures to sniff out, and in parts the thick vegetation was full of a dog's most favorite thing in the world—fresh bones.

Perhaps the hardest work of all already had been done by the time the POWs reached the railhead—that of clearing the route and heaping up the embankment. In places this had involved moving massive quantities of earth to harden the terrain where it was low-lying and boggy. In other places an army of human excavators had had to cut through steep ridges and hillsides using only hand tools. That army consisted of tens of thousands of romushas, and already they were dying at the staggering rate of *one hundred or more per day*.

Unlike the Allied POWs, there were few if any camps constructed for the romushas. The POWs might be painfully underfed, but the romushas received zero rations from the Japanese. *Nothing*. And each night after a day's torturous slave labor they were left to fend for themselves in the jungle. They were literally used as disposable beasts of burden—for excavation, clearance, and transport—and they were discarded once they were too sick or too weak to move.

The bush was littered with the remains of the dead and the dying. Their corpses attracted scavengers: rats, giant iguanas, and tigers. Their skeletons lay everywhere, stripped of what little flesh had remained on their bodies at their hour of dying. For Judy, bones discarded in the jungle were always a temptation, especially as she received zero food rations herself.

But the main issue for Judy was how she could shield her loved ones from suffering a similar fate to that of the romushas.

CHAPTER NINETEEN

The rations doled out at the end of the first day's hard labor reinforced the dominant theme—starvation. The only difference was that the single cup of rice was heaped up and the watery soup had some lumps of tapioca root and okra floating around in it. Just as the sustenance provided by the midday meal had been burned up in a few minutes of lugging iron rails, the evening's repast left every organ in the body crying out for more and every prisoner dreading the long hours of the night that would be racked with hunger pains.

For Judy there was no ration, of course. Yet still Frank and his fellows were unwilling to see her starve. The emotional link between Frank and Judy had become so palpable that many of his fellows feared that if she sickened and died, so would he. Likewise, if Frank was the first to perish, they were afraid that Judy would lose her will to live. It was as if man and dog shared a common life thread. So it was that a small portion of rice was set aside by those with the biggest hearts so that a dog might also live.

Those in Judy's party—sailors, airmen, and foot soldiers alike—had long learned the vital lesson that the outer reflected the inner in any prisoner of war. Those POWs who had let their appearance go had very likely given up on the unequal struggle and were heading for the hospital hut, from where few ever returned. It was vital to try to maintain a modicum of cleanliness and self-respect. But here in the ragged camps along the dark and serpentine railway, the chances of keeping body and mind together were slim indeed.

Camp 4's washing facilities consisted of a slow and muddy river that wound through the forest. The only time allowed for washing was in the evening, and in order to reach the river the prisoners had to flit through the darkened forest, cross a swampy area while balanced on a series of half-submerged tree trunks, and clamber down to the slippery water's edge. It was one hell of an undertaking for men who had been worked half to death already and had only bile and hunger in their bellies.

Such were the grim realities of their first days in the camps that fed the insatiable maw of the railway. With the Sumatran monsoons just around the corner, the SS *Van Waerwijck* survivors would learn soon enough that there was only one alternative to the muddy river as bathroom. It was to wait for a tropical downpour, when the heavens would open and the rain would sheet down, and dash out into the curtains of pounding water for a makeshift shower.

Perhaps inevitably, during those first nights in Camp 4 minds drifted to memories of the comparative plenty of before: of scavenging in the Dutchmen's garbage cans at Padang, of the magical arrival of the Red Cross parcels at Gloegoer One, of the miraculous delivery of the Bible at River Valley Road Camp. At Gloegoer, Frank Williams and his fellows had even felt able to set aside a little of their daily sugar ration—coarse brown native sugar but sugar nevertheless—to sabotage the Japanese war effort.

Whenever a guard's back had been turned, they'd managed to slip a few spoonfuls of sugar into the drums of aviation fuel they were tasked to unload, plus the barrels of gas. Popular folklore has it that sugar provides the perfect sweet revenge—that it can ruin a combustion engine. Sucked along the fuel lines, it gets heated into a sludge that glues up the engine's innards. But the real killer is supposedly when the motor cools and the sucrose slush cools with it, turning rock solid, thus fouling up the engine's arteries for good.

Although those risking it at Gloegoer would have faced a spell in the punishment cell if caught, they were unlikely to have been beaten to death with a shovel on the spot. And whereas the idea of sacrificing a little sucrose to get back at the enemy was entirely feasible at Gloegoer, here on the railway sugar itself was soon to become an impossible dream.

After a long night of sleep tortured by hunger, the next day at Camp 4 began as had the previous, the only variation being what kind of overseer would be assigned to the work parties, for the infamy of the guards went before them. In Camp 4, as in most, the Koreans were by far the most sadistic and vicious. Korea forms part of the Asian continent abutting the islands of Japan, and in 1910 Korea, which was at that time still one country, had been annexed by Imperial Japan.

Most Koreans grew to despise the Japanese occupiers, and those who were recruited into the Japanese military were invariably the dregs of society: they had little to lose by throwing their lot in with the conquerors. Once they were given a uniform, a gun, and the power of life and death over their charges, there was little mercy to be expected from them. By contrast, some of the Japanese showed a grudging respect for the Allied POWs, who were at least fellow warriors and thus men of honor.

In Camp 2—the hospital camp or death camp—Korean guards stubbed out their cigarettes on the faces of the sick and dying. Pencils and other sharp objects were rammed into patients' ears to perforate their eardrums. Every camp had its roster of monsters, whose nicknames betrayed the kind of savagery they excelled in: the Wrestler (a giant of a Korean who challenged the skeletal POWs to wrestling bouts), the Pig (a thickset monster and a brainless savage of a bully), the Basher (a name requiring no further explanation).

But perhaps the worst for those at Camp 4 was a dark-bearded Korean known as the Black Corporal, or more commonly as the Black Bastard. At the railhead the work teams often ran out of sleepers, without which all work would grind to a halt. Some of the *Van Waerwijck* survivors were sent into the jungle with orders to fell trees and craft makeshift sleepers. Among their number was Engine Room Artificer (ERA) Leonard Williams, every inch a gunboat man and the most senior surviving person from the *Dragonfly*'s original crew. Unfortunately, their overseer was to be the dreaded Black Corporal.

ERA Williams was a long-standing fan of Judy of Sussex. He'd been with her on the gunboats, been marooned with her on Shipwreck Island, had drunk the water she'd miraculously unearthed there, and had shared her adventures ever since. He'd often refer to her as the prisoners' "marvelous lifesaver" and "a dog in a million," and he meant every word. But there was only one Judy, and she wasn't able to be with everybody who might need her at all times.

Leonard Williams and a Lance Corporal Smith were in the process of chopping down a particularly large forest giant. The locals normally left such trees untouched because of the menaces they harbored. Some had hairy undersides to their leaves, and as the tree shook under the assault of an ax, the hairs would rain down, causing horribly red and itchy rashes. Other had been colonized by fire ants, a particularly aggressive and painful adversary.

The tree being the ants' home, they protect it ferociously. Within seconds they swarm all over the arms, legs, and head of any ax man until his entire body feels as if it is on fire. The most hated of all the Korean guards had even fashioned his own torture using fire ants. His nickname was Porky, and he liked to tie a prisoner to a post, naked, with his feet barely touching the ground. He'd then collect some fire ants and place them in the man's mouth, nose, and genitals, after which he'd leave the victim to fry in the sun and writhe from the ants' venom.

In time, Porky would threaten to become Judy and her fellows' chief oppressor as they were moved farther down the railway. But for now the Black Corporal was the foremost worry. You had to be very careful when felling the giant trees that made up the deep jungle and even more so when doing so under his baleful gaze.

For a moment Lance Corporal Smith must have let his mind wander from the task at hand, for he'd started to natter away to the prisoner at his side. The simple effrontery of talking was enough to raise the Black Corporal's murderous ire. As Smith swung his ax, the Korean guard smashed his rifle butt down onto the prisoner's unsuspecting head. Smith was thrown off balance by the powerful blow, and instead of hitting the tree as he had intended, he drove the ax deep into his own foot.

To the Black Corporal, Smith was just another of an endless series of victims to be thrown aside when their usefulness expired. A badly wounded British POW was useless for the task at hand, that of building the emperor's railroad. The Black Corporal ordered the injured man—who was bleeding profusely—to be dumped by the railhead. The rail truck that brought the men to work would carry him back to camp. Williams and his team did just that, and while in transit they managed to improvise a tourniquet for Smith's leg to stop him from bleeding to death.

It was seven o'clock that evening when they were finally done with their work, and the poor victim was still lying by the rail tracks. They managed to get him back to camp, but by that time Corporal Smith was at death's door. His life could be saved only by amputating the injured leg, a process that the British camp doctor had to perform with practically no surgical instruments, medicines, or even painkillers—and all because Smith had had the temerity to talk while working on the Black Corporal's labor gang.

This time Judy hadn't been there to shield a fellow prisoner from the savagery of one of the guards, but the time was fast approaching when she would—and then battle would be joined.

As remarkable as it may seem, hardly any of the *Van Waerwijck* survivors had yet lost the will to fight or their spirit of resistance. Their earlier shock and anguish at being brought to the hell of the Sumatra railway was starting to wear off. In its place there bubbled up the typical bulldog spirit and grim humor of British soldiers everywhere and the burning desire to find a way to hit back at their oppressors in however small a way possible.

The men of the devil's own railway began to joke among themselves. They would form the Pakan Baroe Rail Workers' Union, or the PBRWU for short. All were welcome to the PBRWU regardless of nationality and species: four-legged comrades were as appreciated as two-legged ones. They would demand higher wages, shorter working hours, better conditions, and legal holidays. They would have a canteen and a social club with a bar, plus an annual conference with a few short speeches and the best beer and sandwiches money could buy.

Such humor served to raise morale, and with it the idea of sabotaging the railroad even as they built it began to crystallize in the minds of those most inclined to the spirit of resistance. Frank Williams, Leonard Williams, Jock Devani, Peter Hartley—all knew that by deliberately damaging the Japanese emperor's railroad they were putting their lives in great danger, but they faced death on a daily basis anyway, so what of it? And in her own inimitable fashion Judy of Sussex was going to play a vital part in such a perilous enterprise.

The method of sabotage that Judy's gang hit upon was ingenious yet simple. When not laying the iron rails, they very often formed up the gang that fixed them to the sleepers. Normally, this was done using long bolts that fastened the iron to the wood below. However, because the Japanese were in an impossible hurry they opted to use massive metal spikes instead. The spikes were hammered through lugs in the rail and driven deep into the wood, using heavy sledgehammers.

Spike driving under a burning sun proved backbreaking work, but it also offered a delicious opportunity for sabotage. The spikes were like large, blunt-ended chisels. If the chisel edge was driven into the wood in line with the grain, a weakness could be formed. Under the weight of a passing locomotive the wood might well split, breaking the sleeper in two. In the best-case scenario it might even cause a derailment.

Of course, this was something of a double-edged sword, for the workers rode the rail truck to and from the railhead, so they would very likely be such sabotage's first victims. But so be it. Risks aside, a little sabotage was better than no sabotage at all.

Alternatively, when working as a sleeper-laying gang, Frank Williams and his team could choose to place the wooden crossbeams on a soft or uneven patch of ground in the hope that those sleepers would be forced sideways by the weight of a speeding train, thus buckling the track.

Somehow, Judy always seemed to sense when such skullduggery was afoot. All her thoughts of hunting in the forest would be instantly forgotten. Instead, she'd take up the post of chief sentry, positioning herself between the saboteurs and the most likely direction of a guard's approach. From a distance she'd appear to be fast asleep, resting her belly on a sun-warmed sleeper and with her head cradled on outstretched forepaws.

Yet long before a guard might be visible she'd have inched open one watchful eye. Moments later she'd be up on her haunches, ears pricked forward and nose vacuuming up the scent as she detected the Wrestler, King Kong, or the Black Corporal's approach. Just as soon as she was certain one of them was coming she'd let out her signature growl—the one that she only ever used to warn of the approach of a hated guard. And never had Judy of Sussex been known to cry wolf. If she growled, you could be certain a Japanese or Korean was inbound. Time and again it proved a lifesaver.

Yet it was nature itself that would prove to be the greatest collaborator in helping the saboteurs derail the devil's railway. As September 1944 blew around, the monsoon rains began to sweep down from the dark mountains, massive cloud banks piling up into the heavens over raging tropical storms. The lightning flashed and the thunder roared, and with it the largest of the animals began to move, heading for the drier ground of the highlands.

The jungle was teeming with life. Judy had often sniffed out the spoor of what had to be a big cat around the railhead. At one time a group of prisoners had even been saved from a vicious beating by a huge pile of elephant droppings. They'd begged their guard's permission to go into the forest to answer the call of nature. In truth, they were desperate for a smoke. Just occasionally, a little tobacco found its way into the camps, and Peter Hartley had found his Bible in correspondingly high demand, for the wafer-thin pages made excellent rolling paper!

There was a serious side to this craving for a smoke: for a while at least it dulled the pangs of hunger. The smoking party must have dawdled too long, for the guard came looking for them. Catching the scent of tobacco smoke, he'd demanded to see the evidence that they had indeed needed to defecate. It was then that one of the prisoners had spotted a pile of fresh elephant droppings. He'd pointed it out: *There—wasn't that proof enough?* The guard stared at it incredulously. "Many-man *benjo*," the prisoner explained—"Many-man crap." The guard scratched his head in amazement before ordering the prisoners back to work.

As the rains came in ever more ferocious downpours, herds of elephants were on the march, seeking drier ground. They soon ran into this strange linear formation that unexpectedly barred their path. They instinctively shied away. But there was no way around it and no way under it, and so the bull elephant leading the herd clambered up and over with his charges following. In the process, sleepers weakened by sabotage spikes were pounded into matchwood and badly laid rails were left twisted and misaligned.

Other animals that had previously kept away were driven closer to the camps. One evening the Japanese guards yelled out a warning that a tiger had gotten into their livestock and taken some of the Japanese pigs (they kept livestock in an effort to supplement their own meager rations). In spite of the prisoners' exhaustion, there were howls of laughter from the huts and cries of "Which guards have the tigers got, then?"

Yet in spite of such rare moments of levity the monsoons brought added suffering. The rain that fell like a waterfall from a dark sky was surprisingly icy. A sustained belt of storms drove down the temperature, rendering the nights chilly and damp. For healthy, well-fed adults equipped with proper sleeping gear this would have posed little problem. For starving, emaciated prisoner-slaves who were lucky if they had one blanket to sleep under it could be a killer.

More than ever food became paramount. All conversations dealt with it, all dreams featured it, all schemes concerned how to get one's hands on it. Finding enough calories to drive out the cold and stave off death had become all-consuming. Anything even remotely edible would be caught and eaten, and the absolute master in all of this was an English pointer called Judy of Sussex.

Not for her the pointing out of prey anymore, or at least not normally. Every day they were at the railhead, and every day she would be off in the jungle hopping, dancing, and darting forward to snatch her prey. Often it was a snake. The Sumatran jungle abounded with them, and many were highly venomous. She'd dance a duel with the serpent until it was exhausted and disoriented, and then she'd dart forward to strike. She'd snatch it by the tail, shake the body violently like a whip until the neck snapped, then carry it proudly to lay at Frank's feet.

Judy proved such an accomplished hunter that even the guards learned to appreciate her talents. They did so because they might profit from it. Most prey she was happy to take on herself, but just occasionally she'd come across something that was too hot even for her to handle. There were wild pigs, deer, bears, and tigers in the jungle. Whenever she encountered something of that size, she'd start to bark ferociously. The guards soon learned what that signified. They'd come running with guns at the ready in the hope of bagging some fresh meat. Of course, they'd keep the best for themselves, leaving the offal, the hide, and the bones for the prisoners.

Each evening at Camp 4 dozens of hobo stoves—small cans rigged up to cook in—would be balanced over wood fires. The prisoners would cluster around whatever brew was cooking, fanning the flames like witches at a cauldron. Snake proved to taste a lot like chicken, and it made delicious soup. But the jungle harbored a plethora of other exotic prey—giant cane rats, giant lizards, monkeys even—and nothing escaped a ravenous dog's attentions or that of her half-starved human companions.

The prisoners themselves learned to scavenge during the midday work breaks. Fungi, roots, berries, fruit—anything that was remotely edible was harvested. From the Dutch, who had inhabited this wild country for generations, they learned about what was poisonous and what was best avoided. But it was from the romushas that they learned the most about what was edible and could be used in an effort to supplement their starvation diet and so up the chances of survival.

It was not long after the Black Corporal's murderous actions on the tree-felling gang that Leonard Williams found himself working at the railhead again, along with Judy and her fellows. He'd noticed that the dog they all cherished hadn't been herself of late, and he'd surmised that she must have been bitten by a snake. He and his fellow prisoners were ordered to work alongside a group of romushas, clearing vegetation.

Leonard Williams watched them closely, hoping that perhaps they knew of a native cure for a dog suffering from snakebite. In the process he noticed how the romushas had these odd, bright green tips to their fingers. Via sign language, he managed to ask them why. By way of explanation one of the romushas took the British sailor to a certain shrub and ran his forefinger and thumb down the stem. The leaves peeled away, and he caught them in the bottom half of his hand.

The romusha mimed cooking and eating the leaves. There was iron in them, he explained. Iron was one of the many vitamins lacking in the prisoners' diet. Leonard quickly spread the word. The leaves didn't taste very pleasant, but even so, from then on his fingers and those of his fellows would often be stained a bright green.

While plucking the odd leaf or mushroom was tolerated by the guards, barter with the locals was not. Shipwreck victims who had lost practically everything would at first sight seem to have little left to trade. But many still possessed a precious ring—perhaps an engagement ring, a much-cherished wedding ring, or even one handed down from parents—and gold has a value everywhere. The trouble was that any contact with the locals was strictly against the rules and would attract savage retribution if found out.

Again, in bartering along the railway Judy was to play a key role. She'd lope along beside the rail-laying gang, alert to anything of interest. Frank Williams had learned to read her body language quite perfectly, and one particular form of behavior signaled that an opportunity for barter was at hand. Judy would stop and sniff at a bush, then stick her head and shoulders right into it, her rear end still apart from her long white tail swishing gently to and fro. This indicated that there was a local hiding in there, awaiting the opportunity to trade.

Jock Devani proved to be the ace bargain hunter, but once again the incredible thing was how such trade was conducted under the very noses of the guards, with both sides sticking to the terms of the deal. One day a prisoner offered up a battered gold ring. It was worn and broken, but it was still a band of gold. Over repeated passes by the bush that Judy had directed him to, a whispered deal was struck.

In exchange for the ring, the prisoner received what to him was a king's ransom in tobacco and coffee, plus a clutch of eggs and bananas to boot. Tobacco and coffee were highly valued because they were the unofficial tender of the camps. They could be traded with others for whatever they might have on offer, ideally edible and nourishing food.

Barter and scavenging were vital to staving off starvation and death. Sabotage was vital to staving off the death of the spirit, after which the body would surely die. But all such activities were punishable by death in the eyes of the worst of the guards.

Skeletons laboring under a merciless sun—this had become the life of the *Van Waerwijck* shipwreck survivors. The weeks became months, and the inhuman conditions took an increasing toll. As the prisoners weakened, normal bodily functions began to fail.

Yet illness was no excuse for avoiding the never-ending toil on the hell railroad.

CHAPTER TWENTY

One sick prisoner, Tom "Geordie" Scott, found himself on the rail-laying gang under the watchful eye of Judy, plus Frank and their fellows. But they were cursed with the very worst of guards as their overseer—the Black Corporal. In his emaciated, weakened condition Tom Scott was desperate for a pee. He was forced to do it right where he was standing, on the rail embankment. Unfortunately, the Black Corporal caught him in the act and flew into a terrible rage.

"The prisoner has desecrated the emperor's railroad," the Black Corporal howled. "For that he deserves to die!"

The enraged guard took his rifle in the one hand, and brandishing a thick bamboo pole in the other, he charged toward the guilty figure, murder in his eyes. Tom Scott stood there petrified, believing that his last hour on earth had come. His knees were shaking, and he felt utterly unable to move. But the Black Corporal charged right past him and pounced instead on the gang's honcho, whose responsibility it was to stop his prisoners from urinating on the esteemed emperor's railroad.

The Black Corporal set about the honcho—a sergeant in the RAF—with wild yells of rage, repeated blows from his bamboo pole slamming into head and shoulders. He was screaming invective as he evoked the name of the Imperial Japanese Armed Forces, plus His Imperial Majesty Emperor Hirohito himself, both of whom had been irrevocably insulted by such an act of wanton desecration.

Once he was sweaty and breathless from his exertions, the Black Corporal demanded that the honcho in turn beat the offending prisoner. British POW was forced to face up to British POW as an enraged Korean guard continued to crack the honcho over the head while demanding that he in turn punch the living daylights out of his fellow prisoner. The honcho made a few halfhearted swipes at Tom Scott, but this only served to enrage the Black Corporal still further, and he redoubled his blows with the bamboo stave. In the Black Corporal's eyes the honcho was supposed to deliver his beating with the greatest possible enthusiasm, for he had the honor of punishing the offender.

If something wasn't done soon to save him, the honcho was in danger of buckling under the blows, and everyone knew what happened to prisoners who went down. If you couldn't stand and take it, a guard like the Black Corporal would very likely proceed to kick you in the head until you lost all consciousness.

Tom Scott stepped closer to the bloodied, swaying victim. "Hit me, Sarge!" he yelled. "For Christ's sake, hit me!"

At last the RAF sergeant began to respond as the Black Corporal intended, landing powerful blows on his fellow prisoner with clenched fists. Now it was Tom Scott who went staggering backward under the onslaught. It was clear that someone was going to end up very badly injured or even dead unless . . .

To one side of all of this a figure was watching. Judy was growing increasingly agitated. Her lips had curled into their signature snarl, and her eyes glowed red at the horrors she was being forced to witness and her fellow prisoners were being forced to endure. All of a sudden she whirled around and darted off into the bush. Moments later there was that unmistakable bark—*aroof-roof-roof-roof-roof*— the one she reserved for when she came up against a large animal and needed a guard with a gun to help her bring it down.

Somehow, the fierce yelping seemed to cut through the Black Corporal's blind rage. The blood-smeared bamboo pole froze in midair. The Black Corporal glanced off into the bush, his brain trying to process the new information that was reaching him and to make a choice between competing priorities: to uphold the emperor's honor by beating the prisoner to death or to shoot the animal for meat.

His sense of hunger clearly won over his sense of duty to the emperor, for he dashed off into the bush in the direction of the barking, rifle at the ready. The two victims of the beating needed no further urging. Covered in blood and badly bruised as they were, they stumbled off toward the railhead, aiming to get as far away from the Black Corporal's savagery as humanly possible.

Of course, there was no large animal in the bush. There never had been. Judy had witnessed the savage beating, realized a diversion was needed to save the victims, and decided to provide it. She'd taken a major risk in doing so. A guard like the Black Corporal might opt to shoot her once he realized that she'd put one over on him. But it was in her nature to come to the aid of the little guy, and here on the hell railway the underdogs were very much her fellow prisoners of war.

This time at least Judy managed to dart through the jungle unseen. She gave the Black Corporal the slip and was soon back with her work gang. But here on the trans-Sumatran railroad it felt as if she was very much living on borrowed time. She had cheated death in so many ways and for so long, and eventually everybody's luck runs out. It always does some day.

Judy had first defied death as a tiny puppy when she'd snuck under the Shanghai kennel wire; she'd done so next as an adolescent dog tumbling from the deck of the *Gnat* into the Yangtze. She'd done so again in Hankow harbor, at the wrong end of a Japanese sentry's rifle; when trapped in the *Grasshopper*'s flooded mess deck; when gnashed by a crocodile's hungry jaws on the Indragiri River; when smuggled out of Gloegoer One in a sack, under pain of death; when posted out of the porthole of a sinking SS *Van Waerwijck*; and upon arrival in Singapore harbor, when she was spotted by Captain Nissi's murderous eye.

By anyone's reckoning she was eight lives down by now, and it was anyone's guess as to how much longer she could keep cheating death along this railroad steeped in blood.

As if to remind the SS *Van Waerwijck* survivors of all that they had endured, another group of shipwreck victims was about to join them. If anything their story was even darker and more replete with tragedy. In mid-September 1944 the Japanese cargo ship the *Junyo Maru* had set sail from neighboring Java with around 2,300 Allied POWs crammed into its hold, plus some 4,200 romushas. All told there were some 6,500 slave laborers packed into that rusting relic of a hell ship, more than nine times the number that had boarded the *Van Waerwijck*.

On September 18, 1944, the *Junyo Maru* was torpedoed by the British submarine HMS *Tradewind* off the coast of Sumatra. The ship, hit by two torpedoes, sank stern first in a matter of minutes. Some 5,600 POWs and romushas perished, making this the single greatest maritime disaster in terms of confirmed loss of life to this day.

On September 22 just over 400 of the *Junyo Maru* survivors turned up at Camp 4 to join their fellow shipwreck victims as slave labor on the hell railroad. They stumbled into camp like a legion of the damned. Among their number was one Rouse Voisey, a young British soldier captured at Singapore. Rouse had already served as a POW-slave under the Japanese on the island of Haruku in the Moluccas—the so-called Spice Islands—hacking a runway out of the bare, dust-enshrouded, sandpaperlike coral terrain.

He had survived the *Junyo Maru* sinking by hanging on to a raft cobbled together from a glass-fronted cabinet that had floated free of the ship with some planks lashed to its sides. He'd looped his arms around a length of rope and tied himself to the raft as the only way to keep afloat. After forty-eight hours at sea, the rope had rubbed him raw under the armpits and he was hallucinating. He swore that he could see a vision of an earthly paradise calling him— bright lights ashore, with music and laughter and dancing. He was finally saved by a Japanese ship, on which he was brought to Pakan Baroe and the railway.

On seeing the terrible state of Rouse and the hundreds of other shipwreck victims at Camp 4, the established POWs volunteered to take the heavier workload out on the railhead. The *Junyo Maru* survivors were given lighter duties around camp—fetching water, cutting wood for the fires, and digging latrines. It gave Rouse plenty of time to get accustomed to his new surroundings, which in some ways resembled the jungle-clad island of Haruku that he'd come from. The one thing that amazed him about Camp 4, however, was that they had a dog.

Rouse, like Frank Williams, was an incurable devotee of animals, and even the recent hell that he'd suffered hadn't managed to kill his greatest love of all. But to see such a striking, comparatively healthy-looking, and so clearly *edible* dog still alive here in this hellish camp—well, it defied all comprehension. How on earth her protectors had kept her from someone's cooking pot Rouse didn't know. It was such a daily struggle for survival that *anything* on four legs was being eaten, and that made Judy a walking miracle.

Back on Haruku, to his eternal regret, Rouse himself had eaten a cat. The gnawing hunger had driven all normal considerations out of a man's mind. Here on the hell railway prisoners were being forced to eat anything that came to hand. In Camp 4 every living thing had its price, no matter how small and seemingly inedible. A mouse was worth one guilder (the local Dutch currency), a rat two and a half guilders, and in an extreme perversion of the natural order of things, even flies had their price.

In the topsy-turvy nightmare world of the prison camps, the Japanese had decreed that those too sick to work had to catch two hundred flies per day to receive a *half ration* of food. The Japanese reasoned that sick men needed less sustenance, for they were doing no work—hence the reduced calories. Flies spread many of the diseases that were rife in the camps, and so the sick were tasked with making themselves useful and catching their allotted quota—or no food.

A sick man who needed proper rest had to buy his peace by paying another to catch his allotment of flies. Some prisoners had even managed to cobble together ingenious fly traps so as to have excess bugs to sell. Others made a little money on the side by carving whatever a fellow prisoner might need—wooden-soled sandals being the most common item. Several of the *Junyo Maru* survivors had lost their dentures during the sinking. A certain prisoner became an expert at carving custom-made dentures out of lumps of hardwood cut from the forest.

Shortly after the *Junyo Maru* survivors joined the railway gangs, Les Searle was taken off the forward camp construction and rejoined his old colleagues. He was shocked by the scenes of horror that he found at the railhead. Dreadful skeletal figures heaved, toiled, sweated, and groaned until the day was done or they dropped where they worked. Those injured on the construction or rendered too sick to continue were sent to the dreaded Camp 2—the so-called Death Camp.

In the terrible conditions and with such extreme levels of malnutrition, the slightest injury or cut failed to heal. Practically every prisoner had developed ghastly tropical ulcers, some as big as saucers. They ate flesh right through to the bone. Malaria, dysentery, beriberi, and heat exhaustion were rife. But at Camp 2 there were few if any medical supplies, and in spite of Wing Commander Davis repeatedly pointing out to the Japanese how desperately they were needed, nothing was ever done.

In fact, the Japanese commanders appeared perfectly content for the injured and sick prisoners to die. This led many to suspect that the Sumatran railway was as much an extermination project as it was a construction one. By October 1944 POWs were dying at a rate of ten or more a day. On average, each kilometer of the cursed track claimed another twenty Allied lives and those of some four hundred romushas.

Yet incredibly, some four months into their time on the railroad the spirit of the Allied POWs had yet to be broken. As Les Searle observed, "We grimly joked, and we encouraged each other. Somehow we hung on to the slender thread of life." And as luck would have it a much-needed morale boost was about to fall into the laps of those slaving in that living hell.

As there had been at Gloegoer One, here on the hell railway there was a secret prisoners' radio. News was disseminated along the line as rumor in an effort to disguise its timeliness and accuracy. The radio was thought to be operated by one of the officers, who had a hollow leg in which he kept it hidden. It was an aluminum prosthetic, and supposedly each night after use the radio was dismantled and the parts carefully wrapped up and hidden inside his leg!

It was toward the end of October 1944 when the rumor mill began churning big time, courtesy of the secret radio. Camp 4 had in it one of the few American POWs on the Sumatran railway, a Captain George Duffy. Like Frank Williams, Duffy had served as a merchant seaman until his vessel, the *American Leader*, was sunk by a German warship. Taken as a POW by the Germans, Captain Duffy had in turn been passed to the Japanese, which was how he had managed to end up in Camp 4. For Duffy and the handful of other Americans their nationality was about to become both a blessing and a curse.

One night in the last week of October 1944 the Japanese guards held a drunken party. The sake—Japanese rice wine—was flowing, and wild celebrations and what sounded like victory songs echoed across the camp. In the morning the guards were boasting about a decisive Japanese naval victory. The Battle of Leyte Gulf, the largest naval battle of the Second World War, had just taken place in the waters off the Philippines. According to the guards, His Imperial Majesty's Navy had sunk a string of American warships, including one light aircraft carrier, two escort carriers, two destroyers, and one destroyer escort.

The prisoners' clandestine radio soon gave the lie to the guards' claims. In truth, Leyte Gulf had constituted a crushing defeat for the Japanese. Though the losses boasted about on the Allies' side were true, those suffered by the Japanese Navy were far worse. One fleet aircraft carrier, three light carriers, three battleships, ten cruisers, and eleven destroyers were sunk, with the loss of 12,500 lives. Twenty-eight Japanese ships had gone down, as opposed to six Allied vessels.

As tight as it doubtless was, the Japanese propaganda machine couldn't keep such losses secret from its troops, not even those living in a world lost in time. The Japanese and Korean guards couldn't fail to notice the changed atmosphere around the camps. The supposedly invincible Japanese war machine had suffered a major defeat at Leyte Gulf, and thanks to their clandestine radio the prisoner-slaves knew all about it.

It was around now that those at Camp 4 were moved to Camp 5, at Loeboeksakat, twenty-three kilometers farther along the railway. The move was to keep pace with the onward progress of the railhead. Frank Williams, Les Searle, Padre Peter Hartley, plus Judy joined the relocation, as did the American Captain George Duffy. In Camp 5 were gathered together around a thousand POWs, the majority being Dutch, British, and Australians, plus a handful of Americans—those who had achieved the seemingly impossible and crushed the Japanese forces at Leyte Gulf.

Over time George Duffy had taught himself to speak Dutch from the prisoners in the camps. As a result, he was often mistaken for a Dutchman. At Camp 5 he was appointed honcho for a group of mainly Australians, who were tasked with loading gravel into small open-topped wagons along a spur track leading into the jungle. When the wagons were full, the rail truck would pull them up to the railhead to be emptied.

Duffy had allocated a place beneath a certain tree for those who became too ill to work. By midmorning there were six skeletal figures lying in the shade, and he noticed a Japanese guard approaching them. He hurried over, explaining that the men were far too sick to work. This irritated the guard. He demanded to know if Duffy was an Australian. Duffy pretended that he didn't understand the question.

"*English-ka?*" the guard asked—"Are you English?"

Again Duffy shrugged his shoulders, acting as if he didn't understand.

"*Blanda-ka?*" the guard demanded, *Blanda* being the Malay word for "Dutch."

When Duffy tried to claim that he still didn't understand, the guard went to unsling his rifle, a sure sign that the American was about to be clouted. Seizing the moment, Duffy leaned forward and stabbed the guard in the chest with his finger before pointing at himself.

"America! America!" Duffy announced. *"American!"*

The guard's eyes practically popped out of his head. He clearly had no idea that the dreaded American enemy was anywhere near his railway. He waved Duffy back to his task, but word soon came down the line that the guard was working himself up into a towering fury. When the break came for midday meal, the guard struck. On some imagined provocation he grabbed his rifle by the muzzle and swung it like a baseball bat into Duffy's torso, hitting him with all the force he could muster, just below the ribs. The blow was powerful enough to fell the American. Knowing he was in danger of being kicked unconscious, Duffy scrambled to his feet. He was knocked down two further times before the guard finally decided he had had enough.

After eating their lunchtime ration, some of his fellow prisoners tried to persuade Duffy not to go back on the work gang, for he was still in considerable pain and the guard clearly had it in for the American. But Duffy refused to back down, and oddly it was the Japanese guard who failed to return to work, so boosting the confidence of the American that in defeat, the Japanese could be faced down.

A resurgent spirit of defiance swept through those Brits, Aussies, and especially the handful of Americans resident in Camp 5. As the monsoon rains strengthened and even as the floodwaters rose throughout the forest, the prisoner-slaves were buoyed by further news of U.S. victories emanating from the railway's secret radio.

Camp 3 was flooded out completely and had to be relocated. At Camp 5 work gangs were sent out to shore up the rail embankment near a swollen stream. All of a sudden a pair of forest buffalo appeared on the far bank of the watercourse. The nearest guard, a Korean, raised his rifle excitedly and fired. All his shots missed.

Standing next to him was an American POW. Unable to bear the thought of so much potential food going to waste, he wrested the weapon from the unsuspecting Korean guard, dropped to one knee, and fired two shots in quick succession, felling both animals.

The American thrust the rifle back at the startled guard, after which he proceeded to take charge of the meat-retrieval operation. He called for a rope, slung it around his skeletal frame, and waded into the fast-flowing water. Perhaps the Korean had heard of the Americans' military prowess and was starting to worry about whether he'd chosen the right side in this war, but for whatever reason he let the American continue with his mission until both carcasses had been loaded aboard a rail wagon. That evening, in an unprecedented show of evenhandedness, the buffalo meat was divided between guards and prisoners alike at Camp 5.

But such shows of solidarity were rare indeed, and they were destined to become rarer still as Imperial Japan's fortunes in the war worsened. Much as it might defy belief, as defeat stared them in the face the Japanese would drive their prisoner-slaves ever more remorselessly, forcing them to work ever longer hours on ever decreasing food rations—or die in the process.

Christmas Day 1944 was fast approaching, and for the SS *Van Waerwijck* survivors it would prove their darkest in nearly three years of captivity.

CHAPTER TWENTY-ONE

Six months had passed since the SS *Van Waerwijck* survivors had first laid eyes on Pakan Baroe, the starting point for a railway whose progress would be measured in the futile sacrifice of so many lives. Repairs to the bridge damaged in the monsoon had been completed, and a huge quantity of new sleepers and rails was being shipped down the line. It seemed as if the railway's taskmasters had redoubled their efforts to finish the line come what may.

Such was their urgency to drive the iron rails onward that Christmas was almost canceled. But sensing a revolt among the POWs, the Japanese commander declared a rare holiday for December 25, 1944. Each camp had two cookhouses, one for the guards and one for the POWs. The prisoners' kitchen was staffed up by those assigned to light duties—more often than not the recovering sick or the walking wounded. On Christmas Eve 1944 rumors abounded that the cooks at Camp 5 had something special in store for the morrow.

Not for the first time all thoughts turned to food.

For weeks now the cooks had hoarded supplies, and sure enough that Christmas morning breakfast proved to be an impossible feast: five ongol balls per man, plus—joy of joys—coffee. Ongol balls were nothing more than the standard tapioca flour, but fried into "doughnut holes" and flavored with cinnamon and precious sugar. Lunch was more impossible still: ikan daging, nasi goreng, and more coffee. Nasi goreng is stir-fried rice, and ikan daging is a dish made of tiny dried and salted fish.

But it was dinner that proved the real miracle: from somewhere the cooks had rustled up brown bean stew, sambal katjang—hot peppered beans, plus trassi balls—smelly but decidedly tasty golf-ball-sized nodules of fish paste, and . . . more coffee. But though the feast was as fantastic as it was unforeseen, the increasingly jumpy and resentful Japanese guards still found a way to pour cold water on the festive spirit.

Christmas itself wasn't canceled, but they decreed that *singing* was. There were to be no carols.

There would be no repeat for Judy of her yowling serenades at the Strong Toppers Club on the Hankow Bund or even of her performance at the Gloegoer One Christmas pantomime, when she had howled out a wild accompaniment to the merrymaking. As for Padre Peter Hartley, though he insisted on holding a Christmas service, by now he was so sick that he had been consigned to Camp 2, the hospital-cum-death camp, and it proved a sorry and joyless affair.

In Camp 5 the healthy joined the sick and immobile, cramming themselves into the hospital hut, where a service of sorts had been cobbled together. It was one in which carols would be played by musical instruments in an effort to get around the singing ban. Wretched skeletal forms packed together on the rough-hewn sleeping platforms, spluttering lanterns throwing eerie shadows across the flimsy leaf walls.

When the musicians struck up the tune for "Silent Night, Holy Night" the hollow-eyed walking dead could no longer hold themselves back. The hut was filled with a soft, gentle humming to accompany the notes that the prisoners knew so well . . . but that was all. Not a voice could be raised in full song.

In spite of the day's feasting it turned many a man's stomach and brought tears to many an eye. It beggared belief that in the upside-down crazed world of the hell railway the Japanese had even banned singing.

Four days later the entire population of Camp 5 was on the move again. This time they were heading for Camp 7 at Lipatkain, some fifty kilometers farther along the railroad. Lipatkain actually translates as a rather poetic name for such a hellish location. It means "fold in a sarong"—sarong being the traditional multicolored wrap-around skirt worn by the residents of the region.

It was the kind of garment most of the shipwreck survivors would have given their eyeteeth for right now. Very few had any clothing left apart from the single dirty gray loincloth that the Japanese issued to all prisoners.

Camp 7 proved similar to those which had gone before, only it was more remote and the huts were even less substantial. There was a new accompaniment of guards, each of whom came with a peculiarly apt nickname: King Kong, Slap Happy, Howling Monkey, and so on. Among their number was Porky, the guard who specialized in using fire ants to torture his victims. Porky was the very worst—a stocky, fat beast of a man with nearly invisible eyes, his buckteeth sticking out below a thick and fleshy upper lip. He radiated an evil cruelty from his pockmarked wedge of a head to his flapping ears.

But as luck would have it, Porky was about to get his comeuppance, and before he could visit too much of his malice on the new arrivals at Camp 7. He was sent forward to Camp 9, the railway storage depot, to collect a new consignment of rails. In the middle of the loading a heavy storm blew up. Fork lightning stabbed out of the heavens. Fearing that the iron rails might attract a strike, all moved into the fringes of the jungle, to shelter.

Suddenly, there was an unearthly scream followed by a volley of rifle fire. Porky had been relieving himself in the jungle, only to be set upon by a tiger. He was badly mauled before his fellow guards managed to drive it off. He was evacuated down the line to Pakan Baroe and the Japanese medical facilities based there, which in contrast to the POWs' hospital camp were lacking in very little. But Porky was too far gone by the time he got there, and he died from his injuries.

Upon hearing of his passing, there were few at Camp 7 who shed a tear. In fact, Porky's death would inspire some remarkable mimicry. There were one or two prisoners who managed to perfect an utterly convincing tiger's snarl. Upon a dark, moonless night they'd start their roaring, which would send the guards into paroxysms of worry. With the Japanese and Koreans refusing to leave their huts, the prisoners would sneak into the livestock pens and steal a chicken or a goat. All signs of the purloined animal would have utterly disappeared come morning. If any questions were asked, the livestock theft was blamed on the tiger that had supposedly visited during the night.

On January 10, 1945, the first direct signs of the turning fortunes of the war appeared in the skies above Sumatra. The sleek, silvery form of an American B-29 Superfortress—a massive, long-range bomber that was superadvanced for its time—was spotted over Pakan Baroe, returning from a bombing run over the nearby port of Padang. Finally, this island lost in time was back on the radar of the Americans, the long-hoped-for liberators.

Few of the guards were able to ignore the fact that the American enemy was able to operate such a sophisticated warplane over the territory of the railway, and seemingly with impunity. Consequently, they started carrying tin hats and gas masks wherever they went . . . and the prisoner work parties started to catch hell.

The men would be woken by the seven o'clock bugle call, often not to return to camp until past ten o'clock at night. They'd be out on the work gangs for fourteen hours, being driven relentlessly by their merciless taskmasters. Yet the more the Japanese and Korean guards upped the pressure, the more ingenious became the methods the prisoners adopted to sabotage the thing they hated most— the railway that was killing so many of their fellows.

With Judy standing fierce guard, Frank Williams, Les Searle, Jock Devani, and crew set about packing an earthen embankment that they were tasked to build with rotten wood, which they patched over with a thin layer of mud and sand. From a distance it looked firm enough, but when a fire-snorting Hanomag locomotive tried to pass over it, the embankment should crumble, sag, and disintegrate into a mini-landslide.

In recent weeks Judy's gang had also learned how to break off the heads of the iron spikes used to secure the rails to the sleepers. Hammering in just the head gave the impression that a spike was in place, whereas in truth there was nothing substantial holding the rail in place at all. This was a surefire way of causing havoc with the rail alignment, but being caught with a supply of deheaded spikes or just the heads themselves would be a one-way ticket to the grave.

More news of Allied victories percolated down the eighty-odd kilometers of the railroad to Camp 7. This time the secret radio, which was located at Pakan Baroe's Camp 1, was reporting British and Commonwealth forces in action, as Bill Slim's fabulous 14th Army drove the Japanese out of Burma. The guards were faced with news of defeat on several fronts, and at the hands of almost all of the nationalities that made up the prisoners in their charge.

Unsurprisingly, tensions were reaching a fever pitch.

There were signs that the Japanese were moving vital matériel out of the area: tanks and field artillery, plus trucks loaded with military equipment, were driven east on the first stage of the long journey to Singapore. It looked as if the Japanese might be preparing for a major defense of what had once been Britain's island fortress. It was a delicious prospect for the POWs, so many of whom had been driven out of that island stronghold as a lost and vanquished army, a defeat for which they had for too long hung their heads in shame.

By February 1945 some 120 kilometers of the railway had been completed, but there remained 100 kilometers or more to go, and this final stretch would have to cut through the most difficult terrain of all—the Barisan Mountains. The death rate began to accelerate terribly. During March, forty-one POWs died at Camp 7 alone. The next month proved even worse. In the first seven days of April, twenty-five of the Camp 7 prisoners passed away. At such a rate all the POWs in Camp 7 would be dead inside ten months, and the death rate just kept rising.

The Allies might have been winning the war, but the worry of all in the camps was whether victory would come soon enough for any of them. There weren't enough able-bodied men to keep pace with the need for grave diggers, pallbearers, or burial parties. Those on light duties gathering firewood to fuel the kitchens were redirected to carry bodies to the cemetery or to dig the graves themselves.

Yet somehow Judy and her core of fellow prisoners endured. Having clawed himself back from the dead—miraculously he had escaped Camp 2, the Death Camp, and returned to the railhead— Padre Peter Hartley found himself called upon to officiate at burials. During the nightmare weeks at Camp 2 the self-taught padre had come close to losing his faith even in God. Twice he'd been consigned to the Death House, the hut reserved for those who were destined for the other side.

The lack of medicines, painkillers, sterilizers, or any proper surgical instruments at the Death Camp was so acute that the doctors had taught themselves to use fly maggots to treat tropical ulcers. They'd pack a wound with them, bind it with a rag, and let the grubs eat out the dead and infected flesh until the ulcer was rendered clean. With no malaria drugs, they'd also taught themselves to make a form of quinine using the bark of the cinchona tree that grew abundantly in the surrounding jungle.

Ground up and formed into a paste, the foul-tasting and nauseating DIY medicine could be mixed with the morning ration of ongle-ongle to make it vaguely palatable. The nasty skin infection scabies was rife, and lice and fleas were everywhere. The DIY cure for scabies was to use raw sulfur dissolved in old motor oil. The oil was drained from the sumps of some disused Japanese Army trucks, and the dark, gluey ointment had to be smeared over the body from head to toe and left on for forty-eight hours.

Tropical ulcers, scabies, malaria, beriberi—Padre Peter Hartley had had just about every disease going. Yet still he had done the seemingly impossible and twice beat the Death House—and in large part thanks to Padre Patrick Rorke, a Roman Catholic priest who, oblivious to the risks of infection, had spent hours squatting on a homemade wooden stool, comforting the sick and dying regardless of whether they were believers. That Catholic padre had helped restore Peter Hartley's faith and given him the strength to perform his funeral duties as the graveyards along the railroad swelled to overflowing.

Whenever a man died, he was taken to the preparation area, where his body was washed and wrapped in a straw mat. If he possessed four good and able friends, they could request a formal burial service for that evening. If the dead man possessed too few able-bodied buddies, his body was laid outside the morgue. The wood-cutting party would pick it up after its lunch break—along with any other corpses, and invariably there were several—and carry it to the cemetery, whereupon the grave diggers would bury it without ceremony. Such was the casual nature of death on the bestial railway.

Losing life had become so commonplace that those who survived had become inured to the loss. But the Grim Reaper was also stalking the ranks of the enemy as the Allies closed the noose around the Axis powers. Mid-April brought a rash of rumors flying along the railway. Via the secret radio there were reports of landings by Allied forces on Kyushu and Honshu, two of the main islands of Japan, plus news of the death of the American president, Franklin Delano Roosevelt (FDR), from a a stroke.

Roosevelt had indeed died, but in fact there had been no Allied landings on those Japanese islands. Even so, such rumors, which couldn't fail to reach the ears of the railroad's overseers, only served to up the ante still further. Unbelievably, on April 23, 1945, the Japanese ordered that the POWs' daily rations be cut to 200 grams of tapioca flour and 270 grams of rice for workers and less for those who were too ill to labor.

Four days later the death toll in Camp 7 was seventy-nine individuals for the month, and April wasn't even done yet. The prisoners were struggling to bury the dead fast enough as the sick and the incapacitated were starved into their graves.

In desperation, one of the camp doctors had an inspired idea. He figured they could secure a free and protein-rich source of food. He'd watched the camp chickens growing fat foraging around the latrines, and he realized they were eating maggots. In due course he and his fellows started to haul maggots out of the latrine by the bucket load. They were washed, cooked, and fed to those who were at death's door. For many this revolting but protein-rich diet would prove an absolute lifesaver.

But in the tense and febrile atmosphere of the railway there was little that could be done to defend against the guards' growing predations. As they stared defeat in the face, their tolerance was at near zero while their aggression levels were soaring. At the same time—and perhaps sensing that the end was near at hand—Judy of Sussex was becoming ever more defensive of her flock.

Judy never had been able to hide her hatred of the guards, but now she seemed determined to do everything in her power to bring the worst of the savagery to an end—at least on her patch. Whereas once she had been content to dodge a kick leveled at her flank from a guard's jackboot, now she stood her ground. She'd crouch low, barely feet away from her adversary, muscles tensed and ready to spring, her jaws a row of yellowing fangs and a deep snarl issuing forth from her throat. With blatant daring she'd face down the murderous bully. But Judy was up against those for whom a POW's life meant little, and even less when the prisoner happened to be a dog. And with guards armed with rifles it was an unequal contest that, if continued, could only end badly for the dog that had for so long refused to die. Judy's fellows could sense that their railway hell had to end sometime soon now, and none could face losing their miracle dog at the eleventh hour.

Over the months that they'd been together Frank Williams had developed an unspoken, almost telepathic means of communication with Judy. He was always able to reach her. She seemed permanently on the prowl now, almost deliberately seeking confrontation with the guards, but at one word or a gentle touch from Frank her fierce red eyes would soften, and a potentially deadly altercation would be brought to an end.

Sensing the way the wind was blowing—that Judy was on a collision course with one or other of the guards—Frank developed a new trick in an effort to protect her. It was a variation on the jump-into-the-sack routine that he had employed when smuggling her out of Gloegoer One and onto the SS *Van Waer-wijck*. At the soft click of his fingers Judy would disappear into the thick jungle at the rail side. There she would remain, utterly silent and obscured from view, until the coast was clear, where-upon a gentle whistle from the one she loved the most would bring her back to his side.

But the day inevitably came when Judy went a step too far. Frank Williams, Judy, and her gang were out at the railhead, the prisoner-slaves as usual being driven to the brink of collapse by their guards. Perhaps there was nothing specific that had triggered it: in the dark spring of 1945 the railway's overseers needed little provocation to unleash their worst. For whatever reason one of the guards set upon a prisoner, screaming obscenities and slamming him around the head with the thick bamboo pole that he carried.

The prisoner's head whipped backward with the first blow. More followed. The horrific scene had become all too familiar, as a fig-ure who was barely skin and bone staggered under the onslaught and fought to remain upright. He flinched under an extrapowerful swipe and looked sure to lose his footing, when into his place sprang a four-legged champion. Snarling and barking with undisguised ferocity, her hackles raised and her eyes blazing, Judy stopped the guard in his tracks.

Hitherto all-powerful and utterly unprepared for any kind of resistance, the guard's brute confidence momentarily wavered. Then one hand lowered the bamboo pole as the fingers of the other curled around his long-barreled Arisaka rifle. Many a time Judy had witnessed the effects of these oddly shaped thunder sticks. She's seen them fell any number of beasts that were far larger and more powerful than she was. She'd come to appreciate both the thunder stick's range and its deadly effect.

Judy knew instinctively that it was time to make her getaway. In any case her work here was done: she'd turned the guard's aggression away from the prisoner onto her own gaunt and fleshless shoulders. In a flash she whipped herself around and fled, racing for the cover of the thick bush at the bottom of the embankment. But even as her thin white tail disappeared into the dense undergrowth, the guard leveled his rifle and took careful aim.

The long bolt-action rifle barked once, the muzzle spitting fire. A bullet tore after the fleeting figure of the dog. It had all happened at such speed that Frank Williams and his fellows had been powerless to intercede. They were horrified at the prospect that the bullet might find its mark. Thankfully, there was no canine cry or yelp of pain from the undergrowth, and it looked as if Judy had yet again escaped unscathed.

Either that, or the bullet had killed Judy stone dead, silencing her forever.

Chapter Twenty-two

It was a long time before Frank felt able to risk a faint, low whistle to call her back to his side. Several hours had passed, and their work party had moved a good way along the embankment. When finally Judy came to him, Frank noticed that she was limping. He was shocked to discover an angry and bloodied furrow running across her shoulder. The 6.5-mm bullet had missed Judy's head by a bare few inches, her heart by just a few more.

In the dark and malevolent world that was the hell railroad there was no reward fit for a dog as brave or as spirited as Judy apart from Frank Williams's boundless affection and love. Yet Judy went ahead anyway and found one for herself. A while later there was a bout of sustained and excited barking from within the forest. Frank went to investigate, fearing that Judy might have come up against some animal too large for her to handle or maybe even the same vicious guard.

Instead, he discovered his dog with an utterly goofy expression on her features as she tried to drag the world's biggest bone into a hole that she had been digging. She paused for a moment to give him that look of hers—*guess what I've found?*—before going back to her task. It was so large, it could only be an elephant bone, Frank reasoned.

It was certainly a reward big enough for a dog of Judy's enduring spirit if only she could manage to get her jaws around it and give it a good gnaw.

On April 29, 1945, the guards marked the birthday of the mikado, the emperor of Imperial Japan, with a drunken feast. The POWs of Camp 7—Judy of Sussex included—marked it with a grim milestone, the deaths of ten of their number on that day alone. To celebrate the auspicious occasion, the Japanese deemed it worthy to give a gift of a pig to the camp inmates, but just as quickly they decided to take it back again, leaving only the head and guts for several hundred prisoners to share between them.

Bitter resentment and hatred seethed back and forth between the guards and the POWs. Across the camps the means of sabotage became ever more desperate and full of bile. Prisoners who were able to get access to the kitchen spit infected mucus into the drums of porridge being prepared for the guards. Feces from the dysentery patients were even slipped into the guards' food.

One prisoner learned that the hairs from a certain type of bamboo bush were toxic and would cause internal injuries if ingested. He slipped some into the coffee being prepared for a newly arrived team of Korean guards. Those who drank the poisoned brew became critically ill. Within days they were seen stumbling around camp with wet rags tied around their horribly inflamed throats. A week after they had drunk the evil brew they were removed and replaced en masse, for nothing could be allowed to impede the construction of the railway.

But by early May 1945 progress on the railway had slowed to a painful crawl. During the first two months of construction twenty kilometers had been built. Now a few dozen yards were being completed a day. Weakened though they were, it wasn't the labor force that was failing: the prisoner-slaves were being driven even harder than ever. POWs and romushas alike were forced to work round-the-clock shifts, the railroad lit by smoky, spluttering rubber flashlights that drove away the darkness, allowing the torture to continue even during the night hours.

It was the rugged terrain that was the problem. Teams of romushas were sent ahead to cut a route through the most impossible ground of all: the cavernous gorge lying ahead of Camp 11 at

Medikoel, which was the 200-kilometer mark of the railroad. There the Kuantan River had cut deep through the heart of the Barisan Mountains. This was the very area that had claimed the life of W. Ijzerman, the Dutch engineer who had first surveyed this route over fifty years before.

In May and June 1945 it would claim countless more lives.

For the surviving POWs emotions seesawed between ecstasy one moment and utter misery the next. Stunning news of Allied victories would raise the collective hope that surely this had to end soon, only for there to be no change in the camps or at the railhead. The lethal, soul-destroying, and utterly futile work continued day after night after day, seemingly without end. It was all so entirely pointless—for what could be the point of continuing with the railroad when the Japanese were so clearly losing the war?

In the second week of May the seemingly indestructible Jock Devani was able to deliver the most incredible news yet. He returned to Judy's crew's hut after a hard day's labor, complete with a quantity of fresh fruit and vegetables hidden on his person. As he handed the unexpected goodies around to the old faithfuls—Les Searle, Frank Williams, and Judy among them—he revealed to man and dog that a special celebration was in order.

Somehow, Jock seemed always to be the first to hear of any news, and today he'd hit the jackpot. The war in Europe was over, he announced. Germany had surrendered, and all across Europe the Allies were victorious.

"And as a very special treat," he added, "I've brought you the fruit to celebrate!"

He had liberated the fruit and vegetables from a Japanese grave, he explained. One of the camp guards had died recently, and in keeping with Japanese tradition and beliefs his fellows had piled his burial place high with fresh bananas, mangoes, cassava, and the like.

"It would all have been gone by the morning any road," Jock remarked with a grin, "and who is there more deserving than us lot?"

At first the prisoners refused to believe Jock's news. But of course, it was true: May 8, 1945, was the day of victory in Europe—VE Day, although it had taken a while longer for the news to filter in through the POWs' clandestine radio and to make its way down the accursed railway line to Camp 7.

With Nazi Germany having capitulated, the rations deteriorated still further. There was less food handed out, and what there was seemed of an ever poorer quality. General Saito, the supreme Japanese commander in Southeast Asia, had issued orders to reduce the food rations of all Allied POWs. They were to be fed only enough to keep them functioning as prisoner-slaves. They were to be deliberately deprived of any levels of sustenance that might encourage them to launch a prisoner uprising.

Just days prior to VE Day, the prisoners in Camp 7 had been forced to sign a similar declaration to that which they had already agreed to at Gloegoer One—a second non-escape contract. It stated that under no circumstances would they attempt any kind of breakout. In short the Japanese position was characterized by paranoia and not a little schizophrenia: the prisoners needed to be worked like slaves to finish the railway but starved to death to keep them docile and incapable of rising up against their masters.

By mid-June the overall camp leader on the Sumatran railroad, Wing Commander Patrick Slaney Davis, was complaining on a daily basis to his opposite number, Japanese Lieutenant Doi, in the most strident terms possible. He confronted the man with statistics proving how the death rate among the POWs was spiraling out of control. Lieutenant Doi's response was that the Allied prisoners were deliberately trying to sabotage the railway and the Japanese war effort by dying.

Increasing numbers of terribly ill prisoners were arriving at Camp 2, but because of the Japanese quota system in which each camp had to deliver a set roster of fit workers, the newly arrived sick had to be replaced by a similar number of recovering patients, who were sent back down to the railhead. Of course, there were few if any remotely healthy individuals left at Camp 2, and so the barely living were forced to rejoin the work gangs.

Then, in mid-June, Wing Commander Davis was presented with an ultimatum by his opposite number, which was as unexpected as it was perplexing. Lieutenant Doi declared an irrevocable finish-by date for the railway. No matter what, it had to be completed by August 15, 1945. Accordingly, every prisoner who was capable of getting to his feet was required to get out and work—no exceptions. In spite of the wing commander's spirited protests a roll call was held, and any skeletal, ghostly figure even vaguely capable of standing was marched off to the railhead.

In every prisoner's mind was now being nurtured the spark of hope that the end really was in sight if only they could just hold on. But the flip side was the fear—rarely vocalized but felt by all in the darkest corner of their hearts—that in truth the Japanese would allow none to survive; that none would be allowed to emerge from this hellish reality and reveal to the outside world all that had happened here. The fear was not without justification.

Work parties were formed to carry out an alternative light duty task. Their orders were to dig air-raid shelters for the camps. The trouble was, they looked nothing like any such defenses any Allied soldier had ever seen before. Air-raid shelters have to be dug narrow and deep, with high earthen walls, and to be roofed over by massive beams and thick layers of earth to provide adequate protection from blasts. What the work gangs were being made to dig along the railway were long, shallow troughs with no roofs whatsoever.

It didn't take a genius to guess what in truth their intended use might be: they had all the right dimensions for mass graves. Most were situated near the parade grounds, where the men stood for their early morning and evening roll calls. It wasn't too hard to imagine prisoners being called out one morning, only to be machine-gunned where they stood and their corpses rolled into the open pits.

Unknown to the POWs, orders had in fact been circulated to that very effect. The Japanese high command had decreed that should the Allies set foot on Imperial Japanese soil and threaten the emperor, then all Allied POWs were to be executed. In other words, if a decisive ground assault was launched against Japanese territory by American and Allied troops, POWs across Japanese-held territory were to be slaughtered.

In these days that were rife with uncertainty, fear, and desperation, Judy proved a rock around which many a prisoner could moor his restive spirits. Frank and Judy never seemed to spend a moment apart. Wherever he went she followed, and vice versa. Frank was down to around half his weight by now—as were Les Searle, Jock Devani, Pastor Peter Hartley, and their other long-standing companions—but together Frank and Judy were somehow still able to remain strong.

Under the growing pressure there were those in Camp 7 who did crack. One was a young prisoner only ever known to all as Catcher. Les Searle witnessed what happened when Catcher snapped. He was accused by a Korean guard of forgetting to salute and bow properly before him. Screaming abuse, the guard proceeded to beat the young British soldier about the head.

When Catcher flipped, he did so in spectacular fashion: the shocked guard fell back under a hail of blows from Catcher's bony fists, which were going like a windmill. Other guards came running to their fellow's aid. Catcher was quickly overpowered and carted away. The following morning his fate was clear for all to see: he had been placed in a tiny bamboo cage, which was positioned in full view at the edge of the parade ground.

Catcher would be locked in there come rain or shine for days on end. He would be starved, beaten, and eaten alive by insects and vermin day and night. It was a fate that would drive many a lesser man to madness and beyond.

On July 27, 1945, a full year had passed since the *Van Waerwijck* survivors had arrived at the hell railway. Many had spent over a thousand days in captivity by now, and still their suffering wasn't at an end. As impossible as it might seem, the iron rails snaking through the Kuantan gorge had all but reached the far side, though few liked to contemplate how many human lives—both Allied POWs and romushas—that dark valley had swallowed.

Batches of prisoners had even been shipped to the far end of the railway, to Moera, so they could start the building from that end. The plan now was for the two ends of the line to meet somewhere in the middle. But practically everywhere were signs that the Allies were closing in. Seemingly a day didn't go by when a U.S. B-29 Superfortress wasn't spotted high over the camps. Many speculated that some at least were reconnaissance flights, helping plan a campaign to liberate all of Southeast Asia, including Sumatra.

But no one could know for sure.

CHAPTER TWENTY-THREE

Then came stunning news. In the second week of August 1945 a bizarre rumor flew up and down the railway. It would become an impossible to believe yet apparently genuine fact. An inconceivably powerful weapon had been dropped on the Japanese city of Hiroshima. Prisoners and guards alike spoke about it in hushed, disbelieving tones: this one American superweapon had apparently flattened an entire city.

It was of course the atomic bomb code-named Little Boy. Little Boy had been dropped by a U.S. Air Force B-29 Silverplate long-range bomber—one specially adapted to carry a nuclear weapon—on August 6, 1945. Three days after the bombing of Hiroshima a second atomic bomb, code-named Fat Man, was dropped over Nagasaki. Together, the two bombs would end up killing as many as a quarter of a million people, but the alternative to using them—an invasion of Japan that would without doubt lead to many millions of casualties—had been equally unthinkable.

After the dropping of the atomic bombs the Japanese guards seemed lost in a blind frenzy. Work gangs were sent out having had only four hours' rest. Some spent days away from camp slaving on the railhead. American merchant seaman Captain George Duffy was one of those sent to the far end of the line, to Camp 12. Rations were so nonexistent there that he and fellow POWs resorted to eating rubber tree nuts, which are full of deadly cyanide. They had to be laboriously prepared—sliced, soaked, washed, and dried—to render them edible. Prisoners who got the treatment wrong died a horrific death of cyanide poisoning.

With Judy's party at Camp 7, odd and unprecedented things seemed to be afoot. With no apparent explanation or ceremony Catcher, the young prisoner who'd turned on his abusive guard, was released from the bamboo cage. Barely able to stand, let alone walk, the mumbling, half-crazed figure was helped to the hospital hut. With food, proper medical treatment, and rest Catcher's body might recover; it was his mind that no one could be certain about.

Then, from out of the blue it was announced that all prisoners were to have their heads and eyebrows shaved to help rid the camp of lice. Rarely had the guards demonstrated the barest modicum of concern for the health of their human charges. Speculation was rife that the Japanese overseers were beginning to accept the inevitable: that the war was lost, that the camps eventually would be liberated, and that they in turn might be held accountable for the unspeakable horrors that had transpired here.

But for Frank, Judy, and their cohorts, the lice-eradication program was to have much darker consequences. The guards announced that Judy, the heroine of the trans-Sumatran railroad, was likewise lice-ridden, and she was to be handed over to them so she could be shot. Frank, Les, Jock, and her many faithful fellows suspected that this was no lice-eradication measure. The guards were more or less starving alongside the prisoners. In their extreme hunger they had their eyes fixed on the hell railroad survivor extraordinaire—its mascot dog—for the pot.

It was now that Frank and Judy's disappearing act truly came into its own. Overnight, she became a ghost dog. At a flick of Frank's fingers she'd dart into the bush and stay there for as long as her master deemed necessary—basically, until there wasn't a starving or a baleful-looking guard in sight, at which point Frank would whistle her out again. In this way man and dog managed to avoid the worst of the guards' famished predations until the day upon which the impossible came to pass: the completion of the railway.

The final few days had been a madhouse. Torrential rains falling for hours on end had turned the last few hundred meters into a treacherous mud bath. Prisoners were whipped until they dropped. Sleep was snatched here and there at the railhead, and meals eaten three in one go as the prisoner-slaves labored around the clock. But on August 14, 1945, the two work gangs—one building from the Pakan Baroe end, the other from Moera—finally met.

The next day, August 15, dawned bright and sunny over the Sumatran jungle. The men in most of the camps were given a rare day off apart from a handful that were required for a special duty at the juncture of the two ways. The atmosphere everywhere was utterly surreal. After the murderous pace of the past few days and the widespread cursing and beatings—not to mention the deaths—the guards seemed abnormally chatty, even friendly.

The vast majority of the prisoners wondered what on earth this might mean. A few were tasked to attend a ceremony at the very point of the joining of the rails.

The prisoners were ordered to set up wooden tables and chairs adjacent to the spot where the final rail lay waiting. Bottles of sake and biscuits were arranged on the table. The prisoners were told to make their way into the bush and remain silent and out of sight. The ceremony began at close to midday. The sun was high, and it was sweltering as a Japanese officer delivered a short speech. When he was done, the last rail was lifted into place, and the officer produced a golden spike—one modeled along the lines of the iron ones used to anchor the entire railroad.

The golden spike was loosely tapped into place, whereupon a Japanese general was handed the ceremonial hammer and invited to hit it home. That done, there was a reverential silence for several seconds, after which the assembled party took up the formal cry of banzai: "*Banzai Nippon! Banzai Nippon! Banzai Nippon!*"

Banzai translates as "ten thousand years," and it was both a traditional battle cry and a call of respect to the emperor.

The Japanese officers' words echoed across to the prisoners crouched in the bush, but they seemed to lack a certain conviction.

It was little wonder. At 0000 hours that very morning Imperial Japan had surrendered to the Allies. On the day of completion of the trans-Sumatran railway—one laid in suffering, degradation, and blood—the war was already over. As they nibbled on their biscuits and sipped their sake, the Japanese officers were aware of this, yet still they had proceeded with the railroad's formal opening ceremony.

Of course, none of the POWs crouched in the bush could know that the war was over, and the Japanese officers weren't about to tell them. All along the railway the guards were keeping very quiet. At their camp, Judy and her fellows knew that all was not as it had been and that change was afoot—but what exactly the nature of that change might be few could tell.

That evening the camp commanders up and down the line made a similar kind of announcement: the railway was finished, the prisoners could rest, and rations would be increased once the Japanese had the supplies to make it happen. And no one was permitted to leave the camps.

Days passed in this weird, otherworldly kind of limbo. There were signs everywhere that the war had to be over, and the rumor mill was working overtime. In several places the Japanese were seen lighting huge bonfires as they sought to burn all the camp documents. British prisoner and *Junyo Maru* survivor Rouse Voisey spotted them doing so in his camp. Were they destroying incriminating evidence? he wondered. It certainly looked that way.

The daily rice ration—the Japanese still had ample supplies of rice, it seemed—was increased to 2,600 grams a day, ten times the starvation ration of the last few weeks. It was too much food for most, whose stomachs were shrunken and shriveled. Padre Peter Hartley could barely believe it when a consignment of Japanese Red Cross parcels arrived, along with the massively increased food rations. There was little of use in the parcels, but surely it had to signify that the war was over and that the prisoners were finally free.

Fittingly, in Judy's camp it would be the miracle survivor dog who finally barked the good news, confirming that liberation had come for those who had survived over a year on the railway.

On the morning of September 4, 1945, the prisoners awoke to another day in limbo, only to hear a very strange sound indeed: it was a loud, insistent, and somehow clearly joyous round of barking. Judy had spent the last few days living as a ghost dog, only risking the occasional appearance whenever Frank whistled for her. But this morning, she was barking her head off unreservedly.

Judy had long learned to keep her counsel in the POW camps. Barking had only ever served to attract unwanted attention from those who might seek to do her harm. But this morning, as the sun rose above the surrounding jungle, she was truly letting rip. Frank hurried out to quiet her down, but he quickly realized that all was somehow different about the camp. No matter where he looked, there didn't seem to be a Japanese or a Korean guard in sight.

It was then that he understood just what it was that Judy was so joyously barking over. She approached Frank accompanied by two heavily armed figures. They were dressed in the smart uniform of British Royal Marines. Judy cavorted around them, knowing instinctively that the good guys were here at last.

Four parachutists commanded by a Major Gideon Jacobs had been dropped from a Liberator long-range bomber near the location of their former prison camp, Gloegoer One. From there they had made their way to Pakan Baroe and up the length of the railway. Incredibly, the Allies had had not the slightest idea that the trans-Sumatran railroad had been under construction until Major Jacobs had parachuted in to discover it.

As skeletal prisoners tumbled out of their huts to greet the newly arrived troops of liberation—some with wild cries of joy, others with cheers and laughter, but many with a quiet and uncomprehending lethargy—makeshift Dutch and British flags were raised above the camp over which only the Japanese rising sun had ever flown.

But even now news of the longed-for liberation proved too much for some. Even now some would prove too debilitated by their long ordeal to survive. Tragically, some who had fought so doggedly to make it through would perish during these final days as the camps of the trans-Sumatran railroad were dismantled. Yet for Frank Williams, Les Searle, Jock Devani, Peter Hartley, Rouse Voisey, and George Duffy—as for so many other Allied prisoners—this day marked the deliverance for which they had so long dreamed. And for Judy of Sussex, the much-loved dog of the hell railroad, this was the start of her long journey home.

Perhaps it was inevitable, but along the way there would be one last hurdle, one final attempt to separate man from dog. When it finally came time for Judy and her fellows to set sail for England, they would be ordered to depart via Singapore on the troopship *Antenor*. For the first time in Judy's life—she was approaching ten years old by now—she was about to board a ship that wasn't under threat of river piracy or bombing or torpedoing by the enemy. But that was only if she was going to make it aboard.

When Frank received his embarkation papers, a footnote read: "The following regulations will be strictly enforced: no dogs, birds or pets of any kind to be taken aboard."

Frank gave Judy a fond look where she was curled up at his feet. "No dogs allowed, old girl," he murmured softly. "Only ex-POWs, and that, of course, means you."

There was no way that Frank was willing to even contemplate abiding by the order, and neither were Judy's fellow ex-prisoners. This time, no sack was required to hide her from a murderous Captain Nissi, but still the operation to smuggle Judy aboard the *Antenor* was organized with the precision, flair, and efficiency without which these resourceful and brave men might never have saved her from a long string of dangers.

Frank waited until the gangway leading onto the ship was largely clear. Leaving Judy hidden between some rows of kit bags, he went aboard, trying to act as casually as he could. Les Searle and the others followed, but they paused at the top of the gangplank and fell into apparently easy conversation with the staff supervising the boarding.

Once all were seemingly engrossed in the chat, Frank gave a faint whistle in the direction of the dockside. In a flash a streak of liver and white had sped up the gangplank and Frank and his fellows were able to welcome Judy aboard.

Finally, the dog that had so many times snuck under the wire was homeward bound.

Epilogue

During their long voyage to Great Britain, Judy was helped by several trusted fellow POWs and others, most notably one of the ship's crew working in the galley. An irrepressible dog lover, he provided her with all her meals prepared by his own loving hands. But man and dog's trials were far from over.

Upon docking at Liverpool, Judy had to endure six months' separation from Frank and fellow POWs in keeping with Britain's strict quarantine laws. Unsurprisingly, Judy was bewildered and upset to be separated from her fellows at the Liverpool docks, where she was taken to the nearby Hackbridge quarantine kennels. But the subsequent reunion with Frank was made all the sweeter in that by then Judy the POW dog had become something of a national sensation.

Reunited, man and dog were feted by the British media and military alike. Judy emerged from the Hackbridge kennels to a joyous reception from the waiting public. As flashbulbs popped, the now very famous POW dog that had survived the hell railway warmed to the cheering crowds. Judy even enjoyed the distinction of being "interviewed" on a special Victory Day BBC radio program in which her barks were broadcast to grateful listeners all across the nation. No one seemed to complain that they couldn't understand what this hero dog had to say.

Judy visited London and was enrolled in the Returned Prisoners of War Association as its sole canine member. She was presented at

Wembley Stadium as one of four war dogs—the "Stars of Blitz and Battlefront"—and featured on the BBC. She was made an official mascot of the RAF and given a flying jacket embroidered with the RAF's crest to wear. Frank Williams won the White Cross of Saint Giles, the highest honor awarded to humans by the animal charity the PDSA, and Judy won the PDSA's Dickin Medal, more commonly known as the Animal VC.

The press ran headlines typified by the following: "Gunboat Judy saves lives—wins medal and life pension." Judy was even given a generous grant from the venerable animal charity the Tailwaggers Club so that she could "enjoy life in peace for the rest of her days." Proudly sporting her Dickin Medal—inscribed with the motto "We also serve"—Judy and Frank toured schools, children's hospitals, and other venues as the great British public feted a truly deserving four-legged heroine of the war.

Judy's uniquely apposite Dickin Medal inscription reads:

For magnificent courage and endurance in Japanese prison camps which helped to maintain morale among her fellow prisoners, and also for saving many lives through her intelligence and watchfulness.

Saving lives through her intelligence and watchfulness indeed. Judy had saved the lives of her fellows—both soldiers and civilians—on so many occasions during her long journey from the Yangtze River patrols to the hell railway and back again.

The ill-fated railway that had been forced through the Sumatran jungles at such a terrible cost in human life was completed the day Japan surrendered to the Allies. What had driven the Japanese overseers to force it to completion in the face of their inevitable defeat remains a mystery. All the research that I have carried out seems to offer no explanation for this pointless and grossly inhumane imperative other than that it was pursued in an effort to prevent them from losing face—something that was seen as being of the utmost importance in the Japanese culture of the time. If the last few weeks of frenetic and murderous construction were pursued in that name, the waste of thousands of Allied and Indonesian lives is all the more reprehensible.

The railway, completed or not, was never going to serve the Japanese war effort, for even as they pushed the prisoner-slaves to exhaustion and death, it was crumbling all around them. There are detractors of the use of the atomic bombs at Hiroshima and Nagasaki. They need to remember this: without their use, the unspeakable suffering of the Allied POWs and the local forced laborers held by the Japanese would have lasted far longer than it did, at a cost of countless more lives. Indeed, as documents have subsequently shown, the Japanese camp overseers had orders to execute all the POWs should the Allies set foot on Japanese soil and "threaten the emperor."

In many of the trans-Sumatran railroad camps prisoners had been forced to dig what were clearly planned to be their own mass graves. This could have been for no other reason than preparation for their mass execution should the feared Allied invasion of the Japanese motherland have ensued. The use of the atomic bombs ensured that such an invasion wasn't necessary. The bombs dropped on Hiroshima and Nagasaki forced the Japanese to the negotiating table to sue for peace—a peace that would grant those POWs strong enough to survive the first few weeks of liberation their right to go home.

As to the railway itself, its impotence and futility were demonstrated most starkly in the months immediately after the end of the war. It was never put to use. After the departure of the vanquished Japanese no locomotives ever ran on that ill-fated railway. Not a year after the Japanese surrender many of the bridges along its route had been washed away in the monsoons, and the iron rails were already being ripped up and sold for scrap.

In 1951 Indonesia's national railway authority did carry out an inspection of the Pakan Baroe to Moera railway, or at least what remained of it. The recommendation of that study was that only a small section from Pakan Baroe to Logan—the first 100 kilometers— was worth saving, a length that would give access to the Sapoe and Karoe coal mines that the Japanese had been so eager to exploit for their war effort.

That recommendation was never acted upon, and today most Indonesians have no recollection of the railway ever having existed. They have no idea how the rusting hulks of locomotives lying in the jungle or in village clearings—those which their children use as makeshift climbing frames—ever came to be there. Nearly all traces of the railway that was hacked and hewn from jungle, cliff face, rock, and mud with the loss of so many lives have vanished.

The railway has been reclaimed by the jungle, along with so many of the bones of those who perished while trying to build it. One fact often ignored by those relating its history is the appalling death rate suffered by the romushas, the local slave laborers who were forced to work on the railroad alongside the Allied POWs. It is over 80 percent, bringing it very close to that in the German concentration camps.

Absolutely accurate numbers will never be known, but the Pakan Baroe to Moera railroad claimed the lives of some 700 British, Dutch, American, Australian, and other Allied POWs and over *80,000* Indonesians. That doesn't include some eighteen hundred Allied POWs who drowned when their transport ships the SS *Van Waerwijck* and the *Junyo Maru* were torpedoed and sank off the Sumatran coast. All of that untold suffering by so many prisoner-slaves had been for naught.

Petty Officer White—the seaman who had rescued Judy from the trap of the *Grasshopper's* flooded mess deck after the ship had been run aground—did complete his epic escape. It took him and his fellows several weeks by small boat to India, but by a process of dead reckoning and navigating by the stars they did make it to friendly landfall and just a few dozen kilometers from the coastal city of Madras. By then of course the main body of survivors from the *Grasshopper* had been taken captive by the Japanese, Judy included.

After the war Judy and Frank spent two happy years in his native Portsmouth. He'd often take her to his local, the Stamshaw Hotel, and regale fellow drinkers with tales of her adventures. But he remained reluctant ever to speak about his own experiences as a POW. The one thing he did discuss was how Judy contributed to saving his own and so many other lives in the camps.

"The greatest way . . . was giving me a reason to live. All I had to do was look at her and into those weary, bloodshot eyes and I would ask myself: What would happen to her if I died? I had to keep going. Even if it meant waiting for a miracle."

By 1948 Frank Williams had grown restless living in Britain and sought wider horizons. He accepted the offer of a job with the Overseas Food Corporation in Tanzania, East Africa, running a large groundnut (or peanuts as we more commonly call them) plantation. Judy, of course, was going with him—and so the man and dog who had survived so much in foreign climes were once again headed overseas.

Unsurprisingly for a dog so well traveled, Judy thrilled to their new adventure. She had her third and final litter of pups in Tanzania, and she grew adept at chasing after the exotic East African wildlife, all except for the baboons. They'd form a troop and dance and cavort around her, daring the distinguished-looking liver-and-white English pointer to single out one of them to chase. More often than not she found it so beguiling that she'd try to dash after them all, and the entire troop would spring away, chattering and laughing.

But there were bigger and wilder things out there in the bush than playful baboons. One evening Abdul, Frank's houseboy, left a tin bath full of water outside their house on the plantation, intending to empty it the next morning. In the depths of the night Frank and Judy were woken by the sound of loud slurping coming from outside their window. Judy rushed to investigate, only to find an enormous muddy-brown animal sucking up the last of the bath water. The elephant took precious little notice of Judy's spirited barking and continued to drain the last of the suds.

Only when Frank joined his dog shooing the massive beast away did the elephant finally decide to leave, its thirst well and truly slaked. But Judy remained incensed. She grabbed the tin bath—now noticeably lighter—and started to drag it into the house. Frank tried to object that there was nothing much left in the bath to save, but Judy was having none of it. Once the tin trough was safely inside, she returned to bark at the receding bulk of the elephant, which was fading into the silvery shadows of the moonlit African plain. Elephant gone, she curled up in the doorway and settled down to sleep, keeping one eye on her master's precious bathtub.

Frank's plantation work took him by air all across Tanzania and wider East Africa. He always tried to take Judy, his faithful companion, with him. On one such flight he was surprised to see her happily squeeze herself into the onboard kennel, a process more normally met by fierce barking and resistance. Frank wondered why she had gone in so easily this time. He was mystified.

Upon touchdown he got his answer. The top of Judy's cage had an opening large enough for her to poke her head through. Above her had been packed a cargo of freshly killed game. Judy had had a veritable in-flight feast, and much of the meat had been wolfed down.

It seemed that the ultimate survivor dog had never forgotten the lesson she had learned in the Japanese POW camps: if there was food to be had, she was best to grab it, and hang the consequences.

In February 1950—with Judy fourteen years old—Frank took her on a work trip in their jeep. There had been heavy rains, and he didn't want to stray too far from their place of abode on the plantation, near the town of Nachingwea. After the short drive Frank and his workers proceeded to make a camp in the bush, as Judy did what she always did when they were out in the field—she darted off to scout for any danger.

At first Frank wasn't particularly worried. But when three hours had passed and still Judy was nowhere to be seen, he got together a search party. His workers joined Frank in whistling and calling out her name, but still Judy wouldn't come. With dusk approaching,

Frank was getting seriously worried. Then one of his local foremen, Abdullah, discovered some tracks in the bush that were clearly those of the missing dog.

Abdullah used his native tracking skills to follow her, with Frank at his shoulder. Frank became all the more alarmed when they noticed a leopard's tracks apparently shadowing those of his dog. They tracked her for miles along a narrow path that led to an isolated village, but when they got there no one had seen any sign of the dog. Her tracks appeared to peter out. Judy, it seemed, had disappeared.

Frank posted a reward for 500 shillings—a considerable amount of money in what was then preindependence Tanzania—for his dog's safe return and sent messages out to all the surrounding villages. Three days passed, and there was still no news. Frank was getting desperate when, on the afternoon of the fourth day, a local ran into the camp and announced to Abdullah that Judy had been found. On hearing the news, Frank and Abdullah jumped aboard their jeep, with the local acting as guide to take them to the missing dog.

A village elder received them and took them to a hut. He opened the door, and there was Judy. But so exhausted was she from her ordeal that she could barely stand. Seeing Frank, she struggled to her feet, wagged her tail weakly, and promptly collapsed again. Wrapped in blankets, Judy was driven back to their homestead. There they treated her by removing the hundreds of cattle ticks that had attached themselves to her during her long sojourn in the bush, bathing her wounds and dousing them with disinfectant.

Judy ate the food Frank gave her, seemed much comforted, and fell into a deep sleep. Over the ensuing days she gained strength, and Frank hoped the worst was past. But on the night of February 16—some days after her disappearance—Judy began to cry and whine. Frank sat with her during the hours of darkness, but whenever she was awake Judy cried and was clearly in pain. Come sunrise. she was unable to stand and in obvious discomfort.

Frank carried her through the streets of Nachingwea to the hospital, his dog still crying as she lay in his arms. Doctor Jenkins, the

English surgeon at the hospital, found she had a mammary tumor and operated immediately. At first the operation seemed to be a success, but a few hours later the dog who had survived so much succumbed to a raging tetanus infection. She was still trying to fight but she was in obvious pain, and it was clear to the surgeon that she was fading fast.

"Let me end it, Frank," he suggested.

Wordlessly Frank nodded his acquiescence, and on February 17, 1950, at 5 p.m. Tanzanian time Judy was put to sleep.

Judy's body was wrapped in the Royal Air Force jacket that she'd been given when she was made an official mascot of the RAF and laid in a simple wooden coffin. She was buried in a grave not far from the home she had shared with Frank in Nachingwea. Using pieces of white stone collected in the bush, Frank and his workers fashioned a polished sarcophagus over the grave, topped off with a plaque that reads:

In memory of Judy DM Canine VC
Breed English Pointer
Born Shanghai February 1936, died February 1950.
Wounded February 14, 1942.
Bombed and sunk HMS Grasshopper
Lingga Archipelago February 14, 1942.
Torpedoed SS Van Waerwijck
Malacca Straits June 26, 1943.
Japanese Prisoner of War March 1942–August 1945.
China Ceylon Java England Egypt Burma
Singapore Malaya Sumatra E Africa.
They Also Served.

A Short Bibliography

Ambushed Under the Southern Cross—The Making of an American Merchant Marine Officer and His Ensuing Saga of Courage and Survival, Capt. George W. Duffy. An American merchant navy captain's memoir of his ship being sunk by a German raider and the Japanese POW camps spread over Java, Singapore, and Sumatra that he survived.

The Animal Victoria Cross—The Dickin Medal, Peter Hawthorne. Compilation of short stories covering the Dickin Medal winners throughout its history.

The Animals' VC—For Gallantry or Devotion, David Long. Compilation of short stories covering the Dickin Medal winners throughout its history.

Beyond the Bamboo Screen—Scottish Prisoners of War under the Japanese, Tom McGowran, OBE. A compilation of articles and stories from the Scottish Far East Prisoner of War Association.

The Conjurer on the Kwai: Captivity, Slavery and Survival as a Far East POW, Peter Fyans. Superb firsthand account of a British POW who used his skills as a magician and conjurer to stay alive in the Japanese labor camps and save countless other Allied lives.

The Defining Years of the Dutch East Indies, 1942–1949, edited by Jan A. Krancher. Contains survivors' accounts of the Japanese invasion of what was then the Dutch East Indies and the incarceration of the European, American, and local POWs and their forced labor on the death railway.

Escape to Captivity, Peter Hartley. The story of a young sergeant in the British Army who refuses to surrender at Singapore and ends up being captured by the Japanese and imprisoned on Sumatra.

The Judy Story, E. Varley. A short but engaging book written with the assistance of some of the Yangtze gunboat crews, telling of Judy's life and adventures.

The Jungle Journal—Prisoner of the Japanese in Java 1942–45, Frank and Ronald Williams. The story of a young Royal Artillery officer who was held as a Japanese prisoner of war in the Dutch East Indies, as told through his diaries.

Marines Don't Hold Their Horses, Ian Skidmore. The story of Colonel Alan Warren, CBE, DSC, who, having helped many escape the Japanese via Sumatra, ended up as a prisoner of war himself.

Prisoners in Java—Accounts by Allied Prisoners of War in the Far East (1942–1945) Captured in Java. As the title suggests, the book contains collected articles written by former POWs, compiled by the Java Far East Prisoners of War Club.

Prisoner in Nippon, Ray S. Stubbs. Tells the story of the author's retreat from Singapore and capture by the Japanese and the years he spent as a prisoner of war.

Prisoners of War—Australians Under Nippon, Hank Nelson. Stories of the Australian servicemen and women held in Japanese prisoner of war camps.

Spice Island Slaves, Leslie J. Audus. Presents a history of the Japanese prisoner of war camps in Eastern Indonesia during the war years.

The Sumatra Railroad: Final Destination Pakan Baroe, 1943–45, Henk Hovinga. One of the very few books telling the story of the other death railway—the one pushed through the Sumatra jungles by POWs. Encyclopedic. Definitive.

Survivors of the Sword—Prisoners of the Japanese 1942–45, Brian MacArthur. Compelling stories from survivors from across the Japanese prisoner of war and slave-labor camps. An excellent read.

Unsung Heroes of the Royal Air Force, Les and Pam Stubbs. A useful and informative record of the RAF airmen held as Japanese prisoners of war.

Yangtze River Gunboats 1900–49, Angust Konstam. Short but excellent book about the Yangtze gunboats, including fine photos and illustrations.

APPENDIX: ORIGINAL DOCUMENTATION

I have decided to include in this book a sample of official documents obtained from the National Archives, the Admiralty, the Imperial War Museum, and other sources capturing the flavor and essence of some of the key moments in the extraordinary story of Judy and her fellows. What is especially striking is the underplayed, deadpan way in which those present at such events—which were extreme, even for a conflict as all-consuming as the Second World War— relate them. They give a real sense of the nature of Judy's comrades during the war, and from reading these and more it seems clear why she was so devoted to her fellow sailors, airmen, and soldiers, especially when they became fellow prisoners of war. Each document is accompanied by a note outlining the genesis and purpose of the report.

Document One

Author's note—this is a report on the sinking of the Grasshopper, *the vessel on which Judy was shipwrecked as they attempted to evacuate Singapore.*

Narrative 7.

Note—There are probably officers, survivors, P.O.W. in Sumatra & Siam.

Prisoner of War Camp,
Mile School,
PALEMBANG.

P.N. Sherd, 9/9/45
4th April, 1942.

STATEMENT BY Mr. H. BARDEN, Eastern Bank, SINGAPORE— Ship "GRASSHOPPER" (800 tons approx.)

We left Singapore 1730 hours on 13th February, 1942, but with Dragonfly: returned about midnight when we sailed again about 1000 hours on 14th February, one aircraft dropped one bomb that missed us. About 1230 hours two waves each about 25 aircraft bombed us. We were hit and the engine room began to flood. The ship was then beached near a small island in the Rhio Archipelago. Stores were offloaded and magazines destroyed. All personnel including 60–80 civilians were taken ashore. The skipper (Hoffman) arranged for us to go to Daboe where we arrived on the 18th or 19th February. Owing to the effect of blast on my back from bombing I went into hospital where Captain Kirkwood, I.M.S., had just arrived. On 23rd of February the Dutch from Djambi took about 40 of us to the hospital there. Another launch containing fit survivors from Daboe followed us, but went through to Padang. They were mostly serving personnel.

On 1st March we tried to go to Padang but the ferry launch had been destroyed by the Dutch as we retuned.

The Japanese arrived in Djambi on 6th March. We stayed in Hospital until 27th March, and after 2 days in the military barracks Djambi we were taken to Palrumbang where I arrived 31st March as prisoner.

In the party which went to Padang were Commander Alexander R.N., and Lieutenant Commander Reid.

Mr. H.M. James (Planter) died in Hospital at Djambi.

We left in Djambi Hospital a Mrs. Parr with a badly injured arm, Dalrymple (R.A.F.) wounded by shrapnel in the leg, Marine Faint (wounded), Miss Hartley, an elderly lady with slight shrapnel wounds in the leg, two Chinese nurses from the General Hospital, Singapore, and two Eurasian nurses. I regret I do not know what happened to the many people who were left in Daboe.

Document Two

Author's note—this is a report on the sinking of the Dragonfly, *sister ship to the* Grasshopper, *which was shipwrecked as they attempted to evacuate Singapore.*

Statement by Capt. R.L. Lyle (now Major) on loss of H.M.S. "Dragonfly" including statement on possibility of survivors landing in other places and a list of names of those known to have embarked, seen killed etc.

I have divided this report into three:

(1) Circumstances under which H.M.S. Gunboat "Dragonfly" was lost

(2) General itinerary of survivors from the place of loss to Colombo

(3) List of names of those seen killed etc.

e. Loss of M.M.S. Gunboat "Dragonfly"

At about 0200 hrs on the Feb 14, 1942, H.M.S. "Dragonfly" in company with H.M.S. Gunboat "Grasshopper" removed detailed evacuation parties of the various Brigades and Divisions which then remained on Singapore Island. At this period both ships were very badly shelled but appeared to sustain little damage and no casualties.

After steaming at probably maximum speed the remainder of the night, at 0930 the same morning (i.e. Feb) 14 a Japanese Flying Boat was sighted which was very obviously on reconnaissance. At this time H.M.S. "Dragonfly" was leading and H.M.S. Grasshopper was following about a mile astern.

The Flying Boat flew over the "Dragonfly" and dropped two bombs of small caliber. Both however were near misses and no damage was done. The ships guns went into action. The Flying Boat paid no attention to H.M.S. "Grasshopper." As this plane was so obviously a reconnaissance aircraft, the Commander of our Gunboat decided to get under the lee of one of the small islands in the vicinity, in an endeavor to evade any aircraft which might be sent after us. To put this into effect our course was changed slightly. The Commander of H.M.S. "Dragonfly" was to the best of my knowledge by name of Commander Sprott. The Commander of the "Grasshopper" being Commander Hoffman. However, before reaching cover of the islands, large numbers of Japanese Bombers were seen to be approaching from a northerly direction and I was informed by the first Officer Lieutenant P.P. Shellard R.N.V.R. that he had counted some 123. On sighting of aircraft the alarm was sounded and all non-naval personnel were ordered below. I myself was put into the corridor between the officers' quarters forrard along with a number of other Army officers, and spare gun crews of the ship's forward guns.

By some means or other the Commander of the ship had been able to supply all personnel with life belts. There had not been a great deal of time to check up on the exact numbers on board the ship or get their names and Regiments, particularly as in getting to the ship on Singapore Island our parties had been very badly shelled and cut up, and many of the other ranks had lost their Officers in charge. It was however estimated that the Naval crew amounted to 73 and that the total number of persons on board was about 225 i.e. 152 Army personnel of various Regiments that were made chiefly of men from 2nd Battalion The East Surrey Regiment, The 1st Battalion Manchester Regiment, my party of Headquarters, 6/15 Indian Inf Brigade, a few R.A.F. and a few miscellaneous people such as Intelligence Corps. The majority of the other ranks were quartered in, what I believe, was the ratings Mess Deck, aft.

From below we soon heard the aircraft circling overhead which carried on for some minutes, and from my position, which was sitting on the floor forrard, the next thing I knew was a colossal explosion and a complete ceasing of all avoiding action by the ship and the immediate stoppage of the engines, which had appeared to be going full out.

It was obvious to us that something very serious had happened and we therefore filed up the companion-way on to the deck.

On looking round I was able to see that the very worst had happened and that the entire ship, aft of the smoke stack, was just a mass of twisted metal, and the stern of the ship had completely disappeared. It is my belief that the depth charges which were in position for use had exploded, causing the chaos. On going closer to the gap it appeared that it would have been impossible for any man to be alive who had been in the after Mess Deck. However, we managed to get one or two very badly wounded men out through a bomb hole. It was not possible to do very much as the ship was by this time a good deal more than half submerged.

One leading seaman by the name of Brennan (I have reported this to the Navy C/O H.M.S. Sultan Colombo) by great presence of mind managed to get the one sound Whaler into the water. We also got clear two small Carley floats. We managed to get the wounded that were lying about the deck into the one boat and a certain number of other able-bodied personnel got into it as well, before it became obvious that we would have to push her away or she would sink with the Gunboat. I along with a number of others remained on deck until Commander Sprott gave the "abandon ship," when we jumped overboard and swam away from her. At this time Commander Sprott was still on the bridge.

It was now a little after half past ten in the morning. I got some 100 yards away from the ship and turned round just in time to see her take the final plunge. As she was going under I saw two Naval Officers jump out of the bridge onto the ship's side, slip down her bottom and into the sea. All that remained of her to be seen after this was a short piece of her bows, and she remained in this position for some hours. The actual period which she took to sink from the time of the bomb hitting her I estimate as being a maximum of 5 minutes.

The next thing I saw was the Whaler on the far side of the wreck from me with a number of people hanging onto her life ropes. One empty khali float and the other with a number of men on it.

All this time large numbers of aircraft were circling round in squadrons and I was able to vouch for well over 60 planes. They had by this time seen our fate and had turned their attention to H.M.S. "Grasshopper." They were doing the same to her as they had done to us. Pattern bombing by squadrons. For a time she appeared to bear a charmed life and never seemed to be hit. Literally hundreds of bombs must have been dropped near her. She was at this time perhaps up to half a mile away from us circling round in avoiding action. It is possible that some of those bombs severely shook some of those people swimming in the water so as to render them unconscious. We eventually saw the "Grasshopper" circle as if in avoiding action and make for an island which we could see in the far distance. I estimated that she had been hit, which turned out to be correct, and she was endeavoring to beach herself which she eventually did successfully before her after-magazine blew up.

I was given to understand later that H.M.S. "Grasshopper" only sustained some 8 or 9 fatal casualties.

To turn back to the plight of the survivors of the "Dragonfly" the Whaler was now collecting those that she could find in the water and she was getting very full.

The empty float had been occupied by large numbers and was seen to be making away in a direction that I presumed to be Sumatra where a very vague outline of coast could be seen.

The other float was making off to the nearest island which I have mentioned before.

There were still a number in the water who were some distance away from the Whaler. I found myself, after endeavoring to collect people into a bunch as I considered that way we should have a better chance of rescue or getting ashore by swimming, the only officer, I took charge of those that I had collected, a number of about 6 and shouted to others to join us. There were a few whoever who swam off on their own in the direction of the nearest island. I only saw one of them again. I should mention here that all the personnel I had been able to collect were Naval ratings.

By shouting and making signs at the Whaler, which was too far away to recognize persons, we were led to understand that she was too full to take more than the men that were in her immediate vicinity. I and my party therefore decided to endeavor to swim ashore which we set out to do.

By this time the aircraft, their mission fulfilled, had flown away, but some half an hour later we saw a squadron approaching us at a very low level coming from a direction which I presumed to be East. Before long it was obvious what they were going to do and that was to machine gun the life boat. They came down to what I believe is termed, naught feet, and machine-gunned the life boat in tiers of 2 & 3 at a time, the whole time keeping formation. They repeated this twice on the life boat and having dealt with them passed on and machine-gunned myself and party in the same manner. It was very obvious, even from the distance that we were away from the life boat, that they had sustained very heavy casualties. We were more fortunate in that no one was hurt.

Having, as already said, repeated this twice they flew off in the same direction from where they had come. We saw no more of them.

We saw the Whaler re-arrange itself and start off for the nearest island for which we were also making.

At about half past six that evening the Whaler which had been waiting behind picking up people, caught up my swimming party and some of us were able to assist the few able-bodied men in the boat to get the last half mile to the shore, which we reached about 7 o'clock that evening.

We took a count and if I remember correctly there were 27 men composed of 22 in the boat and the 5 who had swum with me, about 8 of those in the boat were in a very serious condition. Unfortunately we found the island to which we had got possessed no food or water and nothing very much could be done for the wounded, numbering considerably more than half of those remaining. I do not know the name of the island.

The following morning a Sub-Lieut, whose name I believe was Clarke, a New Zealander, arrived walking along the beach with 8 others. They had been on the second float and had got ashore a little further up to coast. This made the total count of 36. Others may possibly have got ashore by swimming to other islands in the vicinity, but in my own opinion, I am afraid that they must have been very few, as the majority of the ships' total complement, particularly those of the Army, must have been killed outright in the first explosion or were killed during the machine-gunning of the life boat.

The names of personnel that I can remember are give in part III under the heading of having landed or having died in the particular action.

(Sgd.)

General itinerary of survivors from place of loss to Colombo.

c. Referring to the last sentence of War Office Cable which says "state where he landed and possibility of survivors landing elsewhere," I shall give a short itinerary as it is just possible that other of the ships company did land elsewhere.

As I have said in part (a) of this report the name of the island on which I landed is unknown to be but from having talked to the naval crew of H.M.S. "Dragonfly" I gather that it was estimated to be approximately 100 miles south of Singapore in the vicinity of the Sinkep Group of islands about 10 miles from one by the name of Pongpong. I do not know whether this is the correct spelling but to pin-point it, it may be of interest to say that Pongpong was where S.S. "Kuala" foundered with a large number of nursing sisters on board.

As can be seen from the map there are many hundreds of small islands in this area many of which were visited by various officers in an endeavor to collect more survivors of the large number of ships which sank in that area on our about the 14th Feb. 1942. I believe the number to be sunk within a radius of some 40 miles numbered 9 of various sizes, one other of which I believe, was the "St. Briac," which I gather was a tug and was towing barges of explosives.

Having remained on this small island for 48 hours and having endeavored to make the Whaler more or less seaworthy we eventually were able to contact the crew of the H.M.S. "Grasshopper" by means of a native in a small sampan. We were told to go to another small island where they would endeavor to get a few medical supplies to us. The name of this island to which we eventually got was called I believe Pisec [spelling doubtful]. Unfortunately we were not met here by anyone and it is believed that there must have been a number of places of similar name and we had arrived at the wrong one. Between the time of landing and arriving at this island we had lost a number of the wounded, they having died. See part (c) of the report.

We had been on the second island for about 24 hours when a number of large sampans arrived which were sent by a Dutch Controller of another island some 40 or 50 miles away, he having heard of the various disasters. The town from which they had come was a small Dutch settlement by name of Dabok. We took over the sampans, as by this time the Whaler was completely unserviceable, due to its many bullet holes, and we decided to try and find the personnel of H.M.S. "Grasshopper" which after a night's travel we were able to reach. They were on still another island some 10 or 15 miles away from where we had been, the name of which I do not know, as the village in which we stayed was completely devoid of all local inhabitants who had, it was presumed, gone into the jungle for safety.

It may here be interesting to note that a few of the locals which we had met previously had informed us that the Japanese had been round these islands previously dressed as fisherman, warning all the natives that they would suffer very considerably if they gave help to any British personnel.

Shortly after joining up with the personnel of H.M.S. "Grasshopper" a motor launch arrived to take us off to Dabok which had also been arranged by the Controller of that particular island. It took us three nights to clear all personnel from this one island. However, all that were there arrived safely at our destination (Dabok). Here many of us were put into the local hospital inclusive of myself. While I was in hospital a Committee was formed consisting of the Controller, Commander Hoffman and one or two others and it was decided that all able-bodied personnel including a large number of civilians which were on this island should be sent off in large country boats to Sumatra, which we were informed was about 80 miles away. While I was still in hospital large numbers of personnel left Dabok for Sumatra in this manner.

It is interesting to note that of H.M.S. "Dragonfly's" ships company, apart from those which were in hospital with me, I never saw any again. I can only surmise that either they landed on a different part of the Sumatran coast to that which I did or they must have got across the country a good deal quicker than myself and caught a previous boat out of Padang. I have, however, only seen one Naval Officer of our party since I arrived in Colombo, and he being very sick was sent off a good deal earlier than most of the others. The Navy is in possession of all his particulars although I forget his name.

Some days after arriving in hospital I was sent off in a motor launch along with a party of walking wounded to Sumatra. We made for the mouth of the Indragiri River and eventually landed at Tembhilahan. It is my opinion that those who had left before us in country boats probably landed at Jambi, which of course was considerably further south, and it is therefore possible that in view of the fact by this time, the Japanese had landed at Palembang, and were making their way north, that many of them were cut off and unable to make the west coast of Sumatra.

From Tembhilahan we went by river to Rengat and from there on to Ayermulek staying a day or two at each place. From there was were able to get a truck which conveyed us to Sawerleunto and eventually down to Padang. Some of the wounded party which I came over with were not sufficiently fit to complete the whole journey, and a number of them were left in the various hospitals on route. I eventually left Padang in the early morning of the 3rd of March 42 which I believe was after S.S. "Rosenbloom" left the same Port and has been reported lost with all hands. I understood that some 300 persons embarked on this ship although there was no definite method of checking the numbers. I am, however, very much afraid that personnel who left Dabok three or four days before I did may have been unfortunate enough to have embarked on this ship.

I left Padang in the K.L.M. SS "De Weert" and on the day we left, Padang was completely clear of personnel with the exception of a Colonel Warren, Royal Marines, who was in charge of the evacuation from that Port. A wire, however, had been received that same day from the East side of Sumatra, I do not know whether it was Jambi or the Indragiri landing place, but it said that there were some 700 persons still to come through. However, as it would have taken anything up to a week for them to arrive, the "De Weert" could not possibly wait for them.

Documents Three and Four

Author's note—two reports on the sinking of the SS Van Waerwyjck—
renamed the Werweck *by the Japanese—the vessel on which Judy was
shipwrecked for a second time.*

Tranby Lodge,

Hessle,

E. Yorke.

25th May, 1946.

To: The Under Secretary of State,
The   War Office,
        Edge Lane.
        Liverpool. 7.

From: Captain J.G. Gordon,
Royal   Artillery.

Sir,

In answer to your letter of the 24th May. reference M/954 I will
do my best to answer the seven questions, but would point out that
I have issued a full report on this disaster to the Judge Advocate
General's Office and have made several trips in connection with this
and other War crimes to London. However, I will repeat for your
benefit.

The Japanese vessel on which I was sailing was making a trip
from Medan to Singapore, not Palembang as stated by you.

Answers to your questions.

(4) S.S. Van Warweak.
(5) 1400 hours, July 26th 1944.
(6) Two hundred and seven. (Not quite certain).
(7) Sixty-seven including three who died immediately on arrival
     at Singapore as the result of wounds.

(8)

    a. Sixty miles south of Medan on Sumatra side of Malacca Straits, seven or eight miles from shore.

    b. Three enemy ships in the vicinity which picked up survivors. One Tanker which took the bulk, and two Corvettes.

    c. Completely out of sight within five minutes, actually under water in three.

(6) All British were rescued by being picked up by an enemy vessel (to the best of my knowledge and belief).

(7) I regret that this is quite impossible owing to all my records being removed from me on more than one occasion by the Japanese during later imprisonment. However, practically all the information was computed and filed with the records at the base camp at Pakan Baroe, Sumatra, the C.O. of which being Wing Commander P.S. David, R.A.F., the Senior Medical Officer being Lieut. Col. E.M. Hennessy, R.A.M.C. The latter in the final stages of Japanese surrender was responsible until his transfer to Singapore for all records of lost personnel. If these records were not complete and you care to ask me for the particulars of any individual, and I am able to remember, I shall be only too pleased to help.

In conclusion I would add that I personally reached a Fishing trap just off the shore by swimming, and was then picked up by one of the small Corvettes. On getting on board, I went up to the Japanese Captain of the ship to thank him for rescuing my party, and asked as best I could if he would go round the wreckage to see if anybody else was left alive on the spot, the main bulk of survivors having already left the scene of the sinking in the other two vessels. To my astonishment he agreed. We then proceeded to go round all the remaining wreckage and rafts, stopping sometimes to examine bodies thereon, and I am therefore able to state that at approximately 1630 hours on the same afternoon there was nobody left alive at the scene of the sinking.

When I later was transferred back to Sumatra I discovered that four allied P.O.W.'s all of whom were Dutch had been picked up by a fishing vessel and taken to the shore of Sumatra. After careful investigation I could find no other trace of any other allied P.O.W.s who had been rescued in this way or who had reached the shore. It is therefore to be concluded, unless picked up by the Japanese, which was extremely unlikely with an unfriendly local population, and the knowledge that the Japanese brought all Allied P.O.W.s in Northern Sumatra to the base camp at Pakan Baroe; that there were no other survivors other than those contained on the list held at Headquarters Pakan Baroe and at Changi, Singapore, the Changi list being taken to Changi camp by Major P.E. Campbell, Indian Army, approximately a fortnight after the sinking.

J.G.Gordon,
Captain Royal Artillery.
28–5–46.

To: Officer Commanding,
        Command Medical Store,
        Harefield, Middlesex.

From: 7259601 W.O.11. Eckersall, K.P.J., R.A.M.C.
        Det. 12 Company R.A.M.C.,
        Command Medical Store,
        Harefield, Middlesex.

Date: 28th May 1946.

Sir,

In reply to War Office Letter No. MA/OR/954 dated 24th Mar 1946, asking for information on the subject of loss of British personnel, who while P.O.W. in the Far East, were lost by the sinking of

an enemy vessel by Allied action on the 26th June 1944, the following particulars are submitted:

The route was Medan to Singapore and not as quoted in the
above mentioned War Office letter.

(9) The name of the vessel I am not quite sure of, it was something
     like "Kwewegem," which prior to capture by the enemy, was a
     cargo cum passenger vessel of the K.P.M. Line. The vessel car-
     ried the enemies' serial No. P.1406, this number is to the best
     of my knowledge correct however, no doubt the Allied subma-
     rine commander recorded this prior to sinking the vessel.

(10) Time of sinking—1347 hours (Tokyo time) on Monday 26th
     June 1944.

(11) Approximately 300 Allied personnel of British, Americans,
     Australian, and mixed European Nationality, also approx.
     450 Dutch personnel.

(12) A total of 62 Allied personnel (other than Dutch) were found
     to be missing when a check was made at River Valley Road
     Camo, on the 28th June. A further three died as a result of the
     action in the P.O.W. Camp Hospital at Changi Jail, Singapore.
     Their names are as follows:

     Sgt. Fowler, R.A.
     Sgm. Conley. R.C. of Signals.   —This gives a total of 65.
     P.O. Christopher, R. Navy.

The full total missing was approximately 200, including Dutch.

Of the 65 missing I am certain, as after the fall of Japan in August
1945 I compiled a list of all casualties (excluding Dutch) known in the
Pakan Baroe Area P.O.W. Camps, from 1st July 1944 to August 1944.
This list including full details of personnel (Excluding Dutch) lost in
the sinking of the vessel in question. The details were as follows:

     Nationality—Number—Rank—Name—Initials—Officer or
     Other Rank as applicable to the various arms of the service.

Copies of the list quoted above were taken from the Pakan Baroe Allied H.Q. Camp Office by Lieut. Colonel E.M. Hennessey, R.A.M.C. (Regular Army) and handed over to the British Representative at R.A.P.W.I. Headquarters at the Goodwood Park Hotel, Scott's Road, Singapore, in early September 1945.

Further copies of these lists were handed over by me, together with lists of deaths in the Pakan Baroe area and in Medan area, and sick lists categorized for evacuation, to a Captain Carey, R.A.M.C. (Airborne) of the occupying forces, to whom Lt. Col. Hennessey handed over prior to leaving for Singapore in early September, after release. Note: Dutch records were maintained by their own clerical personnel.

All other Allied statistics were compiled by British P.O.W.s.

5a.   Time of leaving Medan—4pm Tokyo time, on Sunday 25th June 1944, steaming at approximately 6 knots. Vessel anchored at dark and proceeded at dawn. (8pm to 5:30am approx). Note: Owing to clocks being advanced to Tokyo time after April 1st 1942, by Japanese Order, it was light until nearly 8:30pm.

Convoy of three of four vessels, other vessels were tankers, and escorted by three small corvettes, carrying depth charges and small A.A. guns. Two Jap Bombing planes also acted as escort during steaming time.

The ship was sunk by Allied Submarine off Tandjong Bali, a small island about 7 Kilometers off shore, at 1347 hours 26th June 1944, by two torpedoes fired into the Port side from possibly a distance of 6 miles away.

The convoy hugged the coastline all the way from Medan up to the time of sinking, steaming about 4 to 5 Kilometers off shore.

There had been sinkings of other vessels in the same area as wrecks could be seen partially above the water level.

This particular ship after sinking had still approximately 12 feet of its masts showing above the water level.

5b.   There were no friendly ships in the vicinity. Enemy ships in the convoy refused to pick up the P.O.W. survivors until Japanese Merchant Navy crew and native crew survivors, also Japanese Military Guards, were picked up.

All P.O.W. survivors were finally recovered from the water by approximately 1645 hours 26th June 1944, either by ships in convoy or small escort corvettes.

This excludes two or three Dutch, one of whom was a doctor, by name A.L. Yurgens, Captain 1st Class, Dutch N.E.I. Forces, who reached shore by swimming and gave themselves up to native police at the nearest village, and were finally returned to a P.O.W. Camp in the Pakan Baroe area at a later date, approximately August 1944.

5c.   The vessel was not longer than seven minutes in sinking after being struck.

6a.   Two or three are stated in 5b.

6b.   Approximately 550 were picked up by the enemy merchant vessels and corvettes.

f.   I have previously stated in answer to question No. 4 where complete particulars of personnel lost, or died as result of the action (other than Dutch) may be obtained.

For your information I have added the following details:

The final destination as a result of this move was Pakan Baroe, Central Sumatra. The reason we were conveyed by sea from Medan to Singapore was, the enemy did not at that time possess adequate road transport to convoy from Medan to Pakan Baroe by road, a 4 day journey.

The solution being, transfer P.O.W.s from Medan to Singapore in a large vessel, transfer at Singapore to small flat bottomed river craft in order to return to Sumatra and navigate the long narrow rivers which have their source in mountain ranges on the west coast of Sumatra, in order to arrive at Pakan Baroe by the sea and river route.

I trust that the information given herein will shed some light on this most unfortunate incident.

I have the honor to be,
Sir,
Your obedient servant,
K.P.J. Eckersall
7259601 W.O.11. R.A.M.C.

Document Five

Author's note—a report on forced labor parties working in the Suma-tran jungle as POWs of the Japanese that captures the stark horror of the camps and the unbreakable spirit of resistance of the Allied internees.

Report of a POW work party in the Gaje Country, S Atjeh, Sumatra

1. On March 3rd 1944 a POW work party of 300 Dutch, 200 British left Glegeer POW Camp, Medan, Sumatra. The Allied senior officer was Capt. Van der Lande. The British senior officer was Lieutenant L. R. T. Henman, the British Medical Officer was Captain P.M. Kirkwood. The whole party was commanded by Lieutenant S. Miura of the Japanese Army.

2. On arrival at Keta Tjane at the end of a day's truck ride Lieutenant Miura informed us that we must on the following day commence a march of 135 kilometers (approx. 85 miles) to Blangkedteren, S. Atjeh. After protest by the senior Allied officers, including medical officers, one more days grace was allowed before the march was commenced. All belongings that could not be carried had to be left at Keta Tjane.

3. This march was made in four stages with one whole days rest on the way. Food supplies consisted of rice, soya beans and meat. Owing to bad organization on the part of the Japanese the proper quantities were not always available at the stopping places. Many of the British particularly had no water bottles and in spite of warnings men drank from streams on the road and thus laid themselves open to attacks of dysentery. The men had not marched for two years or more and on the way suffered very severely from blisters. Nevertheless very few British fell out. The RN party of 45 (under Second Lieutenant H. Hedley, Mysore Regiment) completed the march in fours, with only one casualty in the last stage.

4. After about one month the British contingent (consisting of four parties—RN, Army, RAF and AIF) were finally billeted at a camp at 28 kilometer Blangkedteren Takengong Road. This road was being constructed by the Japanese with POW and native labor. The camp was at a height of approximately 3000 feet and consisted of bivouac attap huts built by POWs themselves immediately after arrival. Lieutenant Hedley, the RN party and some of the Army men had to spend two nights amongst native coolies in hovels made of bracken, in the midst of a sea of mud and excreta (human and otherwise) before being allowed to move into the camp at 28 kilometers. This they built as best they could with a small quantity of attap and wood cut in the jungle.

5. The men were driven out to work as soon as possible and no fit men were allowed to stay in camp other than a bare minimum for cooking and wood chopping. Work consisted of labor on a mountain road, tree felling, bridge building, stone carrying, earth removal with Java hoes and bucket, and metalling of the road surface. Average days work about nine hours in all weathers, and while carrying stones men sometimes had to walk 30 kilometers a day.

6. Sick men were continually persecuted and many men were forced to go out working when they were in no way fitted to do so. A certain percentage of men were required. If these were not forthcoming the sick were paraded (irrespective of what diseases they had) and the Japanese would choose those who in their opinion were fit for duty. Attached correspondence between Captain Kirkwood IMS and Lieutenant Miura gives an idea of the situation. Officers who protested were merely beaten up by the guards in front of the remaining POWs.

7. Food at this period consisted of 300 grams of rice and 200 grams of soya bean per day, salt fish was also provided, approximately 2 bullocks per week (amongst 500 men) and a small quantity of vegetables (see report by Second Lieutenant J. Hedley, Mysore Regiment). Many men could not eat the soya beans as they caused

diarrhea (see report by Captain Kirkwood, IMS). Naturally, the diet was totally inadequate for the work being done.

8. Particularly at first there were many cases of dysentery. Those were treated in a so-called hospital at Blangkedjeeren where a Dutch Army doctor named Duringa did splendid work with practically no equipment. As soon as these patients were pronounced temporarily fit they had to walk back to the camp from which they came (23–28 km.) and bring with them a bullock which was the meat ration for the camp concerned. Delay in sending men to Blangkedjeeren Hospital was in my opinion the cause of the death of Pte. Lahay, AIF, one of the three British casualties in Atjeh.

The two letters were attached to the original of this report submitted to MI5 War Office.

(13) As a consequence many men sold their clothes and with the proceeds bought extra rice, fruit and native sugar. To do this they had to break out of camp at night. When some of them were caught the whole camp was punished by being made to stand to attention in the evening, after the day's work for approximately 2 hours per day. The guards said that they would make arrangements for fruit to be bought legitimately but, having done so once, they would then forget their promise in true Japanese style and so no more official purchases would be allowed.

   g. The spirit of the men during this period was very high, particularly after news was heard of the invasion of Europe, and this was as well, because without it there would have been far worse casualties on the march down into the plains which began on October 6th.

   cii. On October 5th at 18:00 hours I was informed by Miura that on the following day we were to commence a march of approximately 85 miles which had to be completed in as short time as possible (actually the march took 81 hours including all stops for food and sleep and rest).

(8)   Many of the men had no boots, many more were suffering from diarrhea or amoebic dysentery, the roads were steep and shockingly surfaced and Korean guards (until they themselves got left behind) used sticks and rifle butts on any stragglers. Capt. Kirkwood was himself suffering from amoebic dysentery but nevertheless gave every possible assistance to the sick.

13. The worst part of the journey was a night march between the hours of 20:00 hours and 04:00 hours. During this period I was marching with the Navy party and the singing by them and the Army and R.A.F. of songs such as "The Eagle they fly high in Cell," "Lily of Laguna," and "The beer is on the table" helped a good deal.

14. A Korean guard named Matsuoka was especially vicious during the march. On one occasion when P/O. Sparks, W. No D/JX 125134 with blistered and festered feet as being helped along by Capt. Kirkwood and P/O. Northcott, C.J. No. D/JX 137479 his guard used his rifle butt on all three of them, because they were not walking fast enough.

15. We finally arrived at Kota Tjane with 6% of our strength having fallen out against 25% of the Jap and Korean guards. The streets were festooned with bananas—but Lieut. Miura had given orders to his Sergeant that on no account were the P.O.W.'s to be given or allowed to purchase any fruit at all.

16. This man Miura provides a most interesting study. He spoke English (and Malay) extremely well and had apparently been in some large business firm in Japan, where he said he had many foreign friends. He was always anxious to try to convince me that he was trying to do everything in his power for the P.O.W.'s. Had his actual behavior, particularly toward the sick, borne out his fine words I should have been more impressed with his good intentions. "Sick men," he said to me on more than one occasion, "are of no use to the Japanese Army. It is better for them to die." The hospital too he

said, should be made to resemble a prison as near as possible. "You yourself," he added, "complain far too much. It is not gentlemanly."

17. He had no control over his Korean guards who did more or less as they pleased. He did indeed at my request forbid them to take action into their own hands by inflicting physical punishment themselves, but when, as soon happened, they began to disobey this order, he seemed quite unable or unwilling to see that it was enforced. "Do not punish your men," he told me when I asked for some powers of punishment (with regard to sanitary matters), "Always be kind. I never punish my guards." Quite true.

18. Under the circumstances the discipline of the men was very good and for this credit must go to the officers under me (especially Lieut. Hedley and Lieut. D.S. Matthews, G.S.) and equally to the N.C.O.'s of the various parties (R.N., Army, R.A.F. and A.I.F.) These N.C.O.'s had not only to work and live with the other men, but, on return to the camp each evening, had to distribute food, collect money for canteen purchases (when allowed), detail working parties and settle all minor disputes without having any disciplinary powers at all.

R.N. Party	P/O	Northcott, C.J.R.	D/JX 137479.
	P/O	Bosward, F.	D/JX 140525.
	P/O	Sparks, W.	D/JX 125134.
Army Party	Sergt. Maverty, R.A.S.C. (18th Div.)		
	Sergt. Powell, T.F. R.A.		1454735.
	(head cook)		
R.A.F.	Sergt. Appleton, J.G. R.A.F.		522620
A.I.F.	Cpl. Mackay, L.		2/29 Btn. A.I.F.

I would also especially like to recommend Lieut. Hedley for the excellent work he did as ration officer on the march down from Blangkedjeren to Kota Tjane and at other times.

19. Capt. Kirkwood, I.M.S. succeeded under the circumstances in preserving the men's health, or what was left of it, to an astonishing degree (though for most of the time he was sick himself with amoebic dysentery). In all during the eight months period only three men died.

Pte.	Hopson.	A.I.F.
Pte.	Lahay.	A.I.F.
L.A.C.	Willis.	R.A.F.

Although the hard times which the men underwent was probably the original cause of the many casualties which we suffered afterward in the Pakan Baree area. (See report by Capt. Kirkwood, I.M.S. and Capt. J.G. Gordon, R.A.)

20. The whole Atjeh party (Dutch and British) were drafted to Pakan Baree after approximately three weeks rest in a camp (Sungei Songkel) near Medan. On the way we (500 men) were kept at Fort de Kock (Nr. Padang) for four days in two rooms which in normal times formed the police courts of the town in question. During these four days we were given very little to eat, the only sanitary arrangements consisted of a trench dug in the yard, and it was only possible to have a bath by standing in the bin. There was just sufficient room for each man to lie down on the floor. The sick lay in the middle of one room in a space which we cleared for them.

21. At Petai Camp (Pakan Baree area) Lieut. Miura put cost and difficulties in the way with regard to the digging of latrines. He would not allow sufficient time for the work and forbade me to use the timber (for our big latrine) from the jungle nearby. However by disobeying orders we managed to get the latrine completed, upon which he sent for me and congratulated me on its efficiency. A few days previously he had complained that the British, though they always obeyed him, did so "with a sulky face." The next day (Nov. 23rd) he went to Pakan Baree and bought back Capt. Gordon, R.A. as Senior British Officer.

22. This officer, who had worked untiringly on the troops behalf in Medan, took over the duties of Senior British Officer from me. He was faced with the last (and most difficult) period which we went through as P.O.W.'s, and in my opinion carried out his duty until I left him in Legas in August 1945, in a most admirable manner. He has details, which I handed over to him, of the personnel of the Atjah Party and all casualties which we suffered then and in the Pakan Baree area.

23. Finally I would like to say how much the British Contingent in Atjah appreciated the great organizing ability and general efficiency of Capt. J.J.A. Van der Lande and his S.M.O. Capt. Linggen (Royal N.E.I. Army) particularly in connection with medical matters the work done by Sergt. Major Bougels (R.N.E.I. Army) is worthy of the highest praise.

(SGD) L.R.T. HERMAN
Lieutenant, R.N.V.R.

INDEX